DILEMMAS OF A DOUBLE LIFE

series editor, montana katz, ph.d.

We
are fitfully and certainly
moving away from a world in
which women are defined as less than
men, where masculinity and femininity
are separate realms of experience. It is clear
that gender will no longer be as determining
a factor to an individual's personal identity,
choices, and aspirations as it once was. This
cultural shift will affect every aspect of life,
from subtle daily details to broad social
principles. The Gender in Crisis Series
explores the future meaning, construction, and impact of gender on
all of our lives.

DILEMMAS OF A DOUBLE LIFE

Women Balancing Careers and Relationships

EDITED BY

Nancy B. Kaltreider, M.D.

JASON ARONSON INC.
Northvale, New Jersey
London

Production Editor: Elaine Lindenblatt

This book was set in 10 pt. Carmina Light by Alpha Graphics of Pittsfield, New Hampshire, and printed and bound by Book-mart Press, Inc. of North Bergen, New Jersey.

Library of Congress Cataloging-in-Publication Data

Dilemmas of a double life : women balancing careers and relationships
    / edited by Nancy B. Kaltreider.
        p. cm.—(Gender in crisis)
    Includes bibliographical references and index.
    ISBN 0-7657-0091-3 (alk. paper)
        1. Women—United States—Social conditions. 2. Women—Employment—
    United States. 3. Work and family—United States. I. Kaltreider,
    Nancy B. II. Series.
    HQ1421.D55 1997
    305.42'0973—dc21   97-13953

Printed in the United States of America on acid-free paper. For information and catalog write to Jason Aronson Inc., 230 Livingston Street, Northvale, New Jersey 07647-1726. Or visit our website: http://www.aronson.com

to Leah
daughter and colleague
a guide for the road ahead

CONTENTS

Contents

FOREWORD

Choosing a Path with Heart

The underlying premise of *Dilemmas of a Double Life* is that women must juggle roles, make choices, and cope with career and relationship opportunities and limitations. The book was conceived and edited by Nancy Kaltreider, M.D., Director of the Program for Women at Langley Porter Psychiatric Institute and Professor of Clinical Psychiatry at the University of California, San Francisco. Her perspective, and that of all the authors of individual chapters, comes from personal experiences, climbing up the career ladder, therapy hours with women patients, mentoring, friendships with peers, and literature on the subject.

Nancy Kaltreider and I co-led an ongoing seminar for women residents in the late 1970s and early 1980s, when, for the first time (as a result of the women's movement), the number and percentage of women residents had increased substantially from the token numbers in our own classes. Almost all of them were breaking new ground in becoming the first women in their family lineage to become doctors, and in doing so also breaking with expectations of what their lives were supposed to be. Like all women so empowered by the women's movement, they had no footsteps to follow. In this seminar, as in the women's consciousness groups that had shaped the women's movement, the sharing of personal information brought out a commonality of experience. Once shared, what one woman confronted or chose to do became a possibility for the rest. In a very similar way, the chapter authors describe the conflicts and choices for women who enter the professional, business, corporate, or academic worlds.

This is a mentoring book. In her career at UCSF Nancy Kaltreider has been a role model, mentor, and program initiator for women residents and women psychiatrists, as well as held a significant role in the education of medical students. In a real sense, as the editor, she has mentored the writing ability of every chapter author, many of whom she has influenced in other ways in their professional development. They in turn are offering what they have learned to the readers of this book who face similar dilemmas and choices. There is a likelihood that a reader will see herself or a partner's quandary in the stories of other women and then be able to further clarify her own issues if she thoughtfully considers what a woman professional has to say on the subject. Each chapter author then acts as a mentor to the reader; she passes on what she herself has observed, done, learned, and thought about.

It is helpful to have role models who know the terrain. It does matter what the opportunities or realities of a situation are. It is useful to have information from others who are farther along the path, which is what this book provides. But for work and relationships to truly matter to you, decisions need to be deeply personal, subjectively right, and in harmony with your values when it comes to choosing your lifework, or deciding to marry, or whether to have children. In making these decisions, there is one question to ask yourself that only you can answer: Are your heart and soul in it?

If we believe that life has a purpose, then it matters how we respond to unchosen and difficult circumstances and what we do with the talents and opportunities that are given us. I think that each of us is the protagonist in our own lifestory and that only we can know whether we have chosen a path that is true for us. When we are developing innate aptitudes and following intuitive feelings and dreams, or when there is a harmony between who we are inside and what we are doing, then heart and soul are also engaged. Regardless of the hours involved, or the remuneration, or the recognition, the most crucial question is: Do you love what you do?

Prior to the women's movement, many careers were off limits to women. Women were routinely barred from advancement, and were paid less for doing the same work as men. It was assumed that normal women would be fulfilled by their traditional roles as wife and mother, and that dissatisfaction with these limitations was evidence of penis envy, or a masculinity complex. When discriminatory practices and stereotypes were successfully challenged and misanthropic psychological definitions were discredited, it became evident that not all women were fulfilled by being wives or mothers. Then, as the pendulum swung in the direction of careers, it also became clear that not every woman wanted a career. Generalities about what women wanted or were capable of could not be applied to all women as there were obvious individual differences. Even more perplexing, what an individual woman wanted for herself during one period or decade of her life could and often did change.

The diversity and range of qualities among normal women and within individual women called for a theory and an explanation both wide enough and deep enough to account for these differences. Drawing upon the concept of archetypes developed by C. G. Jung, and the images and character patterns of women as personified by the Greek goddesses, I wrote *Goddesses in Everywoman* (1984) as a new psychology of women. When women recognized themselves in these archetypes, there was an *aha!* reaction, a recognition of something symbolically, metaphorically true. When a particular archetype is active in an individual woman's psyche, then its fulfillment is deeply meaningful. Opportunity to express an archetypal predisposition in a personal way may exist or not, depending on circumstances and the particular culture in which a woman lives. When there is an archetypal depth to what one does, it is a path with heart. Then a woman can easily be totally absorbed in what she is doing, true to herself, and spiritually alive as she goes about doing whatever it is. In contrast, lacking such depth affinity between archetype and outer role, a woman may be a mother because she was biologically able to have a child and yet not be maternal. Or a woman may be able to go through graduate school and enter a profession because she applied her intelligence and did well, only to find no joy in the work, which is just a job and not a vocation. Or it may look as if she has a perfect marriage to others, but there may be a lack of emotional intimacy, passion, and any real closeness.

Everyone makes decisions about career, marriages, children, life-style—for even putting off making a choice is a decision. Each choice is a direction, a path taken. If the decision was based on pleasing others, or out of fear of what others might think, or to avoid anger or rejection, or living out the ambitions of a parent, and your heart is not in it, the journey is likely to be joyless.

A mid-life crisis of work, relationship, or health may then be symptomatic of an underlying falseness that comes from beginning on a path that was determined by the expectations of others, or living a life based on someone else's idea of what you should be doing, and the fear or guilt of doing other than what was expected. If so, such a crisis may finally allow or necessitate a course correction onto a path with heart.

There is a short myth about Procrustes and his bed that speaks to the cost of success: travelers on the road to Athens had to pass Procrustes and his bed. If they were too short, they were stretched, as on a medieval rack, until they fit. If they were too tall, or any part of them hung over an edge, that part was cut off until they fit. Athens is the metaphoric destination for anyone on the road to success. Along the way, conformity to expectations is part of the process. To make it to Athens, you may have to stretch some part of yourself to be an acceptable fit. Persona, academic achievement, social skills may come to fill the whole frame and one-sided development may result. Whatever does not fit the picture of what you are supposed to be is often cut off. If the particular road taken demanded that you cut yourself off from developing a natural talent, or rejecting a calling, or doing what was soul-satisfying, then the toll taken on the road to Athens was costly indeed.

There are many moments of choice, and moments of truth, that we come to on our journey. There are some now-or-never choices to make, and other opportunities or forks in the road that will come up again, in a different form but headed in a similar direction. Never before have so many women had access to as much education and opportunities in the first half of their adult lives or as many options to reinvent themselves in the second half of life. Or as many demands to be superwomen. Or as many economic snares based on their restricted earning power, which may keep them from freely following a path with heart, scaling back, changing careers, or dropping out to be a full-time mother.

The economics of choice are not just monetary, but spiritual and psychological as well. The principle I remember from an introductory college economics course that has great applicability to life choices is that *the true cost of anything is what you give up in order to have it*. Every woman with a career and a personal life knows of the day-to-day trade-offs. The larger picture grows out of those small choices as well as the major decisions that end up shaping who we become and ultimately what we did with the gift of life and the talents and opportunities that we had to make a difference, to live authentically, to be ourselves, and to put heart and soul into our commitments.

Jean Shinoda Bolen, M.D.

Acknowledgments

This book exists because the women authors felt that the topic was so crucial that they inserted writing time into their already full lives—time bought by getting up before dawn, recruiting babysitters, negotiating with partners, and giving up coveted weekend hours. Their unfailing enthusiasm, productivity, and friendship was a precious gift for which I am deeply grateful. The symposium that was the source of much of the content was supported by the Friends of Langley Porter and ably staffed by Debra Moore. The Chairman of the Department of Psychiatry, Craig Van Dyke, M.D., gave me the space to write and the courage to do it. Pamela Martin, M.D., Kyra Minninger, M.D., and Kim Norman, M.D., covered other departmental responsibilities to free me to work on the book writing and editing. Sherrill Brooks served as a valuable editorial consultant and Soyeun Choi did a great job on manuscript preparation, even changing "superman" to "superwoman" in the spell check.

The acquisitions editor at Jason Aronson, Catherine Monk, was a steady guide along the way and Cindy Hyden took over in the home stretch. Montana Katz, Ph.D., set the standard as editor for the series with her fine volume *The Gender Bias Prevention Book*.

Life experience and theory are woven together in the pages that follow; I am fortunate to have had a mother who challenged me to think independently and a sister who opened my eyes to survival issues in the macho world of business.

Finally, the real feminist is my husband, H. Benfer Kaltreider, M.D., who has supported my career and interest in women's issues from the beginning in so many ways; it is the relationship with him and with my adult children, Jeffrey and Leah, that has led me to encourage women to attempt the balancing act of career and family because the potential rewards are so satisfying.

CONTRIBUTORS

AnnJanette Alejano-Steele, Ph.D.	Assistant Professor, Metropolitan State College of Denver, CO, Departments of Psychology and Women's Studies
Dorothy Ford Bainton, M.D.	Professor of Pathology, University of California, San Francisco; Vice Chancellor for Academic Affairs
Jean Shinoda Bolen, M.D.	Clinical Professor of Psychiatry, UCSF; author; Jungian analyst
Marcia Canning, J.D.	University Counsel, Office of General Counsel, University of California
Kimberlie L. Cerrone, M.B.A.	Technology Law specialist, Gunderson, Dettmer Attorneys, Menlo Park, CA
Catherine L. Gilliss, R.N., D.N.S.	Professor and Chair, Family Health Care Nursing, School of Nursing, UCSF
Carolyn Gracie, M.D.	Associate Clinical Professor, Psychiatry, UCSF; clinical practice, Kentfield, CA
Mardy S. Ireland, Ph.D.	Graduate Faculty, Santa Clara University; author; candidate, Lacanian School for Psychoanalysis
Nancy B. Kaltreider, M.D.	Professor of Clinical Psychiatry, UCSF; Director, Program for Women
Pamela Martin, M.D.	Associate Clinical Professor, Psychiatry, UCSF; Associate Director of Medical Student Education

Contributors

Marlene Sockol Mills, M.D.	Assistant Clinical Professor, Psychiatry, UCSF; Board of Directors, RESOLVE
Lynn E. Ponton, M.D.	Professor of Clinical Psychiatry, UCSF; member, San Francisco Psychoanalytic Institute
Carole Sirulnick, Ph.D.	Assistant Clinical Professor, Psychiatry, UCSF; private practice, psychology, Mill Valley, CA
Anna M. Spielvogel, M.D., Ph.D.	Associate Clinical Professor of Psychiatry, UCSF; Jungian analyst
Amy A. Tyson, M.D.	Clinical Instructor, Psychiatry, UCSF; candidate, San Francisco Psychoanalytic Institute
Phyllis Tyson, Ph.D.	Associate Clinical Professor of Psychiatry, University of California, San Diego; Supervising Analyst, San Diego Psychoanalytic Institute and Society

1

"To Love and to Work": Balancing Priorities throughout the Life Cycle

NANCY B. KALTREIDER

"It would be easier to live with a greater clarity of ambition, to follow goals that beckon toward a single upward progression. But perhaps what women have to offer in the world today, in which men and women both must learn to deal with new orders of complexity and rapid change, lies in the very rejection of forced choices: work or home, strength or vulnerability, caring or competition, trust or questioning. Truth may not be so simple."

Mary Catherine Bateson (1990, p. 233)

INTRODUCTION

A century ago, Freud was asked what was essential for a fulfilling life. His reply was deceptively simple: "to love and to work." Simple, perhaps, because Freud addressed his dichotomous thinking mostly toward the lives of men while women generally found relationships and work intermingled within the home. Today, women who were profoundly shaped by their psyches and gender role socialization for the work of home and hearth are now free to reach their full intellectual capacity in the professions and the corporate workplace. We are mostly doing that by trying to accommodate our overly full lives to include these new priorities without giving up any of the old ones that still are embedded within our biological and social drives. It is the tension among these competing systems that informs our choices. Women now find that "to love and to work" is an incredibly challenging task for which there are few generational role models. This book is a broad guide to this terrain, using the framework of women's developmental sequence to explore many arenas in more depth. Ultimately, it is the interplay among these zones of self-concept, external work environment, and family context that must be understood in order to design new life plans that are flexible, humane, and authentically feminine.

3

As one of four women entering Harvard Medical School in the Class of 1964, I began my professional career when the first rumblings of feminist social change were beginning to stir deep within the belly of society. Many years later, I feel compelled to share my perspectives on finding the balance as I see the expanded opportunities for professional women potentially creating unbearable expectations, harsh self-evaluations, and competition among urgent priorities. Pushed to the wall, women have developed several innovative solutions in an attempt to resolve these conflicts, each with merit for some but not for all.

For some extraordinarily gifted and energetic women, it is possible simply to "try harder," to adopt a superwoman strategy that diminishes the tension by willfully rising above it, somehow keeping all the balls in the air at once. Personally, however, after admiring the elegance and power of the Olympic rowers, I returned to my own sculling on the bay expecting to be magically transported into their league by my observations; chagrined, I found that my novice rowing skills were unchanged and somehow diminished by their standard of excellence. The superwoman strategy is possible for the elite, but using the gold medalist's form as a goal only increases the tension for most of us.

Another solution to the inherent tension between gender role expectations and the workplace is to "do it like a man." Self-help books enthusiastically guide women on how to talk tough, not blink in a confrontation, and dress for success. Much as the most felicitous travelers adapt themselves to a foreign culture, some women have been able to blend almost seamlessly into the system; their bright faces tantalize us from the pages of *Fortune* magazine. This solution to the tension is effective for women whose socialization and biological temperament are compatible with the choice of "hard ball," but many of the women who have successfully used this strategy to resolutely climb the corporate or academic ladders are now coming into my psychotherapy office complaining of a curious emptiness at their core as they play out their inauthentic roles.

A group of strikingly pragmatic women survey the path ahead early and decide that it is simply too steep to ascend with so much baggage so they jettison part of the load. Chapter 6 author Mardy Ireland talks about the choice not to have children and Pamela Martin in Chapter 9 discusses working part-time. This is a good resolution of the tensions for those flexible women who are not as internally driven by the need to excel in all rings of the circus at once.

4

As women turn off on these divergent paths, there remains a substantial group of us who really do want it all, who reject the forced choices yet intermittently find the totality overwhelming. We are the ones who can learn from an understanding of the rhythm of women's psychological development that allows us to sequence the most prioritized roles, gradually incorporating them all into a rich tapestry of life. The central premise of this chapter and the book it introduces is that it is necessary for women and the partners who love them to know about the essential issues of feminine internal psychological development, the external work environment, and the issues of building relational ties into a family. With that knowledge base, we then need to move up to the next level of integration to see the overview, the interplay and tension among these spheres, in order to chose authentic solutions that are synchronous with the life cycle of women.

Now is the time to consider the design of the new social ecology proposed by Bateson (1990). Recognizing the inherent discontinuities that childbearing brings to women's lives, she applauds the creative potential of interrupted and conflicted lives. "Each of us has worked by improvisation, discovering the shape of our creation along the way, rather than pursuing a vision already defined" (p. 1). "Composing a life," she states later, "involves an openness to possibilities and the capacity to put them together in a way that is structurally sound" (p. 63). As the lifetime work history universally becomes more fluid, the female experience of multiple fresh starts can turn our well-honed chameleon skills into a learning resource for both men and women.

We are molded by the past, and the experience of being a daughter is profoundly different from that of being a son. Yet however much the childhood development discussed in Phyllis Tyson's Chapter 2 prefigures the palette of adulthood, the issues are then reworked repetitively in an interaction with work and family. Many of the chapter authors are psychotherapists and their perspective is drawn from the daily experience of work with professional women; over and over, these women patients' reactions suggest that their current path is understandable only in relation to early experiences affecting self-concept and gender role.

Yet the path chosen is not simply an internal decision but involves an interaction with others along the way, including a society in which gender equality, at work or home, has not been achieved. Explanations for the continuing inequity have varied (Apter 1993, Bateson 1990), ranging from male power in a society that supports male interests to psychological issues that lead women to allow men to have their way and to accept messages of disdain and derogation or to choose different goals and other means of achieving them. As long as the successful woman in the workplace is still regarded as the exception, the concept of inherent group inferiority will be maintained. Bateson comments, "Every failure is more costly if it is accompanied by the implied message from outside, and the hidden belief within, that little more could have been expected" (p. 37).

Much of this chapter is written from the perspective of white heterosexual women who marry and have children because this is still the most frequent path. The conflicts and the choices are altered by being a minority, lesbian or bisexual, single or divorced, or chronically ill. For many readers an essential aspect of their lives both at home and in the workplace is ignored and I regret that; the book would have been strengthened by adding the voices of diversity. Yet being a woman brings a commonality of experience that is relevant to all those in the balancing act and this book is written to try to mine that richness.

Throughout the book we follow the standard established by M. Katz (1996, p. 22) that *professional* implies a requirement of substantial postsecondary education in preparation for work, and *sex* describes the biological role that one is born with. *Gender* is used to describe the social role acquired after birth. I plan first to review how the tensions are created through the contextual issues of psychological development and career theory as applied to women and then to apply that information to the sequencing of dilemmas that unfold across the life cycle. Armed with a microscopic view of each area, I then switch back to see how the issues might be resolved by constructing a life that accepts the rhythms and key themes in women's development.

THE PSYCHOLOGICAL CONTEXT

Life-Cycle Theories

It is important from the outset to think of women's lives not in terms of how they differ from the expectable male path but rather in terms of how they are novel in design. The first major theorist of psychosocial development across the life span was Erik Erikson (1950). He described eight universal stages of individuation but also noted that one's gender determined a unique quality of experience as well as differences in the underlying psychological organization. So it is crucial in the understanding of women to think about gender "in terms of the experience of what one *is* and *has*—not just the experience of what one isn't and hasn't" (Mayer 1996, p. 241).

Levinson and colleagues (1978) expanded the stair-step approach to adult development and extrapolated their studies (initially just of men) into a generic theory. In a book appropriately titled *The Seasons of a Man's Life*, they proposed that the transition from one stage to another is maturational, that is, biological. They identified a set of universal tasks or themes, and viewed adulthood as a series of age-linked stages that alternate between stability and transition. Early adult transition involves separating from one's childhood and exploring the world of adulthood, including formulating a dream. The "Age 30 Transition" is about finding a niche in the adult world and settling down. The "Mid-Life Transition" is about creating balance in life.

So, from Erikson to Levinson and colleagues, development was seen as a process of separating oneself out from the matrix of others, "becoming one's own man," in Levinson's term (p. 9). Yet women's progression seems less orderly with life's tasks and challenges woven inextricably together. They are as interested in maintaining valued connections with others by being an effective nurturer as in individuation based on their own personal achievements.

Development in Relationship

Feminist theory suggests that women's adult lives are different because their journey to adulthood was different. Jordan and Surrey (1986) propose that girls proceed by relationship differentiation rather than through the autonomous individuation emphasized by Erikson and Levinson. In this context, girls and women develop more sophisticated and elaborated knowledge of themselves and others, not by separating but through the pattern of their relationships. The work of Jean Baker Miller (1984) and others at the Stone Center of Wellesley College has emphasized that the girl's sense of self-esteem is based on feeling that she is a part of relationships and is taking care of the relationships. The girl and woman often feel a sense of effectiveness arising out of emotional connections and bound up with and feeding back into relationships. This does not lead to a completely separate sense of self but rather to a more complex sense of self. From this developmental base, women would be expected to show more comfort with closeness, interdependence, and emotion than with separation, independence, and self-aggrandizement.

The sense of opening and possibility evoked by the women-in-relationship theory has been balanced by the realization that girls' adolescence can be a time of limitation and foreclosure, as proposed by Gilligan (1982) and summarized by Terri Apter (1993) in *Working Women Don't Have Wives*. Struck by the behavioral observations of parents and teachers, the researchers tracked the break between the exuberant voices of 9-year-old girls and the carefully regulated self-presentation of adolescent girls whose self-assurance goes underground in conformity to the social realities that inform their relationships. The cost of this choice is a plummeting in self-esteem, self-confidence, and achievement. Now they explain away their successes by saying that the exam was easy or that they were lucky, being exquisitely careful not to offend. At this age, boys are more likely to say that they did well because they are clever or able, beginning the task of building a sense of self-worth and entitlement that will inform future career negotiations. It is as if the usual construction of a feminine sense of identity goes counter to all the leadership skills and intellectual competence necessary for success in the hierarchical workplace environment of the last fifty years.

These issues emerge even in the creative process. Virginia Woolf (1942) describes experiencing a constraint as she began to write based upon her internal model of the social desirability of being the sweetly accommodating, selfless, feminine servant who brightens the homes of men and is forever at their bidding. In a metaphor describing her deliberate determination, Ms. Woolf turns upon the internalized self-critic and kills her. More recently, feminist authors have described their strategies for preserving a confident sense of the self-as-achieving-and-powerful in their adolescent daughters being raised in the current social milieu (Pipher 1995). I expect that there are few professional women reading this book who did not learn early the lessons of disguising the brainy side of the self to maintain social approval as well as stifling more imaginative thinking to maintain credibility in the logic-based academic system. The cost of this relationship-based value system is a sense of alienation from one's accomplishments and a perception that only ob-jective approaches to problem solving are to be valued (Belenky et al. 1986).

Dissonance in Communication Patterns

Debra Tannen has been an acute observer of the way in which the psy-chological and social bases of the development of women's language patterns affect their adult interactions. In "The Power of Talk" (1995), she describes how girls tend to play with a single best friend or in small groups, and that they spend a lot of time talking. They learn to downplay ways in which one is better than the others and to empha-size ways in which they are all the same. A group of girls will ostracize a girl who calls attention to her own superiority and criticize her as "she thinks she's something"; a girl who tells others what to do is called "bossy." Boys tend to play very differently. Boys with high status in the group are expected to emphasize rather than downplay their ascendency. Boys learn to use language to negotiate their hierarchical role in the group by displaying their knowledge and ability and by challenging others. Thus, for women, the skills of negotiation, entre-preneurship, and leadership must be learned as adults because they are not an inherent part of our developmental experience. Guidelines for skill building in these areas are specifically addressed in Chapters 10, 11, and 12.

Tannen goes on to talk about her eavesdropping in the workplace, where she found that men say "I" in situations in which women say "we." Women are more likely to believe that if they blow their own horn, they won't be liked—by self or other. When ideas are generated and work is accomplished in the privacy of the team, the outcome is often associated with the person most vocal about reporting the results. Studies show that women are more likely to downplay their certainty and men are more likely to minimize their doubts. Women ask more questions and men often perceive this as related to not knowing. Women also tend to say "I'm sorry" as a ritualized way of expressing concern and establishing rapport. It's common to observe women who partici-pate actively in one-on-one discussions or in all-female groups but who are seldom heard in meetings with a large proportion of men.

Often in women's groups or with a therapist/patient gender match, even with individual variations in style, there is the sense of a shared intuitive understanding based on a common meaning structure. Outside the home, however, women exist in a world still largely controlled and designed by men, and this interface can be unnerving. M. Katz (1996) talks about the "gaslight effect" in which there is the "disconcerting feeling that one's own perceptions of life, one's observations of facts and events, even simple ones, are subject to doubt and are probably false" (p. 1). When reading this, I laughed out loud remembering a vivid incident of dissonance in my own life.

I was staying in our small cabin on the edge of the sand dunes on the northern California coast. Drawn to the window by the prospect of sunset, I discovered that a campfire had ignited the nearby dunegrass, which was blazing fiercely. I ran to the phone to tell the village fire department of this serious threat. "Are you sure?" a skeptical male voice interrogated. "Yes, I can see it out the window right now," I answered. "Well, put your husband on the phone!" A feminist dilemma. Given the choice between pride and the destruction of our beloved cabin, I got my husband, who reassured him that there really was a fire. The engines arrived promptly.

Here exactly is the issue. As I have done so often in my professional environment, I was complicit in maintaining the bias. Perhaps recalling the lessons of my youth about the superior importance of men, I gave way. In doing so I avoided the possibility of further ridicule or an angry confrontation. The desired outcome of cabin safety was achieved at the cost of my own sense of personal integrity. By opting to protect the preciousness of the cabin that had contained our "family fun" for years, I gave up any illusory power and status that I had expected in the male bastion of firefighters. An understanding of the psychological development of women suggests my choice was highly overdetermined.

The Undulating Path

At the memorial colloquium for Erik Erikson in San Francisco, Elizabeth Mayer (1996) commented, "I recall being especially impressed by Erikson's describing, some time in 1974, how he regretted the early publication of his work on the life cycle, in which he had portrayed the eight stages of life as a linear sequence. Had he (he said) talked more to (his wife) Joan about it early on, he'd have understood what she'd shown him later, when she transformed his eight-stage system into a weaving" (p. 243). In this changing world there is a highly variable interweaving and sequencing of roles; at age 40 a woman can be a grandmother or a new mother, a law firm partner or a law school entrant. Even with an emphasis on relationship and parenthood, a man tends to follow Levinson and colleagues' (1978) incremental stairsteps while a woman's path will be substantially influenced by her reproductive choices. Women will more often interweave several tasks together, with issues of identity, generativity, and intimacy revisited several times. An early understanding of these possibilities can help young adult women to form "five-year plans" of relative emphasis rather than try to assume the mantle of superwoman or the impatient timetable of their male peers.

THE CAREER CONTEXT

Women's Career Experience

How and why are women's careers different from men's? Gutek and Larwood (1989) propose a plausible set of assumptions: there are differential expectations for men and women regarding the appropriateness of jobs for each sex. Husbands and wives are differentially willing to accommodate themselves to each other's careers. The parent role is defined differentially for men and women. Women are faced with more constraints in the workplace, including discrimination and various stereotypes.

From the cost/benefit perspective, the economist Victor Fuchs (1988) suggests that the economic disparity between men and women stems from the conflict between work and family rather than from career investment patterns. The key to female underutilization is the cost to women of combining work and family, a cost not borne equally by men. Astin (1984) says that the basic work motivation is the same for men and women but that they ultimately make different work choices because of the influence of their early socialization experiences and the different limitations on career opportunities. Women's occupational behavior will be comprehensible only when it is viewed from the human development paradigm that emphasizes process, comprehensiveness, and a life course perspective (Perun and Belby 1981).

Family and Career

Once again, the issues are about the interdependence of these two roles for women. Writing in the Gutek and Larwood (1987) text, Valdez and Gutek pose the key question of whether family roles are a help or hindrance for working women. The theoretical choice is viewing the experience from the point of view of role conflict versus role accumulation, in which the costs of the interface tension are overridden by the benefits of having multiple roles that can protect against failure by providing multiple sources of self-esteem. Although there is substantial evidence for both theories, Krener (1994) notes in her review that women seem to prefer the role conflict approach in their analyses. Perhaps in an attempt to simplify the quandaries in these complexly interactive roles, women tend to emphasize dichotomous issues that could presumably be fixed by social reengineering. For example, Bickel (1988) identified the lack of formal program mechanisms for accommodating to childbearing and -rearing as turning these life events into stressful disruptions for young professional parents. Levinson and her colleagues (1989) indicate that both women and men resolutely believe that childbearing and child-rearing slow women's careers. In their study, 67 percent of women holding full-time faculty appointments in departments of medicine said they thought their careers had been slowed by childbearing, although their median length of maternity leave was only six weeks and 86 percent later returned to at least a 52-hour work week. Rather than measuring changes by time apportionment, perhaps these women were describing a shift in priorities toward nurturing that undercut the competitive edge necessary for advancement in the workplace.

In Braun and Susman's (1992) study, women physicians accurately predicted what their women medical colleagues would say about their pregnancy leave, but overestimated the extent of men's negative responses and underestimated their male peers' willingness to provide special consideration for pregnant colleagues. Cole and Zuckerman (1987) showed in their study that marriage and children did not hamper long-term scientific productivity. The strategies of the productive women scientists they interviewed included regulating the number of roles held simultaneously, compartmentalizing their lives, sacrificing discretionary time for leisure pursuits, and choosing institutional work settings with regular work hours. It is important to note that the successful women developed their own unique style of coping, emphasizing boundaries rather than choosing an expansionist superwoman philosophy.

The Work Environment

No matter what the experience of role conflict and accumulation, the workplace itself can be a daunting environment for women. This is most obvious when there is palpable gender harassment and discrimination. Chapter 13 reviews strategies for coping with such difficult situations. On an everyday basis, the woman's experience at work is more commonly the accumulation of "microinequities" as she has to prove that she "belongs" over and over. This experience is even heightened if she is also a visible minority who doesn't look like the expectable professional. Whether one is asked to bring the bedpan or to run the elevator, the subtext is clear.

Writing a piece on "Scenarios for Success," Janet Bickel (1995a) gives a categorization of microinequities based on her experience in the American Association of Medical Colleges. They include *supportive discouragement*: a department chair advises a new faculty member, "You are such an excellent clinician and teacher, you belong on the clinical track" (without exploring with her possible research interests or the tenure track option); *radiant devaluation*: a surgery resident says to a medical student, "You're much too pretty to become a surgeon"; *friendly harassment*: the department chair phones a faculty member at home two weeks after delivery of a child and opens the conversation, "So I've caught you at home goofing off." If she simply ignores the remark, she invites further similar challenges. If she reveals any anger, she is open to accusal of overreacting or of not being able to take a joke. If she is able to respond with a humorous retort, she may be able to educate him about the inappropriateness of his comment; however, sufficient comfort with confrontation to attain this level of spontaneity is an unattainable feat for most women, especially ones who are two weeks postpartum.

Another issue that clouds the workplace is encapsulated in Judith Rosener's (1995) concept of "sex role spillover." She describes this phenomenon as gender role expectations from early childhood that reappear at work as men being expected to control and women to provide service and support. During a time when the models and expectations are in fact changing, there is a good deal of role confusion. Bronstein and colleagues (1989) report a study comparing male and female job applicants for academic psychology positions. For men, having a family was presented as an asset: "His lovely wife and two children are an additional bonus for a department that has any kind of social life (p. 122)"; for a woman it was presented as a burden: "As one might expect from a woman who has returned to graduate school after taking several years off to raise young children . . . (p. 123)." Although women in the sample were at least as well qualified as the men, they tended to obtain jobs with lower status and at lower prestige institutions. The prestige of the first job in academia clearly affects all subsequent positions.

A third factor in the working environment is critical mass. As a member of the class of 1964 at Harvard Medical School, I went through all my training experiences with women being less than 10 percent of my peers. I could enter no classroom unobserved, and the likelihood of my being spontaneously questioned by the professor was substantially greater than 10 percent. My choice of an early marriage to a classmate was viewed as letting down all aspiring women and one professor said, "Well, you got what you came for, so now you can leave." Further along in a well-established academic career, I was asked to be the first woman on the departmental executive committee. There I often found myself uncharacteristically silent or unheard when I spoke. Two years later, when two additional women faculty joined the committee, my voice returned because now I could be heard for my particular point of view rather than "as a woman." It finally became clear to me that substantial representation beyond the level of tokenism is an essential ingredient in making the workplace welcoming and supportive for women and minorities.

A Glass Ceiling?

Recently, the Catalyst research organization stated that women hold just about 2 percent of the power positions in corporate America, no matter how they are defined—by title, by paycheck, or by responsibility for the bottom line (Carlson 1996). Although women are entering medical school in higher numbers than in the past, they advance more slowly and do not attain positions of power and leadership in the field in numbers equal to men (Bickel 1988). In a similar report, the U.S. Glass Ceiling Commission (1995) defined the glass ceiling as artificial barriers based on attitudes and organizational bias that prevent qualified individuals from advancing into management-level positions.

However, in a later paper, Bickel (1995) went on to say that the external focus suggested by the term *glass ceiling* is not sufficient in understanding why more women are not advancing into policy-making and leadership positions. "Ceiling" implies that the powers-that-be are deliberately limiting the number of women moving ahead. In reality, many deans and department chairs are concerned about the paucity of women candidates for top positions. The psychological perceptions and differing priorities of women themselves do play a role in their flattened career paths. It is important to consider whether women are cognitively and emotionally liable to limit their own career choices. As discussed in the earlier section on psychological context, women are acculturated to avoid self-promotion. A woman researcher may defer principal investigator status on grants or consciously put her student's name ahead of her own with negative personal consequences despite the altruistic intent. At any point on the career ladder, women may find the struggle for career advancement no longer worth the price and choose to opt for a more flexible but less prestigious role.

Often women lack the guidance about how to succeed at the senior level. In Chapter 14 on "Senior Management," Dorothy Ford Bainton, Academic Vice Chancellor at UCSF, offers a guide to the decisions and skills involved. She is modeling effective mentorship, which can be defined as *a supportive, growth-fostering relationship between an entering and established member of the system.* M. Katz (1996) notes, "Across professions the mentor–mentee relationship occurs at the point that one's professional development enters a new level of seriousness. It is also the moment when the system that has promised equity begins to break down. This relationship is already one based on power and authority. When one adds the male–female hierarchy to the picture, the situation becomes more complex" (p. 193). In cross-gender mentorships there is often a sexual tension that is usually unacknowledged. Clearly, a woman mentor is ideal as a role model, but she may be overwhelmingly busy or carry gender-stereotypic views herself. The most important issue is that unmentored professionals are unlikely to be able to think strategically about their career path.

Here responsibility should move from the individual to the structure. Unless the workplace shifts toward accommodating the reproductive and family needs of all of their employees, there is little likelihood that the majority of women professionals will reach their full employment potential. Guidance through the expectable steps by a network of mentors is to be expected by any professional to whom a serious commitment has been made.

THE DEVELOPMENTAL CONTEXT

Starting Off

Having surveyed the psychosocial and workplace influences on the work/family interface, the question remains of how it plays out upon the stage of adult development. In interviewing young women applicants for medical school, I am struck by their easy confidence that they can indeed have the whole bowl of cherries. Similarly, Arlie Hochschild (1989) describes the findings of a 1985–1986 survey of women undergraduates at Berkeley done by Anne Machung. Over 80 percent of senior women felt that it was "very important" to have a career. At the same time, 80 percent of the seniors said they definitely planned to marry and have two or three children. They applauded new opportunities at work but seemed vague and disorganized when asked about their plans for managing a home life. M. Katz (1996) believes that young women in the '80s began to feel that gender issues had been resolved. In the conservative backlash, the label "feminist" became something to disavow. As a result, we have a generation of young potential superwomen planning to embark on professional careers while starting a family and maintaining avocations, and they haven't a clue about the realistic obstacles they would face. AnnJanette Alejano-Steele describes the painful choices to be made at the threshold of a career in Chapter 3.

The sustaining of the dream of combining profession and family is complicated because girls have grown up surrounded by models of successful men in the world but with little access to similar stories of women. Perhaps they were glad for their nurturing by home-bound mothers, but these young women are also sensitive about the personal cost in restricted opportunities to their mothers. For most women, moving ahead to profession and family means going beyond one's mother, always treacherous ground from a psychological perspective. A sense of certainty about direction is hard to obtain without models to build from. The experience of a woman who sought psychotherapy from me encapsulates some of the issues. Like all the patient vignettes in this chapter, "Elena" is a composite patient based on recurring themes in my practice.

> Elena is a successful mid-level advertising executive from a close-knit Greek-American family. Her homemaker mother lived "for the children" and her father presented a heroic public image as an attorney/politician while privately terrorizing his family with verbal abuse and alcoholic rages. Elena is bright and artistically talented, but limited her career choices to her home city where she remained in her parents' house, acting as intermediary in their stormy relationship. Eventually an outstanding career opportunity opened up in her firm's central headquarters in New York. At her mother's urging she accepted the position and began the exciting task of forging her own identity in Manhattan. In their daily phone contacts, the mother began to complain of fatigue and shortness of breath but made light of it. There was little preparation for the late-night phone call from the emergency room where Elena's mother was dying from a massive heart attack precipitated during a particularly intense argument with her father. Elena returned home frozen in her grief and racked by guilt for abandoning her mother in order to seek a fuller life. All too quickly, she found herself engaged to her father's junior associate and planning to leave her job to prepare for the wedding. After experiencing her first panic attack, she presented for psychotherapy because "I don't know who I am supposed to be."

Elena had grown up with the familial and cultural model of woman as selfless servant, living to fill others' needs. Leaving home and developing her own voice took courage, but also meant giving up her sense of omnipotent responsibility for her parents. To Elena, the mother's untimely death was as if she had killed her by abandonment and also a punishment to herself for breaking the family rules. She experienced a strong restitutive pull to be a "good girl" and to replay her mother's

17

life script. It was helpful to Elena in therapy to look at how her mother had felt trapped by her own restrictive life choices and would have been happy to see her daughter enjoying a fuller life balancing career with relationship.

Clearly, women's career choices require not only ability and opportunity but also a self-perception as entitled and committed. Terri Apter (1993) hits this question head-on. She found that although there was a reasonable correlation between a man's IQ and his adult accomplishments, there was no such correlation between women's intelligence and their achievements. The question is why so many women fail: why they fail to reach their full potential, why they fail to hold on to their dreams in the face of adversity. Apter comments, "The real tragedy is not thwarted ambition but the failure to develop ambition" (p. 167). When the class of 1975 at Harvard Business School was studied longitudinally (the first class to reach 10 percent women), they had not thrived as much as expected in the business world. The dean explained that the school had not been able to assess the women applicants' drive, but only their ability. Here is the familiar expectation of "do it like a man" without an acknowledgment of the complex interplay of factors involved.

In my psychotherapy practice I have found that some young professional women may present with a powerful, nearly omnipotent sense of the self as able to do almost anything. Their exuberance is like that of a toddler, intoxicated with locomotion, feeling that no bounds can contain her. They have added a world of limitless career possibilities without anticipating any alterations in the family or relationship path. Like the ancient deities, they feel that they can carry the full potential of both sexes. Inevitably this perception collides with an inhospitable workplace, a biological limitation, or a limiting relationship and an agonizing reassessment is often the result.

> Mary is a nationally prominent molecular biologist who sought psychotherapy because of self-doubts precipitated by a disintegrating marriage. She grew up in a sleepy Ohio town in a family that was unsure how to contain her abundant energies and talents. Although she was offered a full scholarship to Yale, her family prevailed upon her to attend the nearby campus of Ohio State. Graduating summa cum laude with a double major in mathematics and chemistry, she finally felt

18

that she could accomplish anything that she wanted. Her East Coast graduate career was meteoric under the mentorship of an assistant professor whom she eventually married. Their relationship was one of shared intellectual excitement and he was dismayed when, on her thirty-fifth birthday, she announced that she wanted to have a child. Mary's subsequent secret cessation of birth control did not lead to the anticipated pregnancy and she feared infertility. She wondered if the infertility was a message that she would be an unfit mother or had gotten her hormones out of balance by pursuing male roles. Her conflict about her female identity was symbolized when she found that her "favor" at the formal dinner honoring the inductees to a prestigious national science honorary society was a golden football. "Maybe I do want too much," Mary mused in therapy, "but there's never been anything I couldn't do if I tried hard enough."

Much like Mary, women in their twenties and thirties are mostly thinking about possibilities, not limits. Yet this is the time of tough choices and the narrowing job market is making them even tougher. A relationship makes life much more fun, but it soon raises troubling issues of job geographic mobility and the division of domestic labor. As M. Katz (1996) notes, a relationship often means that the woman will be expected to assume the role of social director and facilitator of communication. The extension of this is Arlie Hochschild's (1989) concept of marriage as the notorious second shift, where domestic chores become the role without recompense for the woman even if she is bringing home a substantial portion of the couple's income. Hochschild quotes a survey by Catalyst that found that half of the women plan to put their husband's job first and two-thirds of the men say they planned to put their own job first. For those in the front-loaded professions that require years of preparation, decisions about whether to start a family come too soon when the career is insecurely established and the hoops to jump through still lie ahead: attain tenure, make partner, pass the Boards, get a license, get the business in the black, be promoted. Challenging discussions about how career and family priorities will be negotiated need to occur between partners before final commitment to a dual-career relationship. This continual renegotiation of the daily juggling act in a two-career relationship is described in more depth in Chapter 7.

Mid-Career and Sinking . . .

Cornered by the increased demands of a profession and the inexorable reality of the critical periods for reproduction, the career woman finds that the pace is picking up and the work/family paths diverging. Although her professional self-esteem may be rock solid, she may still be uneasy about her capacity to mother. M. Katz (1996) describes how a professional woman must decide whether to have children and then when to have children. If she lets it be known that she wants children, her work colleagues may think less of her commitment and career future. If she does not want children, she may still find herself treated as if she is on the verge of having them. The early demands in law and medicine careers make it logical to postpone these decisions until a time when both relationship and pregnancy may be harder to attain. If she moves ahead to take on the full family juggling act, she may return to diminished status or a dead-end Mommy track at work. Apter (1993) points out that the Zoe Baird career story is grounded in a husband's relocation, in crippling difficulties with childcare, and in the hostile response to a working mother's desperate solution. Think of the legal potential lost to this country because there were no support systems in place to allow her to more flexibly balance career and family. At the point of insurmountable frustration, women are apt to change course suddenly as they once again cast about to find a balanced life or come up short against unacceptable compromises.

Until recently, most serious professional women either stayed or became single and that still remains a reasonable alternative. Denmark (1992) details that today's women are marrying at a later age, that many more marriages end in divorce, and that more women are expected to stay single for their entire lives. There is a growing awareness among women that they can no longer afford to plan on economic dependence on men because it is quite likely that at some point in their lives they will be single. Once again, the emotional impact of these choices and their consequences is strongly influenced by earlier experiences.

Alison sought psychotherapy at age 42 because she felt increasingly desperate about finding a relationship that could contain her vague dreams of a family. When she was in early adolescence, her father abruptly left the marriage and her mother struggled to make ends meet as the school librarian. The father told his daughters that their mother was a "hysterical demanding bitch" and that he had been involved in an affair with his caretaking secretary for several years. Alison learned to be pleasing and was cited in her high school yearbook as "always has a smile on her face." She was fearful of financial dependence and chose a lucrative financial analyst career in a stock brokerage. Attractive and vivacious, she always had a "date" available, but her vigilant anticipation of rejection usually precipitated it. Staying single had allowed her unfettered career choices and a powerful sense that she alone controlled her future. Yet, like her sister who was in a traditional stay-at-home marriage, Alison found herself preoccupied with the road not taken.

Alison had designed her identity in reaction to the troubling parental roles during her adolescence. She developed a career that kept her from feeling financially trapped like her mother, but underneath she still longed for a man to care for her. When a potential suitor appeared, she acted pleasing (like the secretary) and hid her own needs. Then either her building resentment or a hint of his withdrawal precipitated her flight back to the perceived safety of autonomy. Although this may have been a good choice for her, it was far from a free choice. Psychotherapy can often be helpful in finding the right individual balance of work and family.

Another pathway explored in Marlene Mills's "For Whom the Clock Ticks" (Chapter 5) may involve relationship but becomes conflicted when the choice to postpone pregnancy masks infertility. Mikesell (1992) puts this in the perspective of the issues faced by a previously career-focused woman. The 30-something career woman has learned to take charge. Facing infertility shakes up this sense of control. Soon she finds herself planning a treatment procedure. She has come to expect it is her right to have a child by whatever means is available to her. Within the couple's relationship, she is often the expressor of the sadness of the monthly letdown when her period comes. The husband believes it is his role to support her and not to increase her burden. Caught up in the escalating promises of improved technology, both physician and patient find it hard to acknowledge failure or to balance the substantial personal and financial costs against the statistical likelihood of a term pregnancy resulting. There is often considerable relationship stress related to this period of nonconception. Sometimes only a good friend or therapist can help the woman see that there is a limit to what any individual can expend on any given pursuit, including children.

The accounting of the gains and losses in childbearing reconciles differently for each woman. In Chapter 6 on "Constructing a Feminine Identity without Motherhood," Mardy Ireland adds a perspective on the woman who is childless either because of an ambivalently delayed choice, biological limitation, or the perception that other choices are simply more valuable. Her work deepens Erikson's (1950) view that generativity not only refers to parenting but also includes a vital interest in establishing and guiding the oncoming generation and the world that they will enter.

Chapter 4 on "Pregnancy and the Professional Woman" by Amy Tyson gives an internal perspective on the shift in identity and priorities in that process. Felice Schwartz (1992), writing in *Breaking with Tradition: Women, Work and the New Facts of Life*, adds a lucid view of the external workplace realities that clash with the process of bonding to the potential child. She suggests that women often join their employers in denying the impact of maternity, knowing that it would be career suicide to do otherwise. They struggle to conform to the baby-free image that is required for career success, whether it means forgoing motherhood altogether, choosing their concealing maternity dresses with great care, or truncating their parental leave allotments so as to make a rapid-fire return to the office. When the time comes that they must discuss their physical condition with their supervisors, some women feel apprehensive, embarrassed, even apologetic about what should be one of the most joyous events of their lives.

Schwartz goes on to indicate that the reality is that almost any new mother needs a significant amount of time to make the adjustment to parenthood and then to make the transition back to her job, now combined with parenting responsibilities. The truth is that no matter how conscientious, no matter how career-committed, a woman is, she can never know for certain what she'll do until she has given birth and experiences her desire to be with the baby. Given the challenge and restriction of part-time opportunities, many new mothers decide to stay home with the child, even if it involves great financial sacrifice. They make that decision only after they have given birth, long after they have begun their leave.

When it is time to return to work, a typical new mother may welcome the stimulation of her job after six weeks of being at home with her baby. Still, like most new parents, she craves time with the infant who has stolen her heart. Usually her boss doesn't realize that her period of distraction will be finite and begins to think her commitment has fallen off. "She's not the same," he remarks to a peer and silently removes her from the fast-track trajectory in his mind.

Professional women are generally well-organized high-achievers, so when the pace picks up at work and home, the usual reaction is simply to work harder, not to set priorities or to accept a level of performance modified by the sum of what has to be accomplished. Even though they may consciously wish for help from a spouse, there is a psychological payoff in being omnicompetent. McWilliams (1992) perceptively applies this pattern to the role shifts necessary when a newborn arrives in the home. The woman's greater comfort with closeness and nurturance often leads her to act in an unanticipated way with her husband. When she finds herself initially better at comforting their child, she cannot tolerate it while her husband learns the skills of soothing as both father and child go through an initial period of discomfort. Many women are so relieved to have this area of patent superiority to men that they unwittingly spoil the possibility of a new level of cooperation between genders in the household.

Terri Apter (1993) picks up the superwoman theme by observing the need to give a great deal at home to prove that no one is being cheated because of her "double life." The superwoman syndrome allows men to be unchanged at home, and it allows women to support male career priorities unchanged. It provides psychological justification for women to have everything, because they earn it by doing everything. In order to accomplish this feat, awareness of needs and emotions has to be pushed out of consciousness. Consider the story of Juanita, whom I saw several years ago in psychotherapy:

> Juanita was a 37-year-old pediatrician who sought psychotherapy during her third pregnancy with a history suggesting chronic moderate depression. Although she was a third generation Californian, her Latino family of origin strongly embraced traditional gender roles. When her mother developed debilitating multiple sclerosis, Juanita stepped in to raise the younger children and to prepare meals. Her father, also a pe-

diatrician, did his part by working long hours to support the family. In college and medical school, Juanita returned home on the weekends to oversee the domestic chores and to cook special dishes for the father. She married a research scientist whose "cutting edge" work demanded long hours in the laboratory. She was sensitive to his professional stresses and encouraged him to attend frequent international meetings to present his work. In addition to her busy pediatric practice, she volunteered in a clinic for battered children. Returning home around 7 P.M., she would try to spend several hours of "quality time" with her children even if it meant getting up at 4 A.M. to catch up with her charting. She had steady household help but frequently ended up providing support and counseling for them and their families. As her mother's health deteriorated, the frequency of her phone calls increased. An unplanned third pregnancy was the "last straw" that allowed Juanita to seek help so that "I can learn to be a more cheerful mom." Exploration in psychotherapy revealed both guilt that she was fulfilling each of her many roles imperfectly and anger at the absence of supports in her life. She struggled in therapy to learn to speak in an internal "good mother" voice to herself, encouraging the setting of more reasonable standards and seeking support without feeling defective.

A crucial concept for professional women (and men) is that self-care and self-esteem are very closely linked. As women cut back on their personal time for exercise, pleasure reading, hobbies, friends, and time alone, a growing sense of meaninglessness can emerge in their other-directed lives. The focus on getting to the bottom of the list can cover a need to be busy to avoid looking at the emptiness of her marriage or inner life. In this peak time of home demands, if feasible, the choice to find part-time work may be necessary to allow one to savor the family relationships and to nourish the self while maintaining touch with professional competence. The cost of this choice in the workplace will be real until the structures become more flexible, but in Chapter 9, "Part-time Career, Full-Time Life," Pamela Martin suggests that many men and women have found the payoff well worth it as they lead less frenetic lives that make time for relationship and creativity.

Why has Mary Catherine Bateson's (1990) book on *Composing a Life* achieved almost cult status among women? Clearly it met a need for women to make sense out of the hectic juggling of their lives and to believe that balance and wisdom could be achieved over time. Bateson understands the deeply felt issues that are touched by every professional woman who is raising a family. "Conflict between motherhood and career came not from the macho hours demanded by ambition but from the challenge to provide direct and sustained caring in two different places. . . . My mother used to quote a line in a letter written by Harriet Beecher Stowe, in which she says that she is not getting on very well with her novel 'because the baby cries so much.' My mother's comment was that the reason the novel goes so slowly is not because the baby cries so much but because the baby smiles so much" (p. 168).

I learned a great deal from the professional women who crowded into the discussion groups on dual-career relationships and dual-career parenting that were part of our recent UCSF symposia. There, women in the midst of this mad balancing act seemed to find considerable relief in discovering that no one else felt that she had achieved a stable equilibrium. Both Chapter 7 by Kaltreider, Gracie, and Sirulnick and Chapter 8 by Lynn Ponton offer guidelines for navigating this turbulent period, but there is no way to make these dual loyalties easily satisfied. Against all odds, spouses need to work actively on providing nurture for each other as well as the children. Apter (1993) highlights the way in which parenting evokes deep conflicts in career women as the wish for self-fulfillment clashes with the need to create conditions in which others can thrive. Just when it seems that some equilibrium has been achieved, it is difficult to describe the impact of the birth of a second or third child who fills all the interstices of personal time and more.

I still remember my anguish when a psychotherapy hour with a surgery resident who was tearfully describing her suicidal thoughts for the first time was interrupted by an emergency phone call from home. My 12-year-old son, his bravado betrayed by the quaver in his voice, had just returned from school to find our home burglarized and ransacked. My husband was 3,000 miles away and there were no near neighbors. Somehow I calmed the patient and sent her out early with a promise to call me immediately if the suicidal drive became stronger. Then I raced across the Golden Gate Bridge to find my son sitting outside our home clutching his Swiss Army knife "just in case." By evening both situations were under control, but I felt that I had let everyone down by being insufficiently available. This is the emotional cost of the juggling act.

Looking at the stresses inherent in the double life led by an increasing number of women, it is obvious that the structure of both parenting and working needs to change. Bateson (1990) suggests that collaborative marriages, however productive and satisfying they may be, are constantly under renegotiation; women's lives are half independent and half contingent. In child care somebody's still got to be the mommy. "Women take up the slack, making the need invisible as we step in to fill it" (p. 140).

Mid-Life Shifts

Mid-life can be characterized as a period of surrendering illusions. A review of the roads taken and not taken and reflection on the future make it clear that the world is no longer one of infinite possibilities. Preparation for the second half of life may be a time for perceiving creative new directions, with a sense of continuing growth and the interconnectedness of generations. It may also be a period of awareness of vague physiologic changes, a growing sense of time limitation, with death no longer an abstraction and time now measured in years left to live rather than time since birth. Jung (1933) emphasized the concept of individuation: "The serious problems of life . . . are never fully solved. If it should for once appear that they are, this is the sign that something has been lost. The meaning and design of a problem seem not to lie in its resolution but in our working at it incessantly. This alone preserves us from stultification" (pp. 118–119).

Writing in *New Passages*, Gail Sheehy (1995) comments that there is a revolution in the life cycle. "Fifty is now what 40 used to be. . . . 'I don't know *how* to be fifty,'admitted an Oregon psychotherapist, 'but I do know I'm not going to be fifty like my mother'" (pp. 4–5).

Jung (1933) again captures the essence: "Wholly unprepared, [we] embark upon the second half of life. . . . [W]orse still, we take this step with the false assumption that our truths and ideals will serve us as hitherto. But we cannot live the afternoon of life according to the programme of life's morning: for what was great in the morning will be little at evening, and what in the morning was true will at evening have become a lie" (pp. 124–125).

26

Schwartz (1992) reminds us that the generation of women who are now well into mid-life were starting work in the years 1962–1977, the period she describes as "awakening and ambivalence." It was during this period that Catalyst, the research organization studying women in the workplace, published its first book entitled *How to Go to Work When Your Husband Is Against It, Your Children Aren't Old Enough, and There's Nothing You Can Do Anyhow* (Schwartz et al. 1972).

Much of the current work/family literature is written by women researching and living in the most stressful era of young children and high career demand. We need to pay more attention to the satisfactions of the forties and fifties when the richer relationship with maturing children is coupled with new energy and freedom to invest in a well-developed career. As men play an increased role in nurturing, they also will have more access to these later satisfactions, which may be a substantial balance to the mid-life crisis—but the ticket of admission is fuller participation in the daily drudgery of home and child management with all of the personal costs involved!

Notman and colleagues (1991) point out that an important mid-life change is the shift in perspective from the limitless future of the adolescent to the sense of the finiteness of life—in Neugarten's (1968) phrase, the orientation to "life left to live" (p. 149). Gender roles may become more fluid as men become more affiliative and tolerant of their dependent and passive needs and women become more expressive of their assertive and aggressive wishes. Kovacs (1992) describes this as a relaxing of structures, unleashing character plasticity and the prospect for making change. Belsky and Penshy (1988) back this up with research observations by Livson (1984) who studied a subsample of men and women who rated high in psychological health at age 50. Livson found two patterns, those who were highly congruent with expected sex role stereotypes and another type at sharp variance with the traditionals. These mid-life women who were determined "to love and to work" were ambitious, intellectual, and unconventional, freely using anger, relying on intellect to cope with the world. Later life offers more flexibility either to conform to gender stereotypes or not.

Menopause occurs in American women at an average age of 51. Sarrel (1991) quotes Isak Dinesen, one of whose characters proclaims, "'Women, . . . when they are old enough to have done with the business of being women, and can let loose their strength, must be the most powerful creatures in the whole world'" (1972, p. 119). In fact, Sarrel

(1991) found in the Yale Mid-Life Study that two-thirds of the mid-life women working outside the home stated at their initial interview that menopause symptoms had a moderate to severe effect on their capacity to function at work. The most common disruptive symptom was sleep disturbance, followed by hot flashes, anxiety, depression, and memory loss. However, these changes are temporary, generally responsive to hormone replacement therapy, and occur within the context of a shifting family constellation that may free up new time for creativity.

In literature, middle age in women is often connected with unseemly sexuality (think of Mrs. Robinson in *The Graduate*—the song lyrics say, "Every way you look at it, you lose."[1]). It is viewed as appropriate that a woman past the childbearing years would relinquish sexuality; a friend of mine ruefully remarked, "I told someone I was having an affair and he asked who was catering it." Consider Shakespeare's *Hamlet*: the sexual corruption and lack of judgment that make something rotten in the state of Denmark seem to emanate from a middle-aged woman. Gertrude has an "increase of appetite." Hamlet, furious at her too-rapid remarriage, says "Frailty, thy name is woman" (Shakespeare 1980, p. 887) and later confronts her in the bedroom scene: "You cannot call it love, for at your age the heyday in the blood is tame, it's humble and waits upon the judgement" (p. 906).

In the fifties, both body and mind remind us that we are not dealing with infinite resources. As Bateson (1990) describes, none of us is, after all, a superwoman. Increasingly we have to worry about conserving energy, caring for our bodies and minds rather than spending them carelessly.

The fight to get to the top may be more ambivalently viewed if a spouse is winding down. Apter (1993) describes that when women do rise to high places, they invite difficult and unpleasant challenges, so they have to be as tough as men to sustain their "privileges" over time. Many women who stuck out their careers through the most challenging domestic times are apt to opt for early retirement, deciding that the battle to survive in the alien atmosphere is no longer worth it. Apter quotes research by Judi Marshall, studying women in Britain, "Women

---

1. Reprinted from the song "Mrs. Robinson" by Paul Simon, copyright © 1968 by Paul Simon Music, and used by permission of the publisher.

managers hear a positive message—that of equal opportunities—undermined by a covert negative message—that of the repression of female values" (p. 218).

What's it like to be a senior woman? M. Katz (1996) captures some of the flavor: "A professional woman must be female but it shouldn't show. She needs to have exercised her femininity through child bearing and raising, but it cannot affect her on the job. She must work harder for less financial and other recompense than her male peers, she must be an obedient team player, and she must endure sexual harassment and sex discrimination with a smile, all to be told that she is a pawn in an affirmative action scheme that robs deserving white males of their professional rights" (p. 303). Isolation is an increasing factor because her peers consist of a sea of men. Every step up the ladder further removes her from the critical mass of her women peers and sets her up to be the token success story, the ever-available mother figure for all below her. M. Katz cites in the words of one law partner: "'I finally understood. And it was very hard to understand because I was part of the system, and to the end even despite these awful stories of great humiliation, I was still accepted by them as their woman partner. As their *exceptional* woman partner'" (p. 313).

Mentoring, earlier described from the viewpoint of the needs of the junior "mentee," can pose a conflict for the senior woman mentor. In many ways it seems like the essential generative task, yet it robs her of precious hours now available for a career focus, newly energized by freedom from parental duties. For example, in the very pyramidal system at UCSF, I am one of only a few senior women in the university available for this guidance and the need is far greater than I can fill. There is something about my femaleness that increases the expectation of infinite nurturance in both the person being mentored and myself.

At some point it gradually becomes clear that it is time to pass the baton, perhaps to return to the luxury of domesticity without pressure or to pursue a forgotten dream. It is here that the benefits of juggling multiple roles and identities over time are clearer as one reflects on the abundance of life experience and meaningful work achieved. In an echo of earlier life stages, the move toward older life will be smoothest when flexibility is still in place and there is a readiness to redesign the world yet again.

SUMMARY

In writing this chapter on balancing priorities throughout the life cycle, it gradually became clear to me that not as much positive change for women has occurred in the culture of home and workplace as one would have hoped from the sheer size of the social revolution. Society has much to learn from our feminine values and ability to function within a relational context. Instead, women are often co-opted by the traditional male assumptions as we struggle to speak in their voice and to work their hours. Too frequently we simply add in the expectations of career to the responsibilities of family without questioning why it's so difficult, even for superwomen. Socialized to make life easier for others, we avoid the negotiations necessary to make life easier for ourselves.

Understanding the developmental unfolding tells us that there is time for women to lead rich and full lives without trying to do it all at once. The early years of parenting are precious and should not be given away too cavalierly to meet corporate and academic demands. Women in mid-life bring a talent and energy to the professions that society cannot afford to ignore. However, the creative possibilities of a sequenced life are often stymied by the rigid stairsteps of the workplace.

This book and this chapter are not about how to survive your professional and relationship lives, but rather how to find meaning and pleasure in the combination—at least in your saner moments. This is not a trip to be taken without considerable forethought and as good a guide to the shifting terrain as you can find. "To love and to work" will always create periods of conflict and tension for women but, in hindsight, the journey seems worth the investment. In both the family and the workplace, our male peers and partners have something to learn from the essential humanness of this quest. Perhaps together we can find ways to make the road less daunting for the next generation.

2

The Influence of the Early Mother-Daughter Dynamic on Career Women

PHYLLIS TYSON

Many of the themes discussed in Chapter 1, "To Love and to Work," have their origin in early feminine psychological development, especially in the complexities of the mother–daughter relationship. Increased experience in working with professional women has helped clinicians to be more aware of the crucial developmental tasks that must be mastered in order for the adult woman to feel competent, valuable, effective, and able to function independently. A woman's willingness and ability to stand up for herself, to seek realistic goals, and to sustain criticism all begin in the mother–daughter interaction. Indeed, all women approach professional life with the template formed from early experiences with mothers, replayed in the next developmental stage of adolescence to finally emerge as the core concepts about self and others that the woman brings to her professional life.

Women have different styles in the way they approach their profession, and different styles in the way they approach professional interactions. Some approach professional life with confidence, as a challenge to creative and intellectual skills. These women look to those in authority, male or female, as mentors and feel eager to discuss their work and to gain new insights and new suggestions so as to better improve their progress within their profession. They take criticism as helpful and constructive, and try to learn from their mistakes. If disappointed in a supervisor, such a woman might go to another for consultation. These women may feel quite competent in interactions with those of lesser authority, or with their customers or clients, and feel confident that they could more or less deal with every situation that arose, or seek consultation if stymied. These women readily make friendships, sometimes very close and rewarding friendships, with peers.

Other women feel less secure. They may find that the practice of their profession is intimidating. They may particularly wish for encouragement and support from female superiors, yet instead experience them as critical and demeaning. No matter what their actual competence level, these women may worry about any professional interactions, whether they be with superiors, subordinates, clients, or peers. They fear making mistakes, making themselves look incompetent or foolish. New clients or opportunities arouse a fear that their performance will be judged inadequate, and that they will not live up to the organization's expectations. They may also not form the close friendships, especially with female peers, that they long for.

No doubt many women have wondered at one point or another how their relationship with their mother impacts successes or failures in their professional life. They may wonder to what extent their attitudes and behavior with superiors, subordinates, colleagues, clients, and peers are influenced by their relationship, past or present, with their mother. These issues are the focus of this chapter.

Let me begin by stating the obvious. Adult women do not arrive on the professional work scene de novo. Rather, their feelings about others, roles, and patterns of interactions are all influenced by past relationships. Because of this, I focus this discussion on the childhood and adolescent foundations of the mother–daughter relationship. Since a woman's sense of herself as female contributes to the way in which she interacts with her mother and later with others, I will first orient the discussion around the subject of gender identity.

A SENSE OF BEING FEMININE

A multitude of factors contribute to every woman's sense of herself as female. Although I present a broad outline for heuristic purposes, I want to emphasize that there is not one story of female development, but many stories, many intertwining themes, and many possible outcomes. The challenge is to understand the role of the many, sometimes seemingly contradictory, factors that contribute to any woman's sense of herself as female.

First, some definitional clarifications may be helpful. In discussions about female psychology one often encounters the terms *gender identity* and *sexual identity* used interchangeably. More recently, possibly in efforts toward political correctness, the terms *gender* and *gender identity* are used to refer to all aspects of being female. Following Stoller (1985) and the definitions in Chapter 1, I adhere to the idea of separating biology and psychology. Biologically, women belong to the female sex. What we make of that, how we see ourselves as female, our identity, and social role is psychology. Gender identity therefore refers to a psychological configuration; it is that personal sense of identity that combines and becomes integrated with our biological sex. A wide variety of feelings, thoughts, fantasies, ideals, aspirations, and beliefs about being female, as well as the cultural traditions within which we live, all make significant contributions to this psychological configuration we call gender identity. Some refer to this personal sense of female identity as one's sense of *femininity*. While not an ideal term, I emphasize that the definition of femininity is a personal one; although cultural stereotypes may contribute, fantasies, ideals, and conflicts—many of which are unconscious and many of which are formed in early childhood—lead each woman to form a complex belief system about herself in relation to being female. It is this personal myth that I refer to when I speak of femininity.

GENERATIONAL MOTHERHOOD

The mother–daughter dynamic, and the way it influences a woman's sense of herself as female, which will in turn have an influence on her professional interactions, begins before she is born. With the prospect of becoming a mother like her own mother, the pregnant woman often becomes absorbed with earlier and current issues about her relationship with her mother. As pregnancy verifies being like—at least in some ways—her mother, pride and a sense of togetherness may emerge, but so may ambivalence and old conflict.

The degree to which the woman is able to resolve earlier conflicts and integrate earlier wishes and fantasies with current realities has a profound effect on her earliest response to and handling of her baby. It is well known that parents bring to the relationship with their infant girl a variety of verbal and nonverbal messages that convey the meaning of feminine as defined by that family; their attitudes about girls and women as well as their conscious and unconscious fantasies about having a female child will be reflected in their interactions with their daughters. Therefore, once a woman knows her baby will be a girl (before or after birth), her attitudes toward and fantasies about her baby take on a distinct shape. When her own relationship with her mother has been a close, primarily supportive one, she will delight in shared fantasies about her coming daughter. She and her mother, together, may shop and prepare for the baby. On the other hand, if the woman has had to struggle to find a sense of separateness and autonomy from a mother she experiences as engulfing, she may fear that her mother will try to take over her baby; she then may feel inadequate, and approach her baby only tentatively, thereby possibly disrupting the baby's making a secure attachment. When the woman's relationship with her own mother has been fraught with conflict, she may not have good feelings about herself as a woman. The idea of having a girl may then arouse particularly strong emotions. In a worst-case scenario, the mother may identify her daughter with a denigrated part of her own self-representation. She may then relate to her baby accordingly; as one mother said, "The first time I held her she gave me a cold, icy stare, and she turned away!" This mother had little to do with the care of her infant; the baby spent long hours in day care. Another woman may view having a girl as an opportunity to regain or re-create a fantasized, idealized, lost sense of oneness that she feels must have been a part of her own early experience with her mother. While this may set the stage for the establishment of a healthy and firm attachment, it could, less happily, predispose her to attempt to totally engulf her little girl and discourage independence and autonomy, making it difficult for the girl to break away from her mother's grasp and later to function as an assertive career woman.

Because of a variety of unresolved conflicts, pathological fantasies, or experiences with their own mother, women sometimes view motherhood as a masochistic endeavor (Blum 1976). In such instances the woman may see the arrival of a baby as a loss of her autonomy and independence and as a threat to a newly established career. This sets up the daughter to be a perpetrator of abuse; any demand or need of the infant confirms the mother's sense of servitude. A girl with such a mother may find little in the relationship to confirm any sense of her own competence. Instead she feels herself to be a burden to her mother, yet can find no way to please her mother, to lift the burden. She may feel like a failure.

CORE GENDER IDENTITY

Although the infant's sense of being female begins at birth with being identified as female, given a name, and handled by parents who un-

36

consciously convey messages about how she is viewed, concrete evidence that the child has a sense that she is female begins to appear sometime in the second year. Being of the same sex as her closest caregiver, and making early comparisons with her mother, may be an important factor in this. Fantasies of mother–daughter oneness are common in mothers (Chodorow 1978), particularly as many mothers can so easily identify with the body of their infant girl (Bernstein 1983). Although potentially engulfing, these provide a powerful affective "surround" (Spitz 1965), which can foster the infant girl's sense of competence and lead her to make primitive identifications with her mother. As her own sense of self emerges, which seems to be around 18 months, these identifications contribute to her forming a basic pleasurable sense of being female. This basic sense of being female Stoller (1968) labeled *primary femininity* or *core gender identity*. Once established, primary femininity is, as Stoller remarked, "a piece of identity so firm that almost no vicissitudes of living can destroy it" (p. 48). I want to emphasize that although this most basic sense of being female is established in the earliest years of life, a girl's sense of gender continues to elaborate over the course of her entire development. Indeed, it comes to include various masculine elements alongside feminine ones. This is because we all select certain aspects of each parent (as well as same-sex and opposite-sex siblings, and admired others) for emulation. Early attempts at being like mother or father are also elaborated at later stages. In addition, at various developmental stages the girl attempts to dis-identify, to not be like her mother or father (Greenson 1954). These attempts also make a contribution to gender identity. A woman's ultimate sense of gender identity, therefore, represents a blending of many elements from many developmental stages.

Under most circumstances a girl's establishing a core sense of being female is a relatively simple process. Her closest attachment is usually to her mother, and being of the same sex as her mother, primary identifications follow easily. A more complicated issue is the way the girl feels about being female. Is she proud or ashamed of her body? Is she happy to be female? Does the discovery of anatomical differences lead her to form even closer bonds with her mother and give her a sense of pride when she senses ways in which she and her mother are alike? Or does it leave her with a sense of inadequacy?

A woman's pride or shame about her body and herself as female will be reflected in the way she approaches interactions with others as an adult. This sense of competence, confidence, and pride, or shame and feelings of inadequacy, also has its beginnings in early childhood. The infant girl's first attachment is usually to her mother. The mother's own feelings about being female as well as about having a female child will be conveyed in one form or another and will contribute to the girl's sense of value as a female. Optimally, the girl's sense of her self as female emerges from within a sense of being "at one," at least emotionally, with a mother who values herself as a woman. The infant's earliest sense of competence then develops in the glow of the approving, supporting glances she receives from her mother as she takes her first steps toward exploring the outside world. Once primary femininity has been established, the girl looks to her mother to admire, idealize, and emulate. An enhanced sense of pride and an increase in self-esteem accompany her attachment to her idealized mother and her success in achieving some semblance of being like her mother. Although the recognition of sexual differences may sometimes arouse hurt and anger in the little girl, it may also foster idealization of and identification with her mother. On the other hand, if the mother herself feels devalued and lacks confidence in herself as a woman, or if she herself is critical and demeaning of women and wishes her child were a boy, she may have difficulty in helping her daughter feel valued. The little girl may then not feel good about being female, and may think that being female is second best. Stigmatization in a later work environment may be accepted by her as appropriate.

INDEPENDENCE AND RELATIONSHIPS

There comes a time in the girl's development—around the age of 2 or so, that the little girl wishes for more than a sense of oneness with her mother. She wants to be in control, to be independent, to have her way, even if she is not sure what it is that she wants. She may want to push her mother aside (temporarily) to have an exclusive relationship with her father, only to push him away and want only mother. She is caught in a struggle between her wish for a sense of autonomous competence and a wish for dependency; a wish for intimacy, yet a fear of it; a wish to be with and to be like mother, yet a wish to be separate and different. Struggles over willfulness and control between mother and daughter are typical at this age, and angry, hostile feelings toward her mother may be expressed. This is partly because she views her mother as omnipotent—she thinks her mother could give her anything she wanted, make her feel always happy—if mother only would. As much as she views her mother as the source of all pleasure, she also thinks mother is the source of all pain and displeasure. These feelings interrupt her feelings of being at one with her mother. The loss of the sense of intimacy as well as the mounting anxiety that the mother cannot survive her hateful aggression leads the girl to feel painfully alone, helpless, unloved, and unlovable. She clings to her mother for safety and looks to her mother to do something to ease her pain.

A patient of mine remembered that such a feeling dominated her childhood; she always had the sense that her mother could make her feel better if she would only try. She remembered trying everything to please her mother, yet feeling painfully inadequate, thinking that if she were really good enough to make her mother happy, her mother would make her feel special. She also remembered feeling very angry that her mother always failed her. She described a repetitive fantasy of having a hole in her pocket. She went into the forest where the fairies danced for her and gave her a dime. But on returning home she discovered that her dime had slipped through the hole in her pocket. She was always angry that her mother refused to sew up the hole, for she would have been rich had she been able to hold onto her dimes. These themes can replay later in the workplace when women professionals expect unrealistic support from senior women mentors while feeling inadequate to act in their own behalf.

Another developmental dilemma presents itself. The little girl is striving to gain a sense of independence from mother, yet pride in her femininity is built on some sense of mother as feminine. If the mother can tolerate or even be supportive of a certain amount of aggressive assertiveness, the girl can find pleasure in her independent strivings and experience a growing tolerance for frustration. This ultimately helps the girl to feel competent and confident in making her own decisions. Experiencing some success in assertiveness and independence helps the girl separate from her mother, yet continue to view her as a feminine ideal. She is then freer to selectively identify with those aspects of her mother she likes and dis–identify with those she does not like. In this way she can establish a sense of individuality (Mahler 1981) and also confirm her own unique sense of pleasurable femininity (P. Tyson 1986, Tyson and Tyson 1990).

When angry control struggles between mother and daughter become intense, however, and mother feels threatened by the girl's anger and attacks back or collapses in helpless tears, the girl is left to question her view of her mother as wonderful. A stormy, strongly ambivalent mother–daughter relationship may emerge, impeding a girl's pleasure in independent strivings, but also jeopardizing her wish to be feminine like her mother.

A patient of mine gives an example. She described how everybody saw her as sweet and feminine. But underneath the shy, insecure facade she claimed, "I feel like a tiger inside—I'm afraid I'll mess up whatever I try." She claimed that being angry was not very feminine, but, on the other hand, she doesn't feel very feminine. She said she was afraid that she would compromise the relationship with me if I were to know about her angry, hateful side. She questioned, "Am I a pretty little girl, a boy, or a mess? Could I ever be a competent, assertive, feminine woman?" Her musings echo the frequent theme of fraudulence with fear of exposure so pervasive among professional women.

What psychoanalysts call the superego, our inner shoulds and should nots, becomes the heir to the relationship conflicts of early childhood. To avoid the painful lonely isolation that the overt expression of anger might bring about, a girl may make the conflict with her mother an internal conflict. In other words, she may overvalue and idealize what she thinks are her mother's directives. These often say she "should be" good, neat, clean, not hostile or argumentative, and always take care of her mother or the other. Critical and perfectionistic inner voices lead a woman to be self-critical whenever messy, angry, argumentative, or self-centered wishes find expression.

One of the reasons I am giving such emphasis to these early mother–daughter relationships is that the foundations of a woman's adult character structure are formed in the early years of life. The way a woman interacts with others as an adult reflects the template established in the very early years of life. This does not mean that the issues are the same, or that every interaction is a direct reflection of the early childhood relationship with the mother. It only means that patterns form early, and the legacy of inner critical voices from early childhood has a tendency to endure and sometimes interfere with an adult woman's judgment. When particularly critical, and not modified by later experiences, these may prevent a woman from finding a comfortable sense of assertive competence.

Inner critical voices are also easily projected. This means that the criticisms and directives an adult woman may experience as coming from the outside—superior, supervisor, colleague, or client—are partially derived from internal sources. Those who are not able to distinguish inner derivatives of early childhood conflicts from present-day external realities may have great difficulties in relationships with others, professionally or personally. A woman therefore has to make conscious efforts to consider what may be coming from inside, derived from early childhood, and what may be present-day reality to move beyond some of her more problematical early patterns.

FAMILY RELATIONSHIPS

In the third and fourth year new and different pressures are brought to the mother and daughter relationship. Up to now I have not mentioned the sexual impulses of early childhood. Although little girls are often very successful in hiding their sexual impulses and their masturbation, genital sensual pressures and pleasures are alive and well. When the mother–daughter relationship continues to be one of mutual love and support, inner sensual sensations may bring the little girl a sense of pleasure with her body. An outward reflection of this may be in the ways a little girl uses her body—dancing, gymnastics, and the like. At this time the girl also typically makes further feminine identifications with her mother. Increased pride and an elevation of self-esteem come from playing dress-up, trying on mother's clothes, pretending to have breasts, and pretending to "go to work" like mother. At the same time she enjoys pretending to be pregnant, and expresses wishes to be a mother with a baby. In other words, the little girl enjoys sharing in a variety of activities with her mother, and expresses wishes to be like her mother in many ways. The wish to be competent in the world combined with the wish to be nurturing in the family is not conflictual at this age. However, reconciliation of these two roles, both of which have origins in the idealizations, wishes, and goals of early childhood, will be a lifelong task for the adult professional woman.

Freud's idea of the Oedipus complex is probably one of his most well-known concepts. Simply put, the female version is that in fantasy the little girl displaces her mother and imagines herself to be the object of her father's love. Psychoanalysts put a great deal of stress on

41

the importance of this developmental step. Her responses to these challenges have far-reaching implications for her later adaptation. For one, a girl is challenged to find ways to feel safe in interactions with her father. Finding such safety will provide a secure foundation for future interactions with men. Finding father responsive and appreciative of his daughter's wishes and fantasies, without humiliating her or becoming seductive, will go a long way in helping the girl to find pleasure and pride in a more elaborated sense of femininity. A father who can then share in a variety of activities with the girl, helping her to accept the disappointment of unfulfilled oedipal wishes for exclusivity, yet finding value in the ways in which they can share intimacy, also helps the girl to feel valued beyond her sexuality. Many successful career women perceive that they were "Daddy's girl" in the family. Early pleasurable experiences with father help the adult woman feel that relationships with men can be supportive as well as confirming of her competence. Such a woman expects to find reciprocity in relationships with men. She does not think that she has to use her sexuality to seduce, overpower, and manipulate men and she does not have to tolerate sexual harassment.

Ultimately the girl will have to come to some resolution of the conflicts generated by her oedipal dreams. That is, she must come to terms with the differences in sexes and the differences in generations. She may be father's princess, but mother remains queen. She must begin to accept responsibility for her wishes and actions, and responsibility for the way in which she resolves conflict. Feeling cheated and so justified in stealing mother's crown jewels will not make her queen. Recognizing that mother and father also live by certain shoulds and should nots, and accepting ways in which she can responsibly work toward earning what it is she wants, brings her a new sense of independence and maturity. Revising and finding more appropriate goals, and then reaching them, helps her to experience that she can make things happen. She experiences that she can be competent, self-reliant, independent, and effective.

Development is not always so smooth. A sense of loss may be prevalent as the girl feels not only can she not win her father for herself, but also that her angry competition with her mother interferes with any continuing special relationship she may have wished for with her mother. Self-esteem regulation suffers, and the continued ambivalent attachment to the mother may delay, skew, or impede subsequent developmental tasks. The girl may remain frozen in a state of childlike hostile dependency. Feeling angry and cheated, the girl may then fail to find pleasurable ways in which to relate to father as well as to mother. She may also find herself not able to take responsibility for her own wishes and therefore unable to take the challenge of moving on—finding attainable dreams and ways she can make them happen. Holding on to a cheated "Cinderella" view of herself, a woman may never be able to fully give up her mother: throughout life she feels preoccupied with how to please and satisfy other women (Balint 1973). As a working professional, submissive, compliant, and masochistic attitudes then dominate such a woman's professional interactions. Her early developmental experiences act as a severe handicap for her maximizing any potential she might have as a working professional.

ADOLESCENCE: THE REPLAY OF CHILDHOOD THEMES

So far, I have concentrated on the mother–daughter relationships of early childhood. These certainly provide the template for all later relations with others. But let me turn briefly to adolescence, because the active memory of adolescent exchanges with mother more apparently affect a professional woman's self-esteem and sense of herself in relationships.

The themes of early mother–daughter dynamics tend to be revived and become alive and well during adolescence. Menarche and acquiring an adult female body (sometimes almost overnight) tend to make the issue of mother–daughter sameness inescapable. The young girl must now confront her wishes to identify or to dis-identify with her mother and she must adjust her view of herself and her body to accommodate the physical changes.

Essentially, menarche has all the characteristics of a normal developmental crisis; it can provide a stimulus or be an obstacle to development. It serves as an organizer for a more mature sense of femininity and a nidus around which a revised body image is built. At the same time it revives wishes for dependency, closeness, and intimacy as well as for separateness and autonomy from the mother.

The ways in which mother and daughter negotiated or failed to negotiate conflicts over aggression will be reflected in adolescent mother–daughter interactions. If the girl was able to experience that her mother could tolerate a certain degree of aggressive assertiveness and be supportive of her independent strivings within a responsible family structure, the girl will find ways of asserting her independence as an adolescent. A healthy mother–daughter relationship can support growing autonomy at the same time that a certain intimacy is preserved. Yet, even with the best of mother–daughter relationships, certain stress is to be expected. This is because the girl is trying to break away from her early dependency on her mother, and, unaware of her own regressive dependency wishes, she may angrily think her mother is holding her back. With a "good enough" relationship, however, the girl can consolidate a sense of reciprocity in relationships. This helps her to feel supported by her mother as she experiences a mature body, consolidates a confident sense of femininity, and looks forward to increased interactions outside her own family. Such a sense of reciprocity in relationships will support adaptive approaches to professional interactions.

Adolescent mother–daughter interactions are not always successful. The early childhood struggles over willfulness and control between mother and daughter pale in comparison to possible early adolescent mother–daughter control battles. Often the girl's need to be in control causes her to feel angry at any attempt mother may make to set limits. Her anger may arouse her mother's anger. Mother may become so enraged at the girl's provocations that she becomes extra-controlling herself or aggressively attacks the girl. Such outbursts confirm the girl's sense that anger, assertiveness, and a quest for independence is dangerous and she might not survive her mother's retaliatory anger. Sometimes the girl attacks. Does she experience that her mother can survive and tolerate her aggression, or does she experience that her mother feels threatened and unloved by her anger? If the latter, the girl may then feel a prisoner to her own anger, and in passive surrender gives up her attempts at independence and assertiveness, feeling that she has to take care of her mother. This kind of adolescent mother–daughter dynamic will definitely prove to be a handicap to the woman's ability to adapt to professional interactions. Continuing to fear her own anger, she devotes herself to trying to please, being a "good girl." While on the surface this may make such a woman appear to be amiable and cooperative, she may prove incapable of responsibility if she is unable to make decisions, and so she remains dependent on superiors, but feels cheated and disappointed when she does not receive the promotions she looks for.

One of the most important tasks for the adolescent girl is to come to terms with what her mother (and father) is and is not. In that way she can begin to detach herself from the authority of her parents and assume responsibility for herself. Dispelling the myths of early childhood makes it possible for the girl to see that her mother is perhaps not ideal, but not all bad either. Clinging to idealized images, and criticizing parents as disappointing, a woman can escape responsibility for herself, blaming her shortcomings always on her mother (or father or someone else). If the adolescent can come to terms with her mother's inadequacies, forgive her for her failures, and empathize with her weaknesses, she may be able to find a mutually respectful relationship with her mother. At the same time, she detaches from her mother's authority and accepts responsibility for her own failures, inadequacies, mistakes, and weaknesses. As she must deidealize her parents, she must also revise the ideals and demands she makes on herself so that they are within reasonable limits. Being able to excuse herself when she falls short of perfection makes it more possible for her to assume responsibility for her own actions and for her own decisions. Deidealizing early wishes and expectations for others and at the same time assuming self-responsibility is a crucial but often overlooked aspect of adolescent development. So often the difficulties a woman has in professional interactions, and the disappointments she feels in colleagues, peers, and superiors, as well as her life partners, are because of high, unrealistic expectations.

SUMMARY

A woman's early childhood experiences with her mother provide a template for later relationships. Professional success or failure for the career woman in many ways is dependent on the patterns of interpersonal interactions established with her mother early in life, relived again in adolescence. Success in professional life as well as in personal relationships demands that a woman work through and move beyond these mother–daughter conflicts. This chapter has reviewed the basic developmental tasks faced by the girl in her relationship with her mother.

Mastering the tasks that lead the girl to feel competent, autonomous, valuable, and capable of reciprocity in relationships helps a career woman to be willing to stand up for herself, to seek realistic goals, and to sustain criticism. Establishing reciprocity in relationships also helps a woman to build mature friendships that provide support during times of stress. Mastering the developmental tasks associated with the mother–daughter dynamic bodes well for a successful and fulfilling career and a rich interpersonal life.

3

Early Career Issues:
Let the Juggling Begin

ANNJANETTE ALEJANO-STEELE

Professional women often describe their experiences in terms of a balancing act in a three-ring circus comprised of career, relationships, and family; their challenge arises in keeping the three in synchrony. In contrast to women with established careers, early career women are in the position of learning about the ways of the circus and how to juggle; their challenge is to figure out what to hold on to and what to get rid of within each of the three rings. Today, as graduates with advanced degrees embark upon professional careers, they already find themselves in their late twenties or early thirties. They also find themselves urgently making decisions about commitments to companionship, commitments to career, and reproductive choices.

Denmark (1992) coined the term *front-loaded* professions as those that require large investments of time and energy during the early stages of professional careers. This is particularly true for those in academia, medicine, law, and business who pursue professional education and training that take large amounts of time and energy and leave little reserve for other pursuits such as relationships, social activities, and child rearing. At the same time that careers are being established, larger life decisions knock at the door, refusing to wait any longer; often these decisions are made with little information or they just "happen" with no planning (Cook 1990). Each decision comes with its own set of challenges, which are influenced by individual differences in familial, economic, social, and cultural background. For example, here is a typical scenario of a young professional who must make decisions after a lengthy graduate education:

> Isabella is a 30-year-old clinical psychologist who, after four years of college, attended a graduate psychology program for five years and a clinical internship for one year. After a job search proved too competitive once she had completed her

degree, she attended a two-year postdoctoral program. She and her fiancé, Alex (also a clinical psychologist), jointly decided to wait to marry until they had secured jobs. Isabella and Alex both wish to have a family eventually, but Isabella has also noticed that her peers from college are now working on their second child and first mortgage. She wonders about putting their family life on hold for too long. She is strongly committed to pursuing an academic career and gaining tenure. Her mentor told her that combining maternity and the tenure track would lead to a collision course. But can she wait five to seven additional years before beginning their family? Should she try for a less prestigious teaching or clinical position after she worked so hard to attain academic credibility?

For women like Isabella, childbearing may be intentionally or circumstantially "delayed," an option reviewed in more depth in Chapter 5. Professional women beginning their careers and contemplating family see the early career stages as a time of identity-related stresses and unanswered questions, but also as a time of excitement and opportunity. The messages professional women in the late '90s are receiving are about the discontinuity and unpredictability of the career path, and few professional programs provide guidance in making decisions concerning relationships and childbearing. Many women today have parents who balanced work and home in a traditional manner where Mom was a housewife or perhaps worked part-time. New professionals have heard the complaints from their frazzled senior colleagues who attempted to "have it all" and realized they needed external help in the form of housekeepers and nannies to even maintain their careers. They are trying to make sense of the new gender roles still being created. They see that paternal participation is growing, and husbands are gradually taking on greater but still unequal home responsibilities (Nieva 1985). The 1990s have been a challenging decade because precedents are still being established and the options are as yet unclear. The questions seem daunting: Should Isabella continue to postpone family, or should her career go on hold? What if the opportunities they have put off never come by and Isabella and Alex face infertility problems? What are the odds that Isabella and Alex's impending marriage will last anyway in the face of today's divorce rate? How can she make these decisions with any degree of certainty?

To address these questions, this chapter presents the challenges to decision making and the juggling that occurs as professional women are simultaneously learners and participants in career and personal choices. "Front-loaded" professional women face multiple tasks during early career development: completing education, surviving the job search process, learning about the new organization/department and its hierarchies and politics, dealing with expectations for hours of work and productivity, and meeting the standards of the performance reviews that will determine advancement in academia, law, business, and medicine. How do personal life issues fit in during this time? One participant in our symposium discussion group summed it up: "My decisions all seem like trial and error. Finally I'm in a position to focus on the other parts of my life and I don't know how to do it."

This chapter presents the juggling that begins during early career development, in balancing commitments to career, companionship, and reproductive choices. It provides observations and concerns raised at the Developmental Issues for Professional Women Symposium and some direction to help guide decision making for early career women. Out of all the discussions, the central theme was the need for active decision making, rather than victimization or reactive anger. A simple survival focus does not adequately address personal goals or sources of meaning.

Yet making decisions and compromises is an inherently anxietyridden process. It is difficult to know if all the pros, cons, and possible alternatives have been considered. Schwartz (1992) delineates the difficulties inherent to decision making:

1. We can never predict all the consequences of a single decision.
2. Our decisions involve other people, burnt bridges, and forsworn paths and unknown future turns; our commitments and obligations follow from our interactions with other people.
3. Life patterns are not firm and fixed. Personalities and personal needs and individual skills change throughout adulthood, and we should respond to this flexible potential.
4. Some alternatives are never considered because current benefits tend to loom large in people's thinking relative to future costs of which they may be only dimly aware." [p. 263]

Part of being able to make decisions involves knowing your own strengths and limitations. Professional women today need to be aware of their own capabilities and have confidence in their own self-sufficiency, but need also to be able to ask for assistance without feeling weak. The tendency for many career-motivated women is to do everything themselves; part of being aware of their strengths and limitations is also knowing when to ask for help.

EARLY CAREER PROFESSIONAL WOMEN: WHERE ARE WE HISTORICALLY?

The past four decades have seen dramatic changes in the way professional women have been viewed. The prevalent view of professional and working women in the 1960s was conflicted; women were presented the options of (1) having a stay-at-home family and retaining femininity or (2) having a career and being sexless. Career orientations were seen as growing out of personal dissatisfaction so that the career became a frustration outlet (E. Lewis 1968). During the 1970s, the option of balancing work and family emerged, and women chose to "have it all" and become "Supermoms." The image of professional women improved, and they were seen to have more positive self concepts, a greater degree of personal autonomy and self-esteem, more liberated and achievement-oriented attitudes toward women's roles, and a higher level of self-actualization in comparison to nonprofessional women (Yogev 1983).

The 1980s brought about families who had two wage earners. Employment was strongly expected of unmarried women and young, childless wives (Waite, cited in Wilkie 1988), and although it was not required of them, over half (59 percent) of married women with children were employed. The 1980s and subsequent 1990s presented a picture of overloading and overwork experienced when professional women combined their two roles. More women worked out of financial necessity, and issues surrounding division of housework and child care became more evident. In the 1990s, couples that crossed traditional gender-role stereotypes (e.g., the wife having the higher-status career, men taking over as full-time house-husbands) were becoming more common. Today, alternative work schedules such as part-time and shared time are becoming a more common option. Professional women have begun to realize that they need support systems such as nannies and housekeepers to keep themselves competitive in the career market. With the changes of the last four decades, it is no surprise that current young professional women are receiving mixed messages from mentors drawn from earlier decades of women who faced different societal expectations.

PROFESSIONAL WOMEN IN THE '90S

Women now represent about half of all university graduates (Burke and McKeen 1995). In addition, the percentage of women doctorate recipients has increased markedly in recent years, from 14.3 percent in 1972 to 37.1 percent in 1992 (U.S. Bureau of the Census 1995). Professional and managerial women are also making more career progress than women in earlier times and are gaining the work experiences necessary to equip them for more senior positions. At the same time, more women are now available to serve as role models, mentors, and sponsors for more junior women and men. In spite of the widening opportunities, professional women face greater challenges in juggling career and family. McWilliams (1992) makes the less positive observation on professional women today:

> Contemporary women are not only experiencing the kind of tensions that men have suffered for a long time; women are also handicapped by a marked lag in the culture's adaptation to them as equal partners in the workplace (women are paid less well than comparable men and are still given primary responsibility for home and child care), and women continue to have to make accommodations to their biology that men are spared. [Professional women today] have the worst of both worlds: the burdens of limitation and the hazards of opportunity. [p. 30]

Over the last four decades, the increased education and employment opportunities for young women have also changed their aspirations and made them less exclusively oriented toward family roles. Professional women today have gained a wider vision of their future, a greater sense of their control over it, and a greater sense of their responsibility for it (Schwartz 1992). Most professional women plan to work throughout marriage and child rearing, and many have clear expectations about what they want from and what they are prepared to give to, a marital relationship and motherhood, if those are the choices made (Waite, cited in Wilkie 1988). Although they may be clear about their future goals, decisions about the *timing* of career and family are complex.

REALITY OF THE WORK WORLD

Some women in their mid- to late twenties who have completed their degrees and are in the process of transitioning to the "Real World" may feel as though they have been in school so long that they are not quite sure what is Out There. Society immediately places undue pressure on them to succeed and compete with colleagues. Owing to increasing costs of college and graduate educations that have burdened many with debt, some women experience increased urgency to secure positions only to find themselves in a highly competitive job market. One seminar participant in the midst of a frustrating job search said, "You had this assumption that if you put in your time in a good training program and do well, you're all set. It feels like they changed the rules midstream."

With organizational downsizing and employees continuing to delay retirement, universities have been producing a glut of graduates in a world of too few jobs. This creates a situation in which there is competition with peers during the job search, and the possibility of rejection in the face of peers' successes is very real. Competitiveness is not typically a feminine quality, yet with advanced degrees women are placed in positions where competition is fierce. A woman in the discussion group said, "I feel angry that the men who are my competitors just aren't faced with the same biological issues." Other women may feel a different type of competition with peers who chose to put family ahead of their careers, leaving them to feel they are lagging developmentally in "settling down" and having children.

These are the challenges that face young professional women as they begin their careers. How are they to straightforwardly embark upon careers when the three-ring circus of relationship, family, and career is calling for attention? The following sections will address each of these rings and present how many are managing the balancing act.

RING NUMBER ONE: JUGGLING PROFESSION AND PERSONAL RELATIONSHIPS

For many women the first juggling act involves significant others. As their career goals develop, they may find themselves with mates who have gone through the same or similar graduate programs. Decisions are made about the relationships they have developed and want to keep. For some it means marriage or living together, while for others a prolonged educational focus may have left them isolated or inhibited the development of the necessary relationship-building skills.

Choices about Partnership

Increasingly, the choice to remain single has become a more viable option for many professional women. Marriage rates for single (previously unmarried) women have gradually decreased over the past two decades, from 93.4 per 1,000 in 1970, down to 58.4 per 1,000 in 1988 (U.S. Bureau of the Census 1995). Traditionally, women in high status jobs have been more likely to be widowed, divorced, or separated, or, if married, to be childless or have fewer children than women in lower status jobs (Valdez and Gutek 1987). Today, many women decide that the amount of juggling necessary to combine a busy early career with marriage and family would require too great an effort and cause too much tension; thus they opt to postpone marriage until they have established their career success. With postponement comes apprehension and concerns about having to deal with the prospect of the bar scene, setups, and blind dates in a shrinking pool of eligible mates. The challenge then arises for single professional women to create opportunities to meet partners who are intelligent and confident enough to enjoy being with a competent peer, in what many view as another highly competitive marketplace (Kaslow 1992).

Singlehood need not be seen as a negative attribute, especially in the face of the AIDS epidemic and rising divorce rates. The previous 1960s spinsterlike image of single women in their thirties has been replaced by women with

> good self-image and self-confidence. They are bright, attractive, competent, assertive, ambitious, and articulate. They are selective in the men they date, looking for men they can truly respect and

have fun with and with whom they can share their dreams, thoughts and feelings. They are not willing to be emotionally or physically abused, to flatter a man's ego unless the compliments are merited, to act docile and submissive if they are not, or to totally subjugate their needs to the man's. [Kaslow 1992, p. 80]

Women who have made commitments to significant others have often done so with others from the same profession, by virtue of being classmates or colleagues. The juggling act then involves two career tracks and all the challenges that accompany them. Many women choose to live together with their partner indefinitely in order to maintain a sense of freedom and independence. Others may continue to work in different parts of the country, even after they've made their union "official." Timing of marriage seems less of an issue in the '90s, especially when women are starting out professional careers.

When the relationship involves two working professionals strongly committed to career, several factors can cause strain on the relationship. Nadelson and Eisenberg (1977) observed that professional work is not easily contained within a nine to five schedule; they note that the more ambitious the couple is with their respective careers—with meetings, lectures, conferences, and keeping up with career-related literature—the natural result is less time together. Coordinating schedules while maintaining intimacy may be the greatest challenge. Household chores and responsibilities may become a bone of contention for some couples.

An Aside: The Name Decision

For those who *do* decide to make their commitment legal, another decision looms about whether to keep their name, take their mate's name, or hyphenate. Today, many professional women choose to keep their maiden names because it is the name with which they obtained their degrees; many women find that their name is an inherent part of their identity. For others, the option of hyphenating is a public acknowledgment of the union. Alternatively, some couples choose to take on the hyphenated name for both.

Follow the Job or Follow Your Mate?

Of the many challenges facing a dual-career couple, perhaps the greatest arises when the two have to face a separation. During early career stages, it is already difficult finding a job for one; making compromises for two careers presents a more difficult situation. In today's competitive job market, professional positions are dictated by vacancies, retirements, and mortalities. At times it is difficult to predict where the jobs will be available. The challenge to the relationship is in discussing and deciding who will follow the other to new opportunities.

For example, Mark and Martha are a dual professional career couple and are committed to one another. They have been discussing a possible engagement. Mark has been offered a position at a prestigious New York law firm, while Martha has been offered an equally valuable faculty position at the University of California, San Francisco. So who follows whom? Negotiation through open communication between partners is crucial, where all pros and cons for both partners should be weighed and assumptions about the other's opinions and feelings avoided as much as possible. Are they waiting to hear from other positions? Are plans to marry contingent on being in the same part of the country? Is the difference in salary level offered a factor? Traditional beliefs may still be prevalent for one of the partners; after all, they may be influenced by the role models provided by their own parents. Dilemmas like this one can make or break a relationship; often it remains to be seen whether or not it stands the test of time.

Research has indicated that the decision to transfer careers impacts men's and women's careers differently. Markham (1987) noted that although migration does enhance careers, men are more likely than women to move for their own advancement. When women move for their husbands' jobs, their own careers are often set back or interrupted. Often the decision is made based on the greater income of the two, which in most cases is still the husband's. The perceived quality of life in the geographical area and its suitability for raising a family can also be a factor. Many couples prefer to be in proximity to their own parents after their children are born in order to have family support and to develop relationships between grandparents and grandchildren.

An alternative arrangement to maintain juggling career and relationships is the commuter relationship. Research has indicated factors and characteristics of relationships that link couples across the miles. In a study of fifty commuter couples, the precipitating causes of this life choice were poor job opportunities available for the wife and a strong commitment from both spouses to the wife's career aspirations (Gerstel and Gross 1984). In another study comparing commuting and single-residence couples, no differences in stress were found between the two groups, and commuting couples reported less overload than did single-residence couples. Couples sharing a residence had more personal time and more family time but less work satisfaction than those commuting between residences (Bunker et al. 1992). Commuter arrangements are possible and perhaps easier to make when relative commitments to career and the length of time of separation are considered. For some career women the commuting relationship allows them to better delineate the boundaries between weekday work and weekend private life. (Additional discussion on dual-career relationships appears in Chapter 7 including issues of time allocation, stress reduction, communication, intimacy, affiliative needs, and sense of self.)

RING NUMBER TWO:
PREGNANCY AND EARLY CAREER

One of many concerns regarding the decision surrounding childbearing is the impact motherhood will have on the woman's self-identity. For early career women the timing may be such that the development of the career side of self-identity occurs simultaneously with the development of the maternal side of self-identity: "Her concept of herself as a mother, and her ideas of motherhood, are rapidly formed and transformed by her experience, but at the same time she will be drawing on ideas and fears and priorities that are linked to cultural norms [for working women] and to new personal experiences" (Apter 1993, p. 127). Chapter 4 describes both psychological and physical adaptation to pregnancy in career women, along with feelings about returning to work postpartum. In this section the focus is placed on decisions during early career.

Trends in childbearing have changed over time. For professional women the decision to have a family is a deliberate choice, one requiring shared responsibilities and conscientious choices that are fair and acceptable to both partners. The age at which women have their first pregnancy increased by 81 percent between 1980 and 1986, and the average number of children in each family declined from four in the late 1800s to the current level of 1.8 (Aldous and Edmonson 1993). The first generation of businesswomen tended to be unmarried and without children (Maynard 1988). Today, comparisons between men and women indicate that 90 percent of male executives versus 40 percent of female executives have children by the time they are 40 (Erlich 1989). Professional women expect to have and do have fewer children, begin their families later (Waite and Stolzenberg, cited in Wilkie 1988), and are more likely to remain permanently childless than women who do not work outside the home.

When the question of establishing a career arises, the balance between career and family has a large influence on the answer. Two major sequencing patterns emerge out of an array of possibilities: establishment of career followed by family or establishment of family followed by career. There may be a question of whether to attain tenure, partnership, or licensure before having the first child. For these higher-level achievements, there is further delay of the childbearing age into the mid- and late thirties. The decision for one sequence over another may be primarily a matter of the necessary pace to maintain the career. One woman in a basic science postdoctoral program commented in the symposium, "My research funding is based on productivity and I'm pregnant; I don't think that's the kind of productivity they wanted. . . ." If the career pace is slower, more options are possible, such as working part-time or shared-time. Both patterns allow maximum time to spend with children as they develop; the trade-offs lie in the age of the partners when they parent and the predicted impact on career trajectories.

Pregnancy Timing Specific to the Job Search Process

For some women pregnancy during early career may present an unexpected event that may force the decision-making process. Often the concept of unexpected or unplanned pregnancy is reserved for teen pregnancies, when in fact 42 percent of unplanned pregnancies happen to women in their early thirties (Institute of Medicine 1995). For women who discover they are pregnant as they begin the job search process, several questions arise. Do they carry the child to term and slow down the career? Do they pass up the opportunity to give birth with the risk that they might not be able to conceive at a later age? Is there relief that they have a legitimate reason to step aside from the competition, or is there regret and worry about how it will affect the development of their career? If they disclose the pregnancy during

59

the interview process, will it hurt their chances for a position? Will employers discount the accomplishments that originally gained them the interview?

Often the answer depends on the organization and their history and policies regarding pregnant or adopting professionals. During job search preparation, women can gain informal information from women in the organization regarding maternal leave and part-time employment to help them make decisions about the employer. With the substantial increase in dual-career families, child rearing should come to be seen by organizations as part of the expectable employment cycle.

Is it appropriate for a prospective employer to inquire about family plans? What do you tell them if you are pregnant but not obviously showing? Legally, you are not required to disclose; however, it may show commitment to staying in the area (and hence with the organization), a sign of planting family roots. On the other hand, it can inadvertently place women on the so-called "mommy track" or be viewed as bad faith if you do not share the information during employment discussions. It may be most prudent to delay the discussion until you receive a job offer. Such a discussion also allows you to probe how supportive a program will be and give you an opportunity to indicate that you understand your family plans do have implications for the organization.

The "Mommy Track"

The phrase *mommy track* evolved out of discussions and debates surrounding the barriers that women managers face with regard to their productivity and advancement in companies, a recognition that flexibility was needed to encompass motherhood and personal needs, not business needs alone. Demand called companies to action to provide family supports, child care, and alternative work schedules. The term became a euphemism for an alternative career track for women professionals committed to children and career (Schwartz 1992). Some organizations view women who appear to be less interested in climbing the career ladder because of extra family responsibilities to be those on the "mommy track" even when they have not so requested. Women on this track may find that they are less esteemed by their co-workers and employers, that their contributions are not viewed as important, or that they are perceived as having divisions in loyalty between work and family. Since the reduction in time, especially in law and science, may only be down to 35–40 hours/week, the career price can seem higher than the gain.

In summary, the juggling task involving career and motherhood is one of the most challenging during early career. Decisions to pursue a career "full speed" or to pause to consider the implications and risks of delaying childbearing greatly impact a woman's life course. These decisions force women to reflect on themselves, their priorities, and the consensus with the partner's goals.

RING NUMBER 3: JUGGLING ACT WITHIN WORK

During graduate school, professional women in academia, law, business, and medicine are trained to absorb information quickly, prepare for the job search, and prepare for tasks in their respective fields that will take many hours of hard work. One aspect of the juggling act between work and home that is *not* covered during most training programs is learning how to be savvy about the organizations and the hierarchies and politics inherent in each setting. These are the additional tools within the workplace to which professional women need access in order to make the overall juggling more manageable.

Know What Is Being Juggled

Aside from the everyday responsibilities of the career work itself, early professionals need to take responsibility and initiative; a major part of this involves staying informed within the organization and the field as a whole. As professionals begin their careers in various workplaces, part of the transition involves figuring out their place in the organization and learning about the relationships and politics within the organization as well as the proper "etiquette." Staying informed also involves keeping an ear open to mentors, colleagues, and "the grapevine" to be attuned to the changes ahead of you and the challenges that have already been faced by others.

As you enter a new organization, there are always more requests for your time than you can fulfill while maintaining your own professional focus. A clear sense of your professional and personal goals is important in deciding to whom you can say "no." Delegation of responsibility for research or presentations can lead to hidden errors that can be costly in the future. Being "nice" and accepting inappropriate responsibilities early on can worsen burnout later. Declining a new role based on well-articulated career goals is far more effective than treating it as an issue of being liked.

This clarity about goals and values is important in sustaining you over the long haul with a level of commitment that is personally appropriate. Career mentors who see your potential may urge you toward more ambitious goals than you wish, but also can help you to see things in a longer term perspective. At the symposium one woman scientist shared a common dilemma: "There are months when nothing is working right in my research while the personal aspects of my life are so pleasurable. I think, 'I should give this up,' but could I tolerate being a failure? We've all been groomed to go for the gold." Another participant, who has found teaching to be more exciting than research in her academic role, said, "I'm like the television advertisement 'Snapple wants to be number three'; that feels like me. I want to shine in my own way, doing what I'm best at." Less prestigious roles can bring more satisfaction and flexibility but also a nagging concern that you are not fulfilling your own potential, especially if there are few women in your organization.

Early professionals should also learn about the amount of commitment and stress involved in different career paths within the field, what training and development opportunities are available, flextime arrangements, the establishment of support systems through company seminars on stress management, and the availability of help with meeting child-care needs. Some organizations offer workshops in values clarification, time and stress management, decision making, gender-role socialization, family work–sharing, child-care dilemmas, and related topics. Alternative work strategies may be available and encouraged for men as well as women, with provisions of good child-care facilities and parental leave, including paid leave for either parent to care for a sick child. These are all essential measures in any attempt to gauge the attitude and behavior of organizations in acknowledging the importance of family responsibilities.

Network with Other Jugglers

Many successful women seek the guidance of seasoned jugglers to help them understand work responsibilities and where help is available. Ask them not just what they've done, but also how they thought about it. Most early professionals are not alone in learning the ropes. Some organizations create networks with people in similar situations. Women's organizations also provide an excellent way to get an idea of what others are experiencing and what has worked for them; senior colleagues can provide guidance and forewarn other colleagues of changes that can happen down the road. These networks often provide a safe place to voice concerns and fears without feeling intimidated or risking looking less competent. For example, as part of a trainee program at the University of California, San Francisco, a group of early career women gathered weekly to discuss projects and progress of their work goals as well as concerns about career and home. It enabled them to share in their frustrations and successes. Connectedness between women with common interests and concerns can play a powerful supportive role in helping them juggle and eventually balance career and home.

As women are learning the ways of the new workplace, a common suggestion is not to make waves. But as their careers begin to flourish, they can also let their concerns about balancing home and career be heard. They can promote the understanding of home–work dilemmas and provide persuasive suggestions for policies that would support dual-earner families (Crouter 1984), which will help pave the way for other professionals who will follow. Beyond your personal concerns, it is time to be thinking about how to change the paradigm.

CONCLUSIONS

Career women in recent generations are working harder to gain control and responsibility for their choices. Each has an individual way of creating her own path to success. Each successful woman creates a uniquely different one, making it difficult for women to find ready-made paths to career success. Women who begin their careers with male ideals and male images of success eventually recognize the need to change both their personal and their professional lives. Women still are in the midst of this societal transition. When making choices about work, marriage, motherhood, and child care, they face many unknowns. Past experience, observations, and expectations all influence these decisions. Like juggling, it is difficult to know exactly how each toss will turn out; invariably, some balls will drop and sometimes everything will move in a consistent rhythm.

Periodically, women should take time to reevaluate their realistic goals for home and family; flexibility is essential since these goals and decisions are not set in stone to be judged by others. Understanding your personal sources of meaning is the key. Schwartz (1992) offers this decree for professional women, which extends well beyond the early career years:

> We must accept as right and good whatever we determine is right and good for us alone. We must free ourselves from traditional values, define our individual needs and recognize that today, for the first time, we are free to choose. We can truly say, if I as an individual am comfortable with my choice, then it is the correct choice. [p. 282]

4

Pregnancy and the Professional Woman: The Psychological Transition

AMY A. TYSON

Pregnancy has not historically been a choice. Now, with the availability over the last thirty years of birth control and increasing educational and career options for women, the generation who are of childbearing age in the 1990s have grown up *assuming* that it is their choice to pursue a career intensively and ambitiously, as well as to choose the timing of their pregnancies if and when they decide to have children. Given this relatively new reproductive context for women, what do we know about the emotional experience of pregnancy for women with careers? Chapter 1 discusses the external difficulties of the balancing act and the reality that it is extremely challenging to try to "have it all," but what of the internal experience of pregnancy as a developmental stage of life? How can we understand the psychological development and conflicts that might be particular to women who have had a major part of their adult identity already defined by their careers by the time they decide to become mothers? Much of the current psychological literature that explores the emotional experience of pregnancy is written as if the transition of pregnancy is central to the formation of a woman's mature identity rather than a profound shift within an already full life.

In this chapter I use several sources to try to capture the experience of the pregnant professional woman: descriptions in the literature, a composite clinical vignette, observations of the women in the discussion group I led in the Symposium on Developmental Issues for Professional Women, and my interpretations of my own and other professional women's experiences. I will focus my discussion on a specific population of women: those who are pursuing a serious, lifetime career goal because of their own interest, rather than purely out of financial need.

Despite the ideal of "perfect timing," it is nearly impossible for a professional woman to separate the intense psychological transitions required by early career responsibilities and ambitions from the experience of pregnancy. The period of early intense career building coincides with a woman's peak biological childbearing years. When a woman whose primary identity has been involved in many years of education and career building becomes pregnant, she confronts the need to reorganize with her partner, both practically and psychologically, the roles of career and relationship to accommodate the new role of becoming a mother.

The experience of pregnancy means a variety of things to a woman, such as proof of fertility or femininity, social or personal role fulfillment, acceptable avoidance of being an independent adult, retreat from anticipated disappointments in career, or the need to care for another as a way to feel whole (Colman and Colman 1991, Joseph 1983). For a young, healthy professional woman used to being in control of every aspect of her life, pregnancy is the first time she has had to confront the dictates of biology. In order to establish a career, a professional woman usually has waited to have children until her thirties or even forties, all the while haunted by concerns about her aging ovaries. With the new freedoms of reproductive choice and nontraditional career choices giving her a sense of unlimited power, she gradually realizes that in the arena of pregnancy, biology *is* destiny. This realization may mean a variety of things to such a woman. A woman may take pride in being able to become pregnant and feel that it was in her control if it came easily or, conversely, be vulnerable to feelings of intense failure if she is unable to become pregnant. The onset of the physical limitations of pregnancy challenges fantasies of omnipotence and raises dependency issues. Applegarth (1986) emphasizes that we must pay attention to the way in which "realistic obstacles can also be used as the focus of resistance, without at the same time denying their existence" (p. 213).

Applegarth (1986) notes that "work is intimately connected with important identifications and represents a large part of the sense of identity" for both men and women; there is great pleasure in fulfilling work, but she has observed "patterns of conflict over the attempt to reconcile the demands of work and motherhood" (p. 212). There are pressures inherent in trying to achieve multiple goals, and additionally women may struggle with particular internal conflicts. For instance, if a woman is struggling with self-doubt about her abilities and a feeling that she has achieved in her career based on fraud (despite evidence to the contrary), she may feel relief at giving up the struggle in order to have children. This solution to an internal conflict may not come to light as a work inhibition since for women it is viewed as a "normal" path. However, she may continue to feel she wasn't good enough to succeed. She may feel resentful of her children, or unconsciously place the burden of meeting her unfulfilled expectations upon her children, who may be idealized and expected to be perfect.

On the other hand, a woman may choose to curtail her career because she feels the pull of being with her children to be a greater pleasure at the time than that of pursuing her career full-steam. In that case (as discussed in more depth in Chapter 9) she will have to mourn what she is giving up and struggle with the practical challenges of doing both, but will be less likely to resent the choice she has made. Or she may suffer from what Bernay (1982) terms feelings of "competence loss." Support for pursuing career may be more available than support for emphasizing affiliative needs and family; withdrawing to any extent from the familiar competition may lead to a diminished sense of self as competent.

Although managing the practical difficulties of balancing career and children is undeniably challenging, a woman's unconscious fantasies about how she decides to do this will still come into play. Since there is no prescribed "right" balance, her fantasies about the impact of her working on her children, and about the effect of day care on children, will be reflected in how she prioritizes her time and how conflicted she feels about this. She can deal with her uncertainty by trying to be a "supermom" (Applegarth 1986), feeling that she must meet all challenges of home and work life in order to relieve guilt about pursuing her own goals, which she may feel are selfish. Even if she acknowledges that she cannot be omnipotent in this way and is able to delineate a balance for herself between raising children and pursuing career goals, she will still have to cope with feeling sad, frustrated, or even depressed at the loss of the full scope of her work, much as men traditionally struggle with these reactions at the time of retirement. There is both a gain and a loss.

Pregnancy is divided into trimesters for the description of psychological tasks as well as for physical changes (Colman and Colman 1991). These psychological tasks must be reexperienced and reworked with each pregnancy, and may be even more profound in multiparous women (Fenster et al. 1986). Career women trying to decide whether to have a second child may feel an even more intense resurgence of ambivalence at the thought of going through the difficulties of pregnancy and taking care of an infant again. Career goals versus the wish for more than one child and all the meanings of this (ideal of having "a family," of children having siblings, longing for another child) must be reworked again.

FIRST TRIMESTER

During the first trimester, a woman may be feeling ambivalent about the pregnancy and experiencing physical symptoms. Weakness, nausea, fatigue, and the desire or need to restrict normal activities may be the first hints about how unpredictable pregnancy can be. This may come as a shock to a woman who did not expect her daily life or her career to be affected until the baby arrived. A pregnant psychiatry resident (Franzoso 1992) poignantly expressed the state of upheaval and panic that can accompany this role transition.

> The initial months of pregnancy were a constant state of emotional turmoil and physical distress. I had not expected to become a mother so soon, and did not feel like one. I felt nervous and terribly ill. There was no protruding abdomen, no inner movements to signal the presence of another life inside. . . . I was not functioning like my usual self. This feeling made me reluctant to share my news with many people, especially at work. . . . While friends and family expressed their enthusiasm and excitement for me, I struggled to understand how I would negotiate the roles of student, teacher, physician, wife and mother all at once. All I really wished for was a comfortable place to sleep. [pp. 1–2]

In contrast, other women report feeling empowered and newly productive through this additional role, with a sense of "I'm getting my career together *and* producing a baby." Socialized not to act special, the woman learning of her pregnancy has a secret that soon will distinguish her from her male and female peers. Yet if her career trajectory is not clearly positive, she may be concerned that others will think, "Oh, she couldn't get a job so she got pregnant." She may feel panicked about her ability to handle the impact of the pregnancy and future baby on her life and her work. She may wonder if she'll feel well enough to return to work soon after the baby is born. A confident career woman may predict no ambivalence about returning and will competently make all the arrangements to do so, with no plans to slow her professional progress; others may not feel so confident they will want to leave the baby, but don't want to give up their careers. However a woman anticipates she will feel, first trimester illness and ambivalence may be an initial glimpse into the problems of trying to "have it all."

SECOND TRIMESTER

During the second trimester women usually feel better, and the reality of being pregnant is accepted. However, pregnancy inevitably raises concerns for a professional woman about how her career will be affected. There is a seismic identity shift under way as she wonders how making room for her mother-self will affect the professional identity that has defined who she is. Having actively avoided the descriptor "female" in her professional life, she is now clearly functioning biologically as a woman, which may heighten the identity conflict. Some women of leisure are preoccupied with shopping for baby and maternity clothes long before they are needed, but a busy career woman may put this off, or may even try to conceal a pregnancy from colleagues in order to be perceived as continuing to be strong, competent, gender-neutral, and not vulnerable. Solicitous reactions may be irritating. She may notice surprising things: male colleagues may studiously ignore the pregnancy; female secretaries suddenly want to bond, which may raise uneasy role-boundary questions; people suddenly feel quite within their rights to touch her abdomen or offer intrusive advice. Professional women struggle with how and when to share the information about their pregnancy with supervisors, colleagues, and clients. Nancy Franzoso (1992) describes the experience of her second trimester:

> This period involved changes on many levels. Physically, I began to have days of pure elation, accompanied by swells of energy I had not experienced in months. The nausea and fatigue remained, but not on a daily basis. My need for sleep decreased to a more feasible ten hours per day. Although I did not look very different, I began to feel less "sick" and more "pregnant"; there were strange physical sensations that I thought might be fetal movements. An ultrasound allowed me to visualize the presence of a normal, active fetus inside of me.
>
> One day when I was feeling particularly well, I confided my pregnancy in my department director. To my relief, he was delighted and seemed sure that the remainder of my training would not be compromised. I experienced this time as a turning point in my well-

being. I felt more focused, energized, and accepting of the notion of becoming a mother. My growing enthusiasm allowed me to share my news with an increasing number of people. The responses I received were varied and often different from what I expected. [p. 6]

Another psychiatric resident describes a common experience (Brauchey 1983): "The chief resident looked at me in disbelief, asked me where the baby was, and commented that I did not look pregnant at all. . . . My only redeeming quality in the eyes of most members of the administration seemed to be my thin appearance on which I was frequently complimented" (p. 135).

Women express the fear of hostility from their boss or colleagues, especially in settings where their work will fall on others when they are absent. Women worry about how they will be perceived, and sometimes are actually the recipients of others' veiled hostility. Women's tactics in fending off this hostility (hiding the pregnancy, working just as hard or harder, planning to "work until the moment I deliver") may be an expression of the desire to remain in control of their lives and cling to the known self until the last possible moment.

Supervisors and colleagues, both male and female, may react based on their expectation of personal inconvenience or an added workload. In the symposium discussion setting, one woman who came to medicine as a second career and had been married for a decade told how her chairman had exclaimed, "Couldn't you have waited?" Silently, she thought, "But I *did* wait such a long time." Where there was an "outbreak" of pregnancy in a residency program (Auchincloss 1982), the male residents responded angrily, expressing the fear that their pregnant colleagues wanted to "have their cake and eat it too" while the men continued to carry their burden as the drones of the program. In contrast to this experience, a later study (Braun and Susman 1992) reported that women tended to significantly underestimate the willingness of male residents to provide special consideration for their flexible scheduling needs and that men were more likely to expect that pregnancy would interfere with a resident's overall work performance. The author speculates that the pregnant woman resident may deny possible job impairment to minimize fears of hostility or accusations of ineffectiveness. Lack of support or actual criticism must be weathered, but a woman's resilience to it may depend on her internal sense of sureness about becoming a mother. In the cases in which the fears were clearly *not* based on actual experiences, it seems they reflect the women's own extremely high expectations and critical attitudes toward themselves. Perhaps a hypertrophied superego is inevitable in women who succeed at a high level.

For the pregnant woman therapist, the confidentiality wall between her professional and private life is made permeable by this event (Rosenthal 1990). Both transference and countertransference reactions are affected as the therapist's sexuality enters the consulting room. Patients too may deny the reality of the announced pregnancy or struggle to hide their hostility and sibling rivalry with the therapist's future child, fearing the strength of their destructive impulses. One patient asked permission to knit a baby afghan, then brought it in on the therapist's last day before maternity leave; it was beautifully structured but done in harshly discordant colors, revealing her deep ambivalence toward the usurping baby. Women in the workplace may experience more muted but still powerful responses from clients to their pregnancy. There is also the possibility of envy from women colleagues who are not "doing it all." Again, women's feelings about such external responses will vary depending on where they are on the spectrum of ambivalence regarding their own pregnancy.

The most intense emotional experience of this trimester is feeling the baby move. This inner reminder may be a secret pleasure or a distraction from a woman's work. It is a sign that the baby is real, and the woman must begin turning from fantasies about the baby to the impending reality of a major life change. Her body just keeps enlarging and this may feel odd to a woman who likes to be in control. Dependency issues become more intense as she wonders, "Who will take care of me?" She may turn more to her partner, or want women friends with whom to share this feeling. Dependency pulls may feel very regressive to a career woman. It can be frightening and lonely to have these feelings and yet still wish to go on in the same way with her work. If she has valued herself primarily as a professional colleague and competitor, pregnancy may be experienced as a blow, an embarrassment, something to hide or prove she is not affected by.

THIRD TRIMESTER

By the third trimester women have often resolved their ambivalence about having a baby, and may even be enjoying the specialness of their pregnant state. However, it can be a time of hardship for a working woman. If she feels well she may want to work until the last minute, and may not even plan realistically for stopping, a denial of how her life will change. She may feel unsure about how she will combine her roles of mother and career. She doesn't know for sure how she will feel as a mother, and is unable to anticipate this.

Pregnancy is a time of imagining the child to come. Making a place for the child as a person is an important aspect of the psychological work of pregnancy. This process begins with a sense of the child as part of the mother, and increasingly moves to a sense of the child as separate. The daydreaming necessary to imagine and make space for this new person must either take away bits of time and attention during a career woman's day, or she must suppress it and compartmentalize her life. However she manages her emotions, it will be an ongoing struggle. The pregnant career woman has become larger in so many ways: she must make space in her psyche for a new person, while continuing to encompass the demands of her work. Nancy Franzoso (1992) describes her final trimester:

> Towards the middle of the seventh month, my pregnancy began to be physically apparent. While I still had surges of anxiety, they were primarily about labor and delivery and my ability to juggle my various responsibilities. I felt less agile and energetic again, but I knew, and could feel that it was because of the little person being carried around within me. My dreams and fantasies about the baby focused on his personality and appearance. It had become easier to think of myself as a mother. [p. 10]

If she is able to get a maternity leave, the issue of returning to work will be there throughout. Some women look forward to returning to a familiar and certain identity that provides clear rewards, since the social rewards of parenting are not so clear. Other women find they dread returning to work or feel more torn than they had expected when the unanticipated rewards of having a child emerge. Fatigue is always a big concern—how is it possible to cope with a baby all night and work all day? Professional women must face all of these questions.

In our discussion group at the Symposium on Developmental Issues for Professional Women, one participant described her feelings that the physicality and limitations of the pregnancy had bumped up against her sense of omnipotence, while another woman mused, "Am I copping out?" Pulling back in any way was thus experienced as a kind of failure. Auchincloss (1982) notes "a normal, expectable life event creates for her a situation of deviance in which she must either ask for special help or, resenting this, make angry demands" (p. 820). As the professional woman moves forward in her pregnancy, her idealized fantasy of herself as superwoman with a spectacular career and spectacular children begins to be altered by a more reality-based sense of potential limitations, of the gains and losses of being a woman. She begins to search for new mentors, career women with children who can show her the way. Often these women are rare in the generation ahead of her and her near-peers are so busy juggling that they are hard pressed to find time to offer advice. In our discussion, one woman commented, "The mentors didn't help me as much as I had hoped because you have to do it yourself. They said to me, 'Oh, they grow up so fast, take time to enjoy them,' but I was thinking that I'd be eager to go back to work. I didn't have a clue. There has to be a personal unfolding process." Another discussant said, "It's difficult to be a working mother and nothing anyone can tell you will change that; but it's good to hear from someone else that you really can do it."

CLINICAL VIGNETTE

A composite vignette of Alicia, a 41-year-old corporate litigator, captures the complexity of transitional issues. Her choice to bear a child was ambivalent and she worked hard throughout the pregnancy, collapsing on the weekends while her husband became the nurturer. After an easy labor, Joshua was born; when she held him for the first time, Alicia felt incredibly powerful to be both smart and to have produced such a beautiful baby. At home, Alicia experienced a deep sense of bonding to Joshua, much more than she had anticipated. She breast-fed but felt uneasy because it was so "primal" and thought his frequent wish to nurse kept her isolated from the outside world. However, she was proud of what she could uniquely produce and cherished an image of herself nursing the baby while talking to her boss on the phone. She worried about the vulnerability to loss that her love of Joshua had produced and wondered if he was more attached to the nanny than to her.

Alicia returned to the office at three months and felt upset by giving up the natural rhythms and pleasures of her child. She found that shopping for work clothes no longer gave her "the old thrill" and was surprised to find that she didn't want to work full-time anymore. It was difficult to go to her boss and ask for a reduction in hours because she knew that she would no longer be the "star" of the firm. On balance, Alicia felt that having Joshua was "the best thing that ever happened to me."

ROLE SHIFTS

A spousal relationship that was previously based on equality may begin to feel very unfair during the difficulties of pregnancy and new motherhood. A number of women have expressed the fantasy that "this time it's my turn, next time it's his!" and are dismayed by the reality that, biologically, pregnancy is not like a discrimination that can be righted. Pregnancy may be a disturbing reminder that there are *real* gender differences, and that the woman is physically more vulnerable and therefore dependent. Some men may be increasingly involved at every stage of pregnancy, but a woman *has* to be involved. She needs to take care of herself and ask for help from others in a way that she may never have had to do in her adult life.

There is a positive side to pregnancy for professional women, some of whom describe feeling empowered and increasingly productive and creative in all areas of their lives during pregnancy. Like Alicia, they feel they are successfully having both a career and a baby. Feeling special as a woman may be an unanticipated and surprisingly positive aspect of pregnancy. Intense love for a child and the enhanced feeling of partnership with a spouse may open up an unexpectedly positive arena of experience for a woman who had been primarily focused on her career.

Women in training fear that if they take time off to have a child right when they are on the "launching pad" of a career they will have lost "the window of opportunity" forever. They express fears of losing the sense of competency they worked so hard to achieve, fears of being financially dependent on their husbands, fear of turning away from a hard-won, yet still fragile and unconsolidated sense of professional self. They know that jobs are scarce, feel they should be in the national job market, see friends moving ahead, and feel very conflicted. One woman expressed it this way: "I want to stop and embrace the change—but am I missing out—will I ever get back on track?" Yet bearing and mothering children also occurs during a limited window of time. Again, these are real-life difficulties that inevitably reverberate with internal anxieties that will be weathered and resolved in differing ways. One woman may feel that it all has to be done *now*. Another has a calmer sense that things could be done more sequentially, or that relinquishing certain opportunities now was worth it because of the gains of motherhood. However the career woman/mother works out the balance, it will reflect her inner uniquely personal priorities.

Evolving a Relationship with One's Own Mother

One of the most important psychological themes described in the literature is that of a woman's relationship with her own mother (Ballou 1978, Lester and Notman 1986). "The course of pregnancy is above all determined by factors pointing to the woman's earliest experiences with the maternal object" (Ballou 1978, p. 394). If a woman can resolve internal conflicts regarding her own mother, her pregnancy can be a further step in separation-individuation, and toward a positive sense of herself as a mother. Unresolved negative feelings about her mother can lead to repeating similar difficulties with her child (Tyson and Tyson 1990). As described earlier, pregnancy can also increase feelings of vulnerability and dependence, and a woman's reaction to this may have roots in her relationship with her mother. It may be that feeling physically dependent can raise unconscious fears of being merged with a mother from whom one has been trying to pull away.

But if "a woman is going to accept the dependency of her child, she must to some extent accept her own dependency" (Ballou 1978, p. 394). If in pulling away from her own mother she had compensated by becoming superautonomous, a woman might then also expect her child to act very independently. Or a woman who felt she was not nurtured enough might turn her intense longings to be cared for into becoming both autonomous and highly nurturant. A woman with a career may have feelings of pride that she is doing more than her mother ever achieved, and/or guilt for the same reason. One woman expressed the feeling that her mother was a "superwoman," seemingly able to do it all, and she herself felt unable to do as much. Other women feel unsupported in the face of their mothers' envy over seeing their daughters' ability to have children and careers simultaneously, while not appreciating the difficulties faced by their daughters. However her path is similar or dissimilar to her mother's, pregnancy inevitably seems to awaken a reworking of a woman's relationship (real or internal) with her own mother. How she does this may be reflected in the internal priority balance she ultimately achieves.

Becoming a Mother

Of course pregnancy is about becoming a mother. If the desire to "mother" is an unconscious identification with one's own mother (Chodorow 1978), then a woman with an important career whose mother's primary identification was in rearing children may need to struggle in figuring out how to feel competent as a mother for herself, since she is proceeding so differently from her own mother. Career women having a first baby are more likely to have a clear sense of their value in society regarding professional roles, but less certainty about the value of their roles as mothers. If there is no longer clear public affirmation of the importance of mothering, working women are more isolated in having to affirm its importance to themselves personally. Now that women are educated and achieving professionally along with men, they have the same expectations for themselves. They can feel shocked by how torn they find they feel as they discover the reality that it is impossible to put as much focus and energy into both areas of life as if they were only doing one full-time. For the career woman the longing to be with her child interferes with her work; continuing to be fully involved with her work takes time from her child. The pace of being with a child and being at work are completely different, and she may find the transition from one to the other harder than expected.

How is it possible to find an identity as a mother with this ongoing internal struggle?

It may be that the sense of herself as an effective and involved mother may evolve differently for a woman with a career. She is often older when having her first child and already feels competent in other areas. There is evidence that women who already feel secure in their self-identities *are* able to successfully expand their sense of self to incorporate a positive maternal identity (Robinson et al. 1987). She must also come to terms with the reality that although she is privileged in having multiple areas in which she is able to strive, there will also be painful choices and losses involved in prioritizing.

Back to Work

The developmental literature on infants describes that a woman's sense of her child as a still very attached but real and separate person becomes especially powerful at the third month postpartum, the stage of increased mother–child interaction and mutuality (Tyson and Tyson 1990). It is a very gratifying stage, but occurs right about when many career women choose to or must return to work. Women describe a feeling of longing to be with their child as more intense than anticipated. They describe guilt concerning the sense of not doing either job as well as they had hoped. For a new mother these feelings may be exacerbated by the worry about the adequacy of child-care arrangements. She is now responsible for and passionately attached to a new and separate person, and a woman's career, and her life in every way, will be deeply affected. A woman's sense of herself must inevitably change as she becomes a mother and continues to strive in her career.

In the transition back to work, she is undeniably different. A woman could try to deny that a major change has occurred and continue to forge ahead in her career. However, she must make emotional room to love her baby, or she will resent the baby's interference. A woman might feel the preoccupying longing for the baby, but also feel relief at being back at work and regaining a familiar sense of competent self. Women now express the desire for role models of women who appear centered and fulfilled by the experience of combining career and motherhood. But the balance that is fulfilling for her mentor might not be right for her; women must confront how deeply personal and internal the struggle to manage and integrate roles really is. How each woman discovers her unique limitations and balances this with the gratifications of her career and the discovery of the joy and fulfillment of having a child must be very individual.

5

For Whom the Clock Ticks: The Risks and Rewards of Delayed Childbearing

MARLENE SOCKOL MILLS

Over the last thirty years, delay in childbearing has become an increasingly common phenomenon. For example, in 1995, one in five women had their first child after the age of 35, which represents a 50 percent increase of that cohort in the last decade (American Society for Reproductive Medicine 1995). While the number of infants born to women aged 40–44 is still small, this rate also increased more than 50 percent between 1970 and 1986 (Berkowitz et al. 1990). It is now estimated that one percent of births are to women in this age group (Morris 1988) and this percentage is probably higher for professional women.

Women do not make this decision to delay in a vacuum. In this chapter I look at the different meanings of the term *delayed childbearing* and trace some of the technological and social changes that have allowed women more choice about whether to, when to, and how often to reproduce. In focusing on the issue of when to reproduce, I examine different patterns of delay. There are advantages and disadvantages associated with delay from both the mother and the child's perspective that need to be carefully considered. Finally, I explore ways in which the cultural context might evolve to reshape the parameters of delayed childbearing.

WHAT DO WE MEAN BY "DELAY" IN DELAYED CHILDBEARING?

The most common meaning of the term *delayed childbearing* is childbearing after the age of 30. However, the concept of delay is, to a large extent, defined by the cultural context. Defining delay relative to the age of 30 reflects that throughout history the norm has been for marriage and the inception of childbearing to occur during one's teens or twenties. However, when queried, most professional women, reflecting the experience of their peer group, will define delay as waiting until one's mid-thirties or later. In a nonculture-bound sense, delay may be seen as any interval elapsing between the onset of reproductive maturity and childbearing. The earliest pattern for Homo sapiens involved no choice and no delay. The evolutionary imperative was to produce as many offspring as humanly possible. Women were able to reproduce in their mid-teens (the onset of puberty was later due to poor nutrition) and proceeded to do so every two or so years until they were no longer able to bear children, in their mid- to late thirties. They might live a maximum of another ten to fifteen years, just long enough to see their youngest reach maturity (Altmann 1987). A mature woman's life was always occupied with childbearing and child rearing. This pattern persisted until fairly recently. In 1600 the average number of children a woman bore was nine and in the 1850s the average was six. Since that time there has been a robust trend toward smaller family size. In 1950 the average number of children was 2.5, in 1975 it was two, and it is currently 1.7 (Hogan 1987, Rossi 1987).

Patterns of reproduction respond to social and environmental factors. One social factor has been an increasing value placed on the worth of the individual. The decreased fertility patterns that emerged in the 18th and 19th centuries corresponded with the emergence of the new philosophy of the French Enlightenment. The idea that children were to be reproduced in quantity as assets was redefined; children could be reproduced for their quality (Rossi 1987).

More recently, another factor that has had great impact has been the growth in population. The world's population doubled in the first half of the 20th century and now is redoubling every twenty-five years (Rossi 1987). There is no longer the need for humans to reproduce in large numbers to survive. In fact, the planet's survival now seems dependent on population control. Thus, the climate in the 20th century became ripe for attitudinal changes about the desirability of producing offspring.

Other factors that have made delaying childbearing more appealing and reasonable (and have also contributed to overpopulation) are the advances in medical science, public health, and nutrition that have provided the means to lengthen the life span. The life span for women was 50 at the turn of the century. It is now projected that a woman who was born in 1955 and turns 65 in the year 2020 can expect to live to be 85.2 years old (Office of the Actuary 1995).

With the norm being fewer children, and a woman having many more years of life, new options become possible for women beyond those related to childbearing and child rearing. Daniels and Weingarten (1982) figure that the intensive phase of these functions lasts for about 9 of a woman's 85 years. This is the amount of time they calculate it takes from the time a woman conceives two children until they enter school and full-time caregiving is no longer required.

Social factors further explain why women's attitudes toward child-bearing have changed so dramatically in the last thirty years and why there has been such a marked shift toward delayed childbearing. The Feminist Movement gained momentum as contraceptive techniques truly came of age. In 1963 Betty Friedan wrote in *The Feminine Mystique* that biology is not destiny. The contraceptive pill was developed in 1960 and by 1970 one-fourth of American women of reproductive age were using it. This new level of reproductive freedom and the codifying of a feminist doctrine that encouraged women to think of themselves as more than wives and mothers coincided with the culmination of a period of unprecedented economic growth.

Philosophy, contraceptive technology, and economy combined to present a group of women, the baby boomers born from 1948 to 1964, with an expansive array of options. One option taken up in earnest by women was that of higher education and the pursuit of careers. While other variables may be operative, there is a direct correlation between higher education and delayed childbearing. In 1984 Asian-American women averaged over fourteen years of education; 34 percent delayed childbearing until they were 30 and 24 percent delayed past 35. White women averaged 12.6 years of education; 21 percent delayed beyond 30 and 19 percent beyond 35. African-American women averaged 12.3 years of education and 15 percent delayed beyond 30 and 9 percent beyond 35 (Morris 1988).

This notion of limitless options for women would eventually run into the boundaries posed by another definition of delay in childbearing that focuses on delay in relation to the age of maximum fecundity, which is around age 23. Until recently, and some would argue even now, single women or women and their partners were surprised to find out that it is not as easy to have children in their mid- to late thirties or beyond. They also are often unaware of the risks associated with in-creased maternal age for both mother and offspring. Although the baby boom was followed by a baby bust, the vast majority of baby boomers eventually attempted to become mothers. In a 1978 census, 88.8 per-cent of women aged 18–34 planned to have children at some point in their lives (Daniels and Weingarten 1982). Between 1975 and 1979, as baby boomers decided they had delayed long enough, there was a 73 percent increase in first births among women aged 30–35 and a 33 percent increase among women aged 35–39 (Cohen 1985). Many who tried to conceive but found themselves facing infertility did not make it into those statistics. They were to discover, the hard way, that if biology was not destiny, it at least defined the parameters.

THE ADVANTAGES OF DELAY

In 1982 Daniels and Weingarten distinguished five patterns of childbearing, four of which involve some degree of delay that women perceive as advantageous. They term the patterns *the natural ideal*, *the brief wait*, *programmatic postponement*, *the mixed script*, and *unformed*.

The Natural Ideal

The "natural ideal" script is to marry and have children. Often this course of events is religiously based and taken for granted, and the idea of options is not discussed. However, in our changing social milieu, women are increasingly choosing to be "childfree" or to have children outside the structure of marriage, impacting the assumptions about what is natural.

The Prudent Delay

The "brief wait" scenario involves a couple waiting a few years to get their "feet on the ground." The delay is conscious, birth control is used, but elaborate goals to be accomplished prior to childbearing are not part of the plan. The delay is seen more as "prudent" and as a time for the couple to enjoy marriage before taking on a new set of responsibilities.

Delaying to Accomplish Specific Goals

"Programmatic postponement" is a pattern that well reflects the changes in women's attitudes toward childbearing in the last thirty years. Many women now view childbearing as only one part of their life plans. They consider it important to accomplish a number of other clearly articulated goals and will delay childbearing for a significant amount of time to do so. For the purposes of this analysis these goals may be broadly divided into two categories: one goal is the development of the achieving, separate self, that self that is concerned with one's own individual needs, interests, and potential. The other goal, which may or may not be integrated with the first goal, is the development of the affiliative self, the self that compromises on individual needs so as to engage in lasting relationships. Women express this second goal as a desire to achieve a degree of emotional maturity that will prepare them for the important life choices of whether to marry, whom to marry, and, independent of the first choice, whether to become a mother or not.

Looking at one agenda, the actualization of the achieving, separate self, the striking correlation between the pursuit of higher education and the delay in onset of childbearing, has previously been noted. Once a woman has obtained an education, her next objective becomes that of establishing herself in her career. Over the last thirty years many women have been experimenting with ways to reconcile the timing of childbearing with the pursuit of one's career. The urgent and conflicting nature of these early career choices is explored in more depth in Chapter 3.

The idea of delaying to develop the achieving, separate self has led to many advances for women. However, the significant number of women pursuing this lengthy an education is a relatively new phenomenon and many of its ramifications have become apparent only in the last few years. For many this period has felt like an era of trial and error. The importance of knowing and weighing the advantages of delay against the recently discovered disadvantages cannot be overstated.

Women have also chosen to delay childbearing in order to develop their affiliative self. In fact, they have been increasingly choosing to delay marriage as well, perhaps for the same reason. In 1967, 9 percent of married couples delayed marriage until 30; in 1980, it was 30 percent (Rossi 1987). There has also been a decrease in the rate of marriage and in the rate of remarriage. One pragmatic effect of delay in marriage on childbearing decisions is that it condenses the amount of time that couples have to decide and, for many, it eliminates some of the time for "prudent postponement" mentioned earlier.

Women are no longer as certain about the value of marriage or whether they will marry. What does this mean in terms of delayed childbearing? Cohen (1985) explains that women who delay child-bearing while they hope to find a partner are delaying in a way she terms *conditional*. This type of delay is one in which a woman does not choose to do something unless something else happens. The woman is not sure how to make it happen, so actualizing the second dependent goal feels like a question of "if." She contrasts this with what she terms *purposive* delay. In this scenario a woman delays while waiting until she makes something else happen; she has a sense that she knows how to make it happen and it is a question of "when." When it comes to education and career, women delay childbearing purposively. When it comes to marriage, the delay may feel more conditional. In Chapter 6 Mardy Ireland writes about the "transitional" women who, in their pursuit of social and career possibilities, inadvertently delay childbearing until it is seemingly too late.

Although Daniels and Weingarten (1982) and others (Clay 1996, Mercer 1986, Walter 1986) present the view that when women feel more fulfilled with themselves, then they will bring more to a relationship, Rossi (1987) argues against this. The theory she expounds is that a shift toward developing the achieving, separate self results in less importance being attached to marriage and family. The focus on self-reliance, in-dependence, and the attainment of individual goals affects one's will-ingness to enter into or sustain long-term commitments.

Delaying to Buy Time to Decide

Two other scripts to touch on are the "mixed" script and the "unformed" one. Essentially they are similar in terms of the purpose of delay. In the mixed script a couple does not agree on when to have children and delay is a way to buy time so that discussions can continue and com-promise can be reached. In the unformed script neither person, or the single woman considering motherhood, is able to reach a decision. In both cases delay is more conditional than purposive. Childbearing will not happen unless the time feels right and the course toward making it feel right is not clear-cut. Some of the protracted indecision may be because there is not enough support in our culture for a woman to choose to be childless, or, as it is more positively framed, child-free. Richardson (1993) suggests we might just as well wonder why so many women choose to be mothers as wonder why so few choose not to be.

DISADVANTAGES OF DELAY

Infertility

I began working with Margaret in psychotherapy when she was 34 years old. At that time she had earned her MBA and had a successful corporate career. Although her job was demanding, she was good at setting limits and felt that things had recently become more manageable at work. She was beginning to enjoy a balance in her life between work and nonwork-related interests. She had a circle of close women friends, some single, some married. Until that time she had had only short relationships with men. She had always envisioned herself as someone who would establish a career and then get married and raise a family. At 34 the clock was ticking loudly for her.

As we worked together, she uncovered the source of her passivity around meeting men and was able to interact with them more actively. At age 37 she met the "right man," a bachelor named Paul, and they married when she was 39 and he was 45. She felt herself rushing the courtship because she "wasn't getting any younger." After they were married, they both felt that they wanted a longer honeymoon time with just each other but did not want to risk jeopardizing their chance to have children.

Margaret's mother had experienced no problems with her pregnancies. Margaret had no general or gynecological health problems other than having had an ovarian cyst that resolved on its own. She had no other risk factors for infertility. Margaret described herself as being from "hardy stock." Therefore, although she had had abstract concerns about infertility, she was very surprised when she was unable to become pregnant.

After six months of trying, she and Paul met with a reproductive endocrinologist. Diagnostic procedures revealed no abnormalities and the origin of the infertility was unclear. She tried a variety of treatments, including Clomid, then Pergonal, to which she had a poor response; her estrogen level did not rise in the way that was expected. This indicated that her difficulty conceiving was probably age-related. As she was unable to stimulate production of her own eggs, she moved on to in vitro fertilization with an ovum donor. After three unsuccessful attempts and four years of "torture," Margaret and Paul chose to proceed with adoption.

The issue of fertility is of major concern to young professional women. Women over 35 account for the majority of cases of female infertility in the United States (Mosher 1982). In a 1991 report on a large sample of data gathered in 1988, the rate of infertility was 4.1 percent for women 15–25 years of age, 13.4 percent in women 25–35 years old, and 21.4 percent for women aged 35–45 (Mosher and Pratt 1991). Among my peer group of nine women psychiatrists who trained together and chose to have children in their thirties, two-thirds experienced infertility. It looms as the most troubling obstacle faced by many older professional women. The specific nature of fertility in women has only recently been elucidated. While menopause is seen as the red light for reproduction, a new phase, the perimenopause, has now been differentiated. It involves changes in ovarian function that precede menopause by about ten years. These changes, which produce few symptoms beyond difficulty in conceiving, may analogously be viewed as the yellow light for reproduction. Although the early studies showing decline in fertility were done in 1953 and 1961, the word did not get out to the general public (Maranto 1995).

Prior to this knowledge about their reproductive system, the question facing the 35 million baby boomers born in the two decades following World War II as they entered their reproductive years was, "What do we do with our newfound freedom?" The freedom was intoxicating and it appeared unlimited. Many founders of the Feminist Movement had already borne their children. Their idealistic rhetoric was not informed by their own experiences with pushing the limits of reproductive biology. Thus their disciples and women who chose to delay without exposure to feminism were left to grapple with the limits and help to define them with their own bodies. They became a significant cohort of infertile women in their thirties and forties who sought help from reproductive endocrinology.

Information about their biological limitations has reached women as the field of reproductive endocrinology has been dramatically expanding. New methods of assisted reproduction and family building proliferate. Although women now know that fertility declines in the thirties, they also may know that, with assisted reproductive technology, some women have had babies even after menopause. Although the media focuses on the miracles, the reproductive endocrinologists whom this author surveyed emphasized that women should not underestimate the significance of the biological parameters of fertility. The consensus among the fourteen respondents was that delay until 30–34 years was reasonable while further delay carried significant risk. Several pointed to age 37 as a turning point for decline in fecundity but noted that women needed to allot several years to conceive each child. Thus it would be best if they were winding up the process rather than beginning it at age 37.

They advised that women with any known risk factors such as endometriosis, fibroids, a history of smoking or a family history of early menopause should delay less. One specialist specifically noted that in his experience a history of smoking one pack of cigarettes per day for ten years added about five years to a woman's chronological age when it came to fertility rates. A 1992 study does point out increased risk of primary infertility associated with smoking (Laurent et al. 1992).

Finally, several suggested that women who were considering delay could benefit from having their ovarian function evaluated. This involves a blood test done on day 2 or 3 of a woman's menstrual cycle. The test determines levels of FSH (follicle stimulating hormone) and estradiol; both of these become elevated as ovarian function decreases. These elevations begin about ten years before menopause and chart its course. Since none of us can predict when we will reach menopause, these blood tests could serve as meaningful guideposts for women at any age, but particularly for those in their thirties who are wondering how swiftly the clock is ticking for them.

The decline in woman's fertility has been determined by studying populations, such as the Hutterites, in which birth control is not practiced (Tietze 1957). Fertility is highest in the early twenties, declines gradually until about age 34, has a slightly sharper descent between ages 34 and 37, then drops off precipitously until it is virtually gone in the late forties (Arai and Cates 1983, DeCherney and Berkowitz 1982). Among the Hutterites the majority of women have their last child by age 40, an age where only one percent would be expected to be menopausal (Godsen and Rutherford 1995).

There is a multitude of reasons for this decline. Much information about the aging of the reproductive system has been deduced from the results of in vitro fertilization (IVF). This is a technique in which (1) the woman's ovaries are hyperstimulated to produce many ova (eggs, oocytes); (2) these ova are retrieved from the woman's ovary; (3) the ova are then mixed with the man's sperm "in vitro," which means in the test tube; (4) they remain there until fertilization and cell division occur, producing a microscopic-size embryo; (5) the embryo is then transferred into the woman's uterus where it may implant and grow to a full-term infant.

Use of this procedure has indicated that after the age of 37 ova production decreases by about 50 percent and the rate of embryo production decreases by about one-third. There also is a decrease in the rate of implantation, which translates into the rate of pregnancy, from 19.4 percent for women under 35 to 7.1 percent for women over 42. The rate of miscarriages also increases with age from 15.6 percent for women under 35 to 52.7 percent for women over 42. These factors add up and lead to IVF outcome data showing the percentage of ova retrieved that lead to live births is 15.9 percent in women under 36 and 2.8 percent in women over 41 (Lansac 1995). A woman's ova are as old as she is, and they are not replenished. The IVF data reinforce the idea that not only are the ova that remain in a woman's ovaries in later life older and more likely to have been damaged, they are also the ones that have, throughout the woman's reproductive years, resisted the signal from the ovary to mature. They may be the least viable ova, possibly the chromosomally abnormal ova.

There is a clearly established correlation between an increased rate of genetic defects and maternal age. These genetic abnormalities also contribute to the increased rate of miscarriage with age. One defect that is well studied is Trisomy 21, Down's syndrome. The rate is 1/1600 at age 20, 1/885 at age 30, 1/109 at age 40, and 1/32 at age 45 (Cohen 1985, Lansac 1995). Recent research has determined that in IVF-obtained embryos the rate for aneuploidy (an abnormal number of chromosomes) increases from 9 percent in women under 37 to 42 percent in women over that age (Maranto 1995). While prenatal testing by amniocentesis, chorionic villus sampling, or other methods can be done to detect this and other conditions, the fact that maternal age has increased has resulted in the birth of a larger number of infants with chromosomal abnormalities than were born 20 years ago (Lansac 1995). Furthermore, those screening techniques are not without risk.

It should be noted that the development of these tests, which are recommended for women over 35, gave older women more of a sense of security about being able to delay childbearing without having to give birth to an infant with chromosomal defects. Amniocentesis, which is done at around 16 weeks, carries with it a slight risk of miscarriage secondary to the procedure. This risk is usually quoted to be one to 2 percent. Another concern associated with amniocentesis is that, if there is a defect, the information does not become available to the woman until 20 weeks' gestation. Thus a second trimester abortion may be elected, which carries with it risk of complications and is illegal in some states. Of psychological importance is that older women often do not feel that they can invest in their pregnancy until the results are back. This can be almost halfway through the pregnancy and often after the mother has heard the heartbeat, seen the fetus via ultrasound, and even felt the fetus move. This can create strong conflicting feelings for the pregnant woman. Chorionic villus sampling is done at around the ninth week of pregnancy. The risk of miscarriage is about one percent higher than with amniocentesis, but the results may be back during the first trimester.

While infertility does increase with age, techniques such as IVF have been developed, but success is far from guaranteed. A recently developed technique combines IVF with ova donation. In this case the problems of older women related to aged and lower quality eggs, lower rates of fertilization and implantation, and higher miscarriage rates are circumvented by using the eggs of young donors. When eggs from younger women are used, there is a dramatic increase in the rate of success as measured by pregnancies and live births (Redwine 1987). Even postmenopausal women can conceive and bear healthy children with the same degree of fertility as the age of the donor of the eggs. This indicates that "the egg rather than the uterus is the Achilles' heel of reproduction" (Godsen and Rutherford 1995, p. 1585).

Of even more significance to professional women is a technology currently under development. The technology for freezing ova rather than embryos (which require a partner's sperm) has been elusive because of the fragility of the ova. This procedure, when perfected, would give a woman the opportunity to freeze her ova while she is in her early twenties and use them after she has established herself in her career and relationship. It would also reduce some of the ethical dilemmas raised by human embryo freezing and storage. This could be an effective so-lution to the problem of decreased fertility and egg quality for many older women. This procedure, which is essentially IVF in two stages, requires time, medical risk, and expense. It would currently cost be-tween $5,000 and $10,000, which medical insurance does not reim-burse. Furthermore, it does not eliminate other disadvantages to delay.

In addition to the intrinsic effects of aging on the reproductive system, extrinsic factors contribute to decreased fertility. Primarily, there is an increased risk of or progression in gynecological disorders like endometriosis with age (Cohen 1985, Redwine 1987). One in three women over age 35 have a "fibroid tumor." Sexually transmitted dis-eases increase the likelihood of infertility by 7.5 percent. Salpingitis, an inflammation of the fallopian tubes, increases it by 32 percent. Intra-abdominal surgery also increases risk of infertility (Lansac 1995).

Furthermore, as a woman ages there is also increasing exposure to environmental and occupational toxins. Advancing age heightens the risk of the development of or worsening of medical conditions that would have an impact on fertility and pregnancy but are not directly involved with the reproductive system. Some of the most common ones are hypertension, diabetes, and renal disease, which are intricately re-lated to pregnancy risks and perinatal outcome.

Maternal Pregnancy Risks and Adverse Perinatal Outcome

Recent research on the relation of the mother's age to maternal risk and adverse perinatal outcome has produced mixed results. Generally there is agreement that some factors related to maternal risk do increase while there is debate about perinatal outcome. Studies that were done excluded women with preexisting major medical illness or multiple gestations.

Maternal gestational diabetes is shown in one study to double with age (Cnattingius et al. 1992). Pre-eclampsia, a severe complication of pregnancy characterized by convulsions, is also reported as more fre-quent (Lansac 1995). Pregnancy-induced hypertension increases with age. Berkowitz et al. (1990) reports rates of 8.5 percent in women under 35 and 15.3 percent in women over 40. The risk of hemorrhage prior to delivery (antepartum hemorrhage) is also increased for women over 35 (Lansac 1995).

Older women have a higher incidence of prolonged second-stage labor, that is, a second stage lasting more than two hours. This is one factor that contributes to the marked increase in cesarean sections in women over 35. However, it does not explain why the cesarean section rate triples for women over 35 who are having their first child. These women have been labeled "high risk" because of their age even when there are no other risk factors. They have also been called "elderly prime-ips" (*primaparous* means first pregnancy). This labeling and bias may contribute to the higher cesarean rate as well. Nonetheless, the fact remains that about one in three women over 35 will have their baby delivered by cesarean section. This operation is known to increase the risk of maternal mortality by a factor of five when compared with uncomplicated vaginal delivery (Lansac 1995).

Although maternal mortality is a rare occurrence, it must be noted that, despite medical advances, it does exist and it increases with age. The rate goes from 6/100,000 in the mid- to late twenties to 35/100,000 in the early forties and 91/100,000 for women over 45 (Lansac 1995).

Women delaying childbearing also need to be aware of the relationship between maternal age and perinatal outcome. Several recent studies have indicated that the risk of infant complications is not as great as it was presumed to be in studies done a decade or two ago. In 1990 Berkowitz studied 3,917 women who gave birth in a private hospital in New York City. In this study the odds of having a low-birth-weight infant were slightly elevated for women over 35, from 1.0 to 1.3. No significant increase was found in the odds for preterm delivery infants or perinatal death (Berkowitz et al. 1990). Strictly speaking, the Berkowitz study is flawed because it did not sample the heterogeneity of the U.S. population. The women in the study were predominantly healthy, well-nourished, white, married, college-educated, nonsmokers who got early and continuous prenatal care. However, its bias makes the study particularly useful for professional women, who may have many characteristics in common with the women studied. In 1992 Cnattingius and colleagues studied the Swedish birth register for 173,715 women. The study reported higher rates of poor perinatal outcome, citing the odds of perinatal death increasing from 1.0 at under 35 to 1.5 to 1.6 for women over 35. In summary, when looking at the recent studies, it appears that for the professional woman the risk of maternal complications weighs more heavily in the balance than does the risk of poor perinatal outcome. Both these studies were done on women carrying a single pregnancy. The picture changes when multiple births are considered.

The rate of multiple births of nonidentical twins increases with age from 1/100 under age 30 to 1/75 at age 35 to 1/65 at age 40. Interestingly, it drops back to 1/100 for women over 40 (Cohen 1985). The rate increases even more dramatically for women undergoing the many forms of infertility treatment. Medications that induce multiple ovulations lead to a 10 percent incidence of multiple birth with Clomid and a 25 percent incidence with Pergonal (Nachtigall and Mehren 1991). Carrying twins increases maternal complications and perinatal morbidity and mortality. A specific risk is preterm delivery and low birth weight. Larger multiple births carry exponentially greater risk. On a positive note, survival rates for preterm deliveries went from 50 percent in 1970 to over 90 percent in 1980 (Cohen 1985).

THE EXPERIENCE FROM THE PERSPECTIVE OF THE "OLDER MOTHER"

At age 35 Carol sought therapy to address concerns she had about her work and her relationship with her husband, Howard, age 39. She had earned her Ph.D. in economics and was on a tenure track at a large university. She felt pressure at work to teach a heavy class load and to publish. She was in the process of completing a book and was questioning whether such a high-powered academic job was right for her. Carol's husband was highly successful in the corporate world and had to travel extensively for business. She felt he was inaccessible both physically and emotionally. She had an increasing awareness that this was not the life she had envisioned for herself. What she had dreamed of included a successful career, having a family, and having some time to be with them. Her husband and she had discussed having children but were waiting for the right time, if there ever was one. They had both been successful for a while, things were not getting any easier, and she was "almost 36."

At this realization she became more vocal about her concerns at the university and was able to carve out a little more breathing space. She and her husband sought couples therapy and he agreed to find work that required less travel.

When Carol was 37, Howard and she decided that they were ready to have children. She conceived within a few months, had an uncomplicated pregnancy, and give birth to a healthy baby. Four years later, at age 41, she decided to have another child and went through the same uncomplicated process again. At present she and her husband feel "stretched" but anticipate that they will adapt. She feels that being a mom in her forties has not made her feel any less vigorous and "if so, the change is so gradual that you don't really notice it."

There are a few studies (Daniels and Weingarten 1982, Fabe and Wikler 1979, Mercer 1986, Rossi 1980, Walter 1986) of how women feel, specifically, about delayed childbearing, that is, how they feel about being an "older mother." They tend to involve small samples (22–300 participants), and utilize interviews with less emphasis placed on standardized measures for studying responses. In general, these studies reveal that while older mothers have greater psychological maturity, there are also ways in which the delay of childbearing makes the transition to and the experience of motherhood more difficult for older women. In comparing the various studies, there is agreement about the characteristics of older mothers, discussed below. There is some disagreement as to whether these characteristics are seen as assets or vulnerabilities for older women in their role of motherhood.

1. *Older mothers have more financial resources available and a better support network established for themselves.* There was agreement in all studies that older mothers often delayed to achieve a degree of financial security and benefited from this. They could afford to spend more and obtain high-quality child care for their children if they returned to work. Interestingly, the older-mother group was the only one in which the infants of employed mothers scored higher on growth and development factors than the infants of mothers who were not working outside the home. Presumably these mothers could afford to provide a stimulating environment for their infants, which fostered their growth and development. Older mothers also felt that being able to afford babysitting and to continue to get out to pursue rec-

reational activities was important for their state of well-being. They also describe feeling more isolated than younger women do, however. This may be due to a smaller peer group for older mothers or to their earlier career experience of having a high degree of daily contact with peers in the work setting.

2. *Older mothers are more flexible, highly integrated women who score more positively or adaptively on personality traits and child-rearing attitudes.* While younger mothers more often described a "good baby" as one that does not cry, older mothers more often saw the "good baby" as one who vocalizes what it needs and is strong and healthy. Older mothers scored higher on developing ways of handling irritating child behaviors. They also reported less difficulty with the phases of increased infant activity level and individuation. It is speculated that because of their higher level of integration, older mothers rely less on their children for their identity and foster the child's independence. They are less threatened by and more encouraging of their infant's individuality (Mercer 1986). Unlike some younger mothers, they are not seeking merger with their child.

   While younger mothers enjoy playing on the floor with their children, older mothers enjoy "doing things" and "going places." Mothers with higher education tend to talk more to their babies, provide more interesting toys, and use praise rather than criticism when teaching new skills (Cohen 1985). The older mothers enjoy verbal rather than nonverbal communication. Their process of connection is less symbiotic than that of younger mothers. Where there is more distance in the early mother–child relationship, there may be less anxiety and struggle during the child's separation and individuation phase. One vulnerability that is implied has to do with the older mother's degree of attachment and gratification during the early phases of motherhood.

3. *Older mothers tend to plan their desired pregnancies and to be highly motivated to be mothers.* Often, older mothers have accomplished other goals and plan their pregnancies for a time they have chosen deliberately. They benefit from having a broader perspective on where motherhood fits in their lives and their choice is a more informed one. Clay (1996) points out that their mothering skills are heightened by the fact that they

are used to postponing immediate gratification in order to accomplish long-term goals. The strength of their motivation to become mothers is often attested to by the sacrifices older mothers make in their immediate career goals. Clearly, those sacrifices could lead to later ambivalence and vulnerability for the older mother.

4. *Older mothers have had more life experiences.* Older mothers have had more individual experience and freedom so they presumably have fewer regrets about what they have given up to become mothers. Clay (1996) and Walter (1986) report that these older women have fulfilled personal goals such as travel and are less likely to resent having children than women who have never experienced that freedom. The main advantages older mothers reported clustered around their feeling that they knew themselves better, had explored personal options more, and felt that they had not missed out on other things and that this satisfaction contributed to a positive, committed attitude toward motherhood. One stated she felt she had a better sense of time and perspective. If a child was going through a difficult phase, she knew that nothing lasted forever (Walter 1986). The older mothers in Rossi's (1980) earlier study reported a different set of feelings. These women tended to feel older than their chronological age and to long for their past youth.

5. *Older mothers place a high value on achieving and have a high set of standards for their role as mothers.* Older mothers who have achieved success in their careers expect to "do motherhood" well. They approach motherhood with the zeal and ambitiousness with which they approached their career development. However, the level of competence that a woman has reached in her career may be directly proportional to the degree of frustration that she experiences in the initial phases of motherhood. Older career women are used to being goal directed and achieving success. When it came to childbearing, they attended childbirth classes and had high expectations of the birth process. Nonetheless, they experienced a higher rate of cesarean sections and reported higher rates of disappointment in the birth process. At one month postpartum, they reported higher levels of exhaustion, perhaps related to pregnancy complications and longer recovery times.

Related to issues of competency, achievement, and self-esteem, Rossi (1980) found that the self-esteem of the career-oriented women is more centered around her performance in the "outer world" and that her self-concept is threatened if she transfers a portion of her time to being at home with children. These women may experience a drop in self-esteem as they wonder what they are doing with their lives and their professional training. Rossi's view is corroborated by Walter's (1986) finding that there is a significant correlation between age and the effect of motherhood on self-esteem. The younger the mothers were in her study, the more they perceived a positive effect of motherhood on their self-esteem. Still, Walter concludes that achievement-oriented late-timing mothers ultimately do gain a sense of enrichment from the experience of nurturing a child. One interpretation would be that older mothers have already accumulated many different experiences that built their self-esteem so that the addition of motherhood has relatively less positive impact on them.

6. *Older mothers have better problem-solving, organizational, and communication skills, which they acquired through their careers.* These skills have obvious positive applications to mothering and contribute yet another facet to the improved child-rearing skills of older mothers. They do, however, have their downside. Older mothers may feel frustration because they have become accustomed to collaboration and the opportunity to receive positive verbal feedback. Caring for an infant is quite different. Mercer (1986) reaches the conclusion that despite their many powerful assets, the older mothers consistently reported the least gratification during the early phases of motherhood that constituted the scope of her study. Despite their scores of higher competency, this group of older women with high achievement orientation tended to feel that they had not met their own expectations for themselves as mothers.

In looking for generalities about older mothers, the variability of the experience may be lost. Daniels and Weingarten (1982) bring complexity back into focus when they explain that individual older mothers experience motherhood in three essentially different ways. Motherhood may be perceived as a supplement, a new chapter, or a crunch.

Viewed as a "supplement," it is a fulfilling extra in a woman's life and blends well with her previous prioritization of her career and her view of herself. Those who feel as though motherhood is a "new chapter" feel dramatically changed by the experience. They do not necessarily experience a crisis or tension if they are flexible in accepting and adapting to the newly discovered parts of themselves. Many of the older mothers in Walter's (1986) study felt that they were changed by the experience and found themselves feeling more nurturing and affiliative than they had in their careers. They began to pursue friendships more because they felt themselves opening up and becoming warmer. They were often surprised by how much difference there was between their career and mother selves. In all the studies done, a large percentage of older mothers responded to the discovery of this part of themselves by returning to part-time or more flexible work schedules, as discussed in Chapter 9.

Those in a "crunch" experience a dramatic change coupled with an irreconcilable discrepancy between their expectations and the experience. They feel the demands of the situation exceed their capacity to manage them in a way that meets their own standards. The crunch may be a result of time constraints, but it may also result from a poor fit between the temperament of mother and child or the pressure that results from having a particularly demanding child. When it comes to a crunch, Rossi (1980) also noted that some late-in-life mothers at the time of her study were in a mid-life squeeze between their growing, often adolescent children and their aging parents. This is a significant stressor for older mothers, particularly in a society that has been cutting back on funding of social programs both for children and seniors.

Older mothers also worry about being judged negatively by others. They fear they will be seen as selfish for having attended to their own needs for so long before having children or for having children when they may not live long enough to see them reach mid-life. There is some truth to their fears. In the media, older women, or working women in general, are sometimes characterized as narcissistic mothers who occasionally drop in on their children when they are not working. One author believes that in the '90s this myth is fading (Clay 1996). The isolation and sense of being different may also be diminishing. In the 1990s, in many urban areas, older mothers have a lot of peers. At some of the more expensive private preschools the mother in her twenties is the exception. Although there have not been studies of this phenomenon, it would seem likely that a sense of fitting in would reduce some of the older mothers' fears and worries.

For the mothers in Walter's (1986) study, a significant conflict arose because while they felt that they had to struggle to compress more into each day, they also were aware that they had less physical energy than they had when they were younger. Some worried about what it would be like to have adolescents when they were in their fifties. This was the preretirement age, when they had anticipated life would get easier. With child rearing, ease and freedom are inevitably lost at some stage of life.

THE EXPERIENCE FROM
THE CHILDREN'S PERSPECTIVE

One small study has begun to explore the reaction of children to older parents. *Last Chance Children* (Morris 1988) reports the results of interviews with twenty-two grown children. One theme that emerged is that at adolescence these children experienced embarrassment over the appearance of their older parents. This study was published in the '80s and the parents of the grown children she interviewed were part of a generation in which childbearing delay was much more of a rarity than it is today. Another issue related to adolescence had to do with whether there was an intensification of the generation gap when parents are older. The study indicated that this was variable and some children felt a good rapport with their parents throughout their adolescence if their parents spent a satisfying amount of time with them. Although this phenomenon has not been studied, one could hypothesize that women having their children go through puberty at the same time that the mothers reach menopause could make for a lot of hormonal havoc around the house. Rossi (1980) points out that it is difficult for mothers who are winding down to deal with adolescents who are winding up.

Another theme that emerged is that the children of older parents wished they had done the things that younger parents did; an activity frequently cited was camping. Men more often than women expressed regret that their parents, especially their fathers, were unable to join in games with them. Although this is speculative, in our current culture, with its emphasis on youthfulness and staying in shape, it might be expected that older parents are more active. The adult children also expressed that they appreciated that their parents often had the financial resources to provide luxuries unavailable to their peers.

Finally, these adult children experience a significant degree of fear about their parents becoming sick and dying. One woman, who had been an only child, expressed anger at having to care for aging parents while still in her youth. Others felt envious of peers who had younger parents and still appeared to be relatively carefree. Many in the study had experienced a sense of loss and aloneness at the death of one or both parents by the time they reached early adulthood. As a whole, these children have a higher likelihood of becoming the "Omega Generation," the oldest members of the family, before they reach mid-life. Usually young adults have a buffer between themselves and death that reduces their sense of vulnerability and mortality. The adult children interviewed perceived the significant advantages of having older parents to be that their parents had more financial and marital stability and were wiser and more patient.

Delay Squared or Cubed

Older mothers face the same questions facing any mother as she contemplates having a second child. For the older mother, however, the issues may be highly intensified. With a second child, challenges to finding a balance, dividing one's attention, and tapping one's energy reserves abound. Mothers of all ages wonder if the increase in work related to a second child is geometric or exponential. Unlike making the decision the first time round, they now have their own hands-on experience to consider.

DECISION MAKING

This chapter has not focused on making the motherhood decision. An older woman contemplating the decision might find it helpful to consider what various studies have suggested as the assets and vulnerabilities of older mothers. She could then assess her own strengths and weaknesses accordingly.

Cohen (1985) provides several scales for self-evaluation. One, an assessment of expectations of parenthood, involves ranking belief in statements such as (1) a primary reason for existence is to continue the human race, (2) children make you feel important, (3) children make you a more loving person, (4) having children is costly in terms of achieving personal goals, (5) parenthood means the end of flexibility and freedom in most things. Other tools involve ranking feelings about one's career and one's level of social involvement. In these areas a woman is asked to consider how much of her identity she derives from these areas, how much time they require, how flexible she is in terms of her desire to redistribute her time, how flexible the situations and relationships are in terms of allowing her flexibility. Finally, Cohen presents ways in which a woman can assess the different qualities of her personality. Several other source books exist for older women who are considering motherhood for the first time or anew with a next child (Bing and Coleman 1980, Fabe and Wikler 1979, Rubin 1980).

SHAPING OUR FUTURE

Can we take the "delay" out of delayed childbearing? The strategies for incorporating childbearing into a woman's life seem to be very much in transition still. Erica Jong (1994) referred to the "whiplash generation" of women, referring to the Ping-Ponging of models of the ideal woman from Doris Day and Donna Reed in the '50s and Gloria Steinem in the '70s to Nancy Reagan and Princess Di in the '80s, and now back again to Hillary Rodham Clinton in the '90s. The question for the '90s and beyond is more complex than whether biology is our destiny. One way to phrase it might be, "How do we use our knowledge of our biological limitations and our cultural context to optimally shape our destiny?" If women now live thirty-five years longer than they did at the turn of the century, why is everything they want to accomplish compressed into a small fraction of their lives? These questions echo Dr. Kaltreider's sequencing theme in Chapter 1.

As one colleague put it, "We are living longer, but are we doing anything differently and in order to live better?" Rossi (1980) suggests that "American society is undergoing a shift from the lockstep pattern of schooling and job scheduling of mature industrialism, to a post-industrial pattern of greater flexibility, more interspersing of school and work, a more subtle adaptation between family and work patterns . . . a new organizational form is emerging in the advanced sectors of the economy, based on temporary, task-centered teams rather than bureau-cratized job ladders, which will mean far less solidity to expected job promotion, location, even job skills, for future workers" (p. 199). In other words, this may be the age of the free-lancer or independent con-tractor; an age when those who are most adaptable and willing to change will succeed best. While it may mean that it will be more diffi-cult to chart out a life course, for high-achieving professionals it also means the opportunity to develop different aptitudes that may not have been able to be integrated into one job. It may make it easier for a woman to take on a project, complete it, have children, take on a different type of project that is tailored to meet the demands of early child rearing, and then move on to something else that fits her next phase of life. It would allow women many varied opportunities for learning and mas-tery and make their expanded life cycle truly more expansive.

The way things are now, delayed childbearing with its risks and rewards may still feel like a good solution for many women. However, when thinking about maximizing destiny, the fact that there has been negligible change in the span of a woman's reproductive years while her life span has been dramatically increasing suggests that it might be practical for women to explore alternatives that allow them to delay other less time-limited goals. Perhaps what they experience now as "delay" and "juggling" with their associated negative connotations can evolve into a process that is more like "sequencing." New sequences may shift some of a woman's growth and fulfillment to the newly emer-gent thirty-five years available at the end of her life cycle. These years constitute a new and exciting developmental phase.

6

Constructing a Feminine Identity without Motherhood

MARDY S. IRELAND

I thought there must be another way [besides being a mother] to have an identity. When I really sit down and think about it, if I give it serious thought, I always end up back on the side of not having a child. I end up on the side of living with the fear and the aloneness, and getting old, and having to cope with whatever that's going to mean. . . . I think it is exciting to decide not to have a baby and really try to make room for your own creative self, but I also think it's really hard. I don't think it is easy. I think there are agonies involved. But I also think there are agonies involved in being a mother, many of which are never spoken. [40-year-old woman] [Ireland 1993, p. 84]

Toward the end of his life Sigmund Freud wondered, "What *do* women want?" He was speaking about the limitations of psychoanalytic theory to fully explain or elaborate female psychology. One answer to this question is that most women want more than just motherhood. And an increasing number of women simply do not want to be mothers at all; they wish instead to be and to do something else.

Motherhood was considered by Freud, and still by many today, to be the ultimate achievement and the confirmation of adult womanhood. Yet there has been a profound social shift; at the beginning of the twentieth century less than 10 percent of women were childless, and as we near the end of this century that figure approaches 20 percent (Tolnay and Guest 1982). Yet despite this sizable group of childless women, little popular literature was available in 1988, when I began my own research on this topic. There were a limited number of studies in the psychological literature (Houseknecht 1987). Initial research focused on infertility and its psychological sequelae or on exploring whether childless women were somehow more pathological (Kraft et al. 1980, McEwan et al. 1987). The research sample repeatedly consisted of highly educated, professional, white, married women (Houseknecht 1987). To expand the breadth of research sampling, I included women of varying class, race, and educational background in the 100 in-depth interviews. During the course of the five years it took to complete the research and writing of my book the overall interest in childlessness increased in both the popular and academic press.

It is a common phenomenon that when an idea whose time has come begins to emerge from the collective culture, it pops up simultaneously in multiple places and occurs with increasing frequency. Indeed, during those five years leading to the publication of my work *Reconceiving Women: Separating Motherhood from Female Identity* (1993) and in the subsequent years, the articles and books on childlessness have continued to increase (Chan and Margolin 1994, Connidis and McMullen 1994, Lampman and Dowling-Guyer 1995, Lindsey et al. 1994, Perry and Johnson 1994, Roskies and Carrier 1994). What is especially noteworthy in this regard is that the interest in a life without motherhood as a positive choice has incrementally risen. For example, two books published in 1996, *Without Child* (Lisle) and *Beyond Motherhood* (Safer), look exclusively at the lives of women who have made an active choice not to be a mother. In psychological terms, women who opt out of motherhood have historically received projections of emptiness and deviancy from others in society. Today a healthy curiosity is growing about these women and their lives. The stigmatization of this pathway of adult female development is receding slowly, but it is receding.

Common Myths about Childless Women

At least two common social myths about the woman who is not a mother have contributed to stigmatization: (1) she does not value or is not capable of sustaining personal relationships, and (2) she is over-invested in her career or work. In my research and in most other research neither of these stigmatizing myths are fully supported. Let me address each briefly.

The vast majority of the 100 women I interviewed mentioned relationships as one of the most formative influences of the past twenty-five years for their adult identities. In fact, relationships with husbands, lovers, friends, and other people's children contributed significantly to the creation and sustaining of a childless female adult identity. Relationships help a woman confront the limitations of her current ways of thinking about herself. (Is there something wrong with me if I don't want to have children? Must I have children to be a real woman?) Relationships for childless women are thus the mortar that helps to hold their identities together, and also at times a catalyst for change.

Embedded in the myth that childless women are not invested in relationships may be an assumption that women who choose not to become mothers are doing so because their own family experiences were so negative that they are irrevocably relationally damaged. In actuality, more women from dysfunctional families have children than do not. However, bearing children with an unexamined wish to heal childhood wounds results far more frequently in another generation of damaged children. Rather than social criticism for the women from dysfunctional families who decide "the family cycle is going to end with me," they should receive positive acknowledgement for a thoughtful judgment and acceptance of their social contributions in other spheres.

Primary relationships are usually a vehicle of adult development for most women and this is no different for women who choose not to be mothers. However, the primary relationships for women who aren't mothers do underscore a delineation between motherhood and female sexuality that is often either ignored altogether or overstated. This boundary confusion seems to result in women's inheritance of two opposing models of female sexuality: the nonsexual mother or the overly sexual and possibly promiscuous woman who isn't a mother. Mothers and nonmothers alike suffer from this misconstruction.

Additionally, for all childless women (by choice or not), female friendship is crucial to the structuring of the very meaning of "woman" and provides a grounding for their atypical identities. Friendship for women who are mothers is also important but not as essential in grounding their female identities because they have many historical definitions of "woman as mother" to which they can attach their womanhood. Thus, in contrast to the myth that childless women do not value or are not capable of sustained relationships, connection is even more central for women who aren't mothers.

The second common myth about childless women, that they are overinvested in their career or work, actually needs to be challenged. The overemphasis on women's capacity for maternity has diminished social recognition of their capacities for developing other aspects of themselves.

As discussed in Chapter 1, Freud is said to have defined the hallmarks of a healthy adult life as the capacity to love and to work, but this dictum seems to have been applied primarily to men. Clearly, women who are not mothers have their own creative spirits to birth and bring into the world. That these spirits are not in accordance with traditional views of women's creative experience is not necessarily a sign of their deviance, but rather an indication that traditional views are incomplete.

For some women motherhood is not experienced as a personally meaningful expression of creativity; motherhood, however, has been idealized and institutionalized in our society as inextricably linked with women's creative capacity. Nonmaternal activities seemingly continue to be regarded in a "lesser" light. Many, if not most, women harbor some of these negative perceptions, if only unconsciously, and consequently suffer guilt for having impulses to love and to work that are not satisfied by motherhood. The woman who is "childless by choice" actively chooses to focus her creative energy in places other than motherhood; in doing so she makes an important contribution toward dissolving social confusion linking woman's creative energy to her procreative capacity.

CHILD-LESS OR CHILD-FREE: PATHWAYS TO CONSTRUCTING A FEMININE IDENTITY WITHOUT MOTHERHOOD

To put it simply and directly, the woman who chooses a life that does not include motherhood is seeking to take a recognized place beside the woman who is a mother rather than to be hidden by her shadow. In the shadow she is seen not at all or in a distorted way—somehow as deficient, threatening. There are two pathways involving an element of choice for constructing a feminine adult identity without motherhood. Selecting each pathway has different implications for women currently considering whether to have children or not.

Transitional Women

The less proactive pathway and the more ambivalent choice is manifest in women who delay childbearing; as discussed in Chapter 5, this delay sometimes leads to their becoming childless by default or to their making a late decision to remain childless as the biological tick becomes deafening (Morris 1988).

These women, whom I call *transitional women*, are living in the stream of the social changes of the last thirty years. During this era, women have come into unprecedented access to effective birth control, education, and the workplace (Gerson 1985). These are the minimal conditions needed to create a "real" choice for women regarding motherhood and the worlds of career and community. Transitional women want to pursue the new social and career possibilities but they also want, or think they might want, to have children. They usually identify with characteristics of both traditional feminine and traditional masculine gender roles. These women would have been called androgynous in the 1970s, but in the 1990s it is more to the point to say that they express an expanding female identity rather than that they express aspects of a male identity (which is implied by the term *androgyny*) (Taylor and Hall 1982). To a greater or lesser extent, these women are ambivalent about the pleasures and demands of motherhood. Some have difficulty acknowledging this ambivalence to themselves during a period of time, which contributes to their delay (Rossi 1987, Walter 1986).

Most women who do become mothers do so before age 40. The woman who finds herself childless and approaching mid-life who can then *consciously* evaluate her maternal ambivalence has the opportunity to accept and differentiate her life from that of the woman who is already a mother and has put maternity higher on her priority list. Here are the words of one transitional woman about her process of becoming more self-aware.

> I've been split because historically I have seen my woman-self looking for Prince Charming. I have also seen my male-self kicking the world in the ass to a certain extent. It has only been in the last couple of years that I have seen that split and begun to integrate the two selves. So now I empower my woman-self to do what I have allowed my male-self to do, and I soften my male-self to allow myself to "schmooz" through situations and not attack [them] with brute force. That is an integration process of selves that I've had to do. Now I'm getting to the point where I see they don't have to be so separate. [Ireland 1993, p. 59]

Or another 44-year-old woman:

> I always thought of myself as having a child, but someday was always a long time away. . . . There's a part of me that could have

had a child and been happy with that, but I guess it isn't as big as the part of me that felt not having a child was the right way for me. There's been a lot of tension between these two parts of myself. [Ireland, unpublished]

Alternatively, the woman childless at this point in her life may experience her lack of being a mother as an unfulfilled desire. If so, she must begin to address what it is that is really "missing," interpret its meaning, and take some form of action to "fill" that missing space. For example, a woman may choose to become involved with children through volunteer work as a place to focus her nurturance. This other aspect of the maternal ambivalence is similar to that of the woman who is childless because of infertility. The self-evaluative process here involves acknowledging the losses not only of her imaginary children, but of the possible "selves" that might have developed through her experience of becoming and being a mother—selves that are now lost to her (Markus and Nurius 1986). Once these losses are acceded to, another creative focus and/or nurturing activities become possible. As a result, she will be more able to absorb and integrate the loss that is uniquely her own.

The transitional woman illustrates the dimensions of struggle and sacrifice. Struggling to reconcile and fulfill both maternal and nonmaternal desires, and faced with the reality that childbearing is no longer possible if or when she delays too long, the transitional woman needs to consciously understand and accept her own particular childless circumstances, letting go of her identification with her womb as a place to nourish a child. Only then can other kinds of creative "children" be born or simply be more fully acknowledged in those cases in which her creative work is already evident. In the act of conscious letting go of the concretization of birth, a different path is opened. Along this pathway to a child-less or child-free life, a transitional woman learns to release those aspects of her adult identity revolving around motherhood in order to be open to whatever else can be born from the space within.

Transformative Women

The woman who actively chooses a life without motherhood is a trailblazer, creating a path through a thicket of meanings of what a woman "should be." For this reason I call her a *transformative woman*. She is a woman whose identity is often more organized around independence and autonomy; because of this she may be judged by others as having a "masculinity complex." In fact, this kind of woman does often endorse characteristics of assertiveness and leadership capacity—traits more commonly associated with a traditional male sex role. However, research has shown that women identifying with characteristics of a masculine sex role have higher self-esteem and a sense of competency than do women who identify with those traits associated with the stereotypical feminine sex role (Taylor and Hall 1982). As a result, the transformative woman is more able to deflect negative social judgments about her child-free life than is the woman who is ambivalent about motherhood or the woman who is infertile and wants to have children. With a greater sense of self-confidence she is more likely to respond to such judgments with her own query about why a woman's life must be bounded by the institution of motherhood. These women usually feel connected and supported by the social network they create for themselves while at the same time they are aware of how their lives are left out or marginalized in the popular media.

Women who make an active choice to remain child-free are saying to the world that theirs are personal quests in which motherhood plays no part. This is not to say that all child-free women fulfill a frequent assumption that they do not like children. They are, however, making a clear decision to explore other avenues of expression for whatever maternal feelings they have and to mourn the loss of all the experiences of what bearing and raising a child in this culture means. A typical remark from the women I interviewed might be, "I've always thought I would make a good 'father' because I enjoy children, but I've never wanted to be the 'primary parent.' Most men I've met do not want to be the primary parent either."

In this respect I found in my research that not choosing motherhood is more about rejecting a "primary caretaking role" than about not wanting to relate to children. Many women who are childless by choice are not child-free in that they have important attachments to others' children. Additionally, some of these women feel that they have already fulfilled their maternal instinct, function, or desire by having been a caretaker of siblings or needy parents (Bram 1984).

In effect, these transformative women feel called to be and do something else besides being a mother. Most often this is a calling that arises from within more than as a response to an external expectation. Relationships, however, are often a formative versus originating influence in the calling to a different life. Confirming other childless research (Bram 1986), I found the positive quality of the intimate relationship with their mate was a significant factor in the decision by some women not to have children. Indeed, primary relationships among couples who choose not to become parents are more egalitarian and are reported to be more satisfying than are those of couples with children (Bram 1984, 1986, Houseknecht 1978). In short, voluntarily child-free women do not look to men to either give them a child or to "provide" for them in what would be considered "traditional" ways. They appear to seek partners with whom they can be "sojourners" through life.

Egalitarian childless relationships are not necessarily better than traditional relationships in which divisions of family responsibilities are more along gender lines, but neither are they worse or deviant. In the final analysis each and every arrangement of an adult intimate relationship bears its own particular rewards and problems. Interestingly, among the women I interviewed, those transformative women who chose a life without children found that a deeper connection with the self evolved through their meaningful relationships with others as much as it did through their own solitary efforts.

There was a clear pattern here of these women seeking to be open to what was emerging from within themselves concerning the charting of their lives. This means of accessing creativity and the creative space within one's self through intimate connection with others and permitting the self to be filled by what is there seems to represent a little-explored path of adult identity development, one that may be related to "feminine" characteristics in their most positive form but need not be reserved exclusively to women. Perhaps "womb envy" may not be limited just to a woman's reproductive capacity, but to this special way of developing an identity.

RECONCEPTUALIZING THE WOMB

Freud said, "Anatomy is destiny." It has become evident that we need not restrict our interpretation of these words to their literal meaning. The lives of these child-free women are telling us that we need not concretize the metaphorical possibilities of their womb space to the biological meaning of childbearing, nor do the words representing woman need to be restricted to reproduction per se. The varied lives of women who aren't mothers support the idea that motherhood has been more of a culturally embedded mandate than a biological or psychological mandate. The female body, the womb space (or more specifically the woman space), can be viewed as a generalized creative metaphor of holding and bringing forth. Rather than limiting women to their re-productive function, the womb can then be seen as a metaphor for all humanity of the holding of creative seeds and the birthing of genera-tive possibilities. Opening the female womb to its metaphoric potential enables a woman to be seen as complete unto herself in the same way as a man is.

The womb is a liminal space existing at the threshold between real and symbolic offspring. Many of the women in my research perceived that creative work, paid or nonpaid, had an important role in develop-ing and sustaining their adult identities. These women are creating additional metaphors (symbolic offspring if you will) that reflect fe-male themes of interconnection and of a self-in-relation rather than the more masculine metaphors of solitude and conquest. Here is the way one 40-year-old woman described it.

> I think of the feminine as something which is coming from the unconscious, or coming from inside. There is the element of having to open yourself up to what is given rather than deciding what you want. You take what comes. I think that is a very feminine capac-ity for experience. The masculine is more of "I'm going to decide what I want and go after it." The feminine is, "I'm going to open myself up to what might or might not be there and discover what it is." [Ireland 1993, p. 139]

The emptiness attributed to women who are not mothers, because they do not bear children from their wombs, may be reframed now as a lack of adequate social recognition and understanding of femi-nine metaphors. Until quite recently, what has been very culturally absent has been the naming and representation of nonmaternal fe-male experience.

One 42-year-old woman who said her creative self was like "a little ember that somebody blew on and I just had to go with it" is express-ing the experience of many women who are simply following the inner call toward an individual life. This life needn't be exceptional, in fact it may be very ordinary, but it is a feminine life apart from motherhood, which, to some people, is still an extraordinary choice. But for many of the women who are child-free by choice, their view is that "we are healthy women making healthy choices not to have children but to do something else with our lives" (Ireland, unpublished).

WOMEN BUT NOT MOTHERS: CONCLUSION

Searching for historical roots for these thoroughly modern women led me to a creation story that I believe speaks to aspects of female identity and subjectivity that have been present in the unconscious of every past woman and especially present in women who choose not to become mothers. This legend reveals some of the roots of the negative portrayals of women who aren't mothers and of the incipient threat posed by the very "otherness" of their womanhood. Concomitantly, it also points toward a direction for integrating this "other" kind of female energy.

According to the Hebrew legend, Lilith was the first woman created by God from the matter of earth, like Adam, the first man (Begg 1984, Hurwitz 1992). Lilith and Adam soon began to argue over who would "lie beneath" the other during sex. Lilith became aware that neither was listening to the other, so she uttered the name of God and "flew into the air of the word," running away to reside by the sea.

Adam complained to God that Lilith had run away. God then sent three angels to bring her back, saying that if she refused she must be prepared to sacrifice 100 of her sons each day. Lilith refused. She said that she was destined to weaken infants unless they were protected by the names of the three angels who had come for her, or by the image of God. In later elaborations of the story Lilith, on some of her return visits from the Red Sea, would visit men in their sleep and bring them wet dreams.

This creation story of woman and man was later amended to name Eve as the first woman; it is this amended version that appears in the book of Genesis. Eve, being made from the rib of Adam, begins on less than equal footing. Eve's single expression of Lilith's independent, equal nature has catastrophic consequences. It is Eve who first bites the forbidden apple of knowledge, resulting in the couple's expulsion from Eden and a legacy of painful childbirth for all women to come as part of her punishment for breaking the law. Lilith embodies female characteristics that were essentially deleted from the mythic roots of the womanhood as portrayed by Eve. Lilith, who is made of earth like Adam, manifests woman's difference in equal terms instead of woman's difference being defined in opposite and lesser terms of man.

This legend also imparts what the less-than-desirable consequences are when a woman is cut off from a mutual relationship and must live in a patriarchal society that denies her equality. When there is lack of acceptance and support for a woman's independent impulses, the effects upon herself and others are likely to be distorted. Lilith births her own kind of children (not born of man) but is forced to sacrifice 100 of them each day—her own creative contributions are constantly diminished, as it were. In these circumstances she also carries a destructive potential, perhaps associated with a malignant envy, toward other women's children. Because her sexuality is denied, Lilith must cloak her natural sexual desire in the folds of night, seeking satisfaction from unavailable partners.

On the other side of the coin, Lilith suggests a direction to pursue regarding the expansion of female identity. Her legend illustrates both repression and the importance of language in constructing human subjectivity. Lilith spoke the name of God in the moment before she left Adam. Considering the role of language in human experience, one could interpret Lilith's speaking of God's name as empowering her own destiny. Did not God recognize the validity of her claim to individuality on her own terms by not forcing her to return to Adam?

In Old Testament stories related to Lilith, it was said that, in her surreptitious returns from the Red Sea, she promised to forsake her evil ways toward whomever they were directed if that person would call her by one or all of her fourteen names. This seems to be an attempt, through the use of language, to legitimate the process of feminine subjectivity. I would suggest that when the feminine has more access to conscious "names" (words/identities) other than motherhood, the apparently negative aspects of nonmothers, which bear some of the repressed and disavowed attributes of Lilith, will be experienced as less threatening and destructive.

A conscious remembrance and removal of the repression of feminine empowerment and female desire, as metaphorized in the story of Lilith, is needed. Women who are mothers are not really required to integrate the energy Lilith symbolizes into their female identities because the culture supports this partialized female identity. They can remain identified with the feminine energy of Eve but their lives will be less vital without this fuller integration. However, women who are not mothers must reintegrate the nonmaternal feminine energy symbolized by Lilith into their identities if they are to forge and maintain a positive adult identity.

The transitional woman with her maternal ambivalence must open herself to the Lilith side of her nature so that her life unfolds not as a substitute for motherhood but instead as an equally meaningful pathway. She must broaden her identification with the feminine beyond Eve to include features not attached to maternity.

The transformative woman, who more actively turns away from Eve's maternity than does the transitional woman, is aligned earlier in life with Lilith's feminine energy. She is drawn to a quest outside the territory of motherhood. At times, identifying, following, and engaging herself in the realization of her nontraditional interests may make her feel very much like Lilith—a woman alone, if not in exile. As such, she must discern the importance of connecting with others who value her difference. She must know that she will bear a certain burden of other's misunderstanding or nonacceptance of choosing a life of her own.

The legend of Lilith is only one point of departure I have used to think and speak about feminine experience outside of stereotypic notions. It simply offers a name and range of meaning for womanhood not contained in our western Judeo-Christian tradition's story of Eve. Using "child-free" or "child-less by choice" as words to categorize the women who are not mothers by some measure of choice is today inadequate. These words still focus attention on the identity of woman in terms of a child, still define her in relation to motherhood rather than as an individual as a separate adult woman making life choices. Other names and words are needed; slowly they will be birthed.

> The word "childless" is focusing on what you are not. This has been another part of my own healing *journey—the shift from what is not to what is.* [47-year-old woman]

> If I made jigsaw puzzle pieces out of every aspect of my life and I then put them all together, there would not be a big gap in the middle that was somehow the "unborn child" in my life. [43-year-old woman] [Ireland 1993, p. 83]

7

Love in the Trenches: Dual-Career Relationships

NANCY B. KALTREIDER
CAROLYN GRACIE
CAROLE SIRULNICK

This is what it's all about. Dual-career relationships represent a profound social experiment, carried out behind closed doors and with infrequent role models for guidance. Today young people are restructuring their career and family expectations at lightning speed, often under the pressure of the increasing necessity of two incomes for a family's financial survival. This chapter is a translation of the phenomena of this role-in-transition into everyday experience, bolstered by theory and amenable to the development of coping strategies. Overall, this book, *Dilemmas of a Double Life*, examines issues within the context of the interaction of work and family and its relation to well-being; the primary love relationship is the stage upon which this interface is played out.

Dual-career relationships at their best can provide a rich and meaningful life experience as each partner becomes for the other intellectual companion, best friend, and lover (Nadelson and Eisenberg 1977). Because there are few role models of older couples who placed high individual value on both work and family commitment, the care and maintenance of these relationships often involves more stress than either partner anticipates. Traditional gender role expectations no longer fit, yet they lurk close to consciousness, shaping our sense of what we "should" be bringing to the interaction with our partner. Tensions increase as professional women embark in directions far different from the life journeys of their mothers or grandmothers alongside men who have changed less radically, and sometimes less willingly (Hochschild 1989). In addition, many dual-career partnerships are not formalized by marriage and many families are not based on a heterosexual model, yet we hope that most of the themes in this chapter will apply to their lives as well; we also acknowledge the additional stress imposed by these nontraditional choices.

In a descriptive study of the phenomena of a good marriage, Wallerstein and Blakeslee (1995) saw the current dual-career relationship issues as daunting at best: "In today's marriages, in which people work long hours, travel extensively, and juggle careers with family, more forces tug at the relationship than ever before. Modern marriages are battered by the demands of her workplace as well as his, by changing community values, by anxiety about making ends meet each month, by geographical moves, by unemployment and recession, by the vicissitudes of child care, and by a host of other issues" (p. 7).

These are normative dilemmas and the evolving solutions are far from resolution as a new generation, seeing their parents reeling from "having it all," is now working on the design of a more flexible model to contain the inevitable work–family tension. In the research by Wortman and her colleagues (1991), when women and their husbands were asked how often they had experienced conflicts between their work and family responsibilities in the past month, over 75 percent reported experiencing such conflicts "every day." The conflicts include time management, overload symptoms interfering with role performance, and the difference in partners' expectations of effort devoted to home and work. They are heightened by disparate views about gender roles, by perceived inequity of contribution to the partnership, and by limited flexibility in the workplace. As emphasized throughout the book, these conflicts are experienced within a developmental context in which life-cycle transitions, career shifts, and events in the lives of family members will affect the couple's perception of the stressors.

The dual-career life style is demanding but not inherently stressful; the costs may be balanced by considerable benefits, including personal fulfillment and increased income (Lewis and Cooper 1988). The literature is disproportionate in its focus on the experience of women, but its consistent theme is that career women report high self-esteem when the relationship is working well and both partners experience each other as competent (Sekaran 1986). The sense of self is enriched by multiple sources of identity and shared incomes that allow each partner to make individual career choices less driven by financial necessity. Women now bring to the relationship negotiation and compromise skills learned in the workplace rather than in the original family. Although challenging, the work–family conflicts are not necessarily any more stressful for women than the traditional limited roles but simply require new skills to maximize the rewards.

The shift in societal expectations and gender role models offers some exciting possibilities for both sexes. Men, especially, are still adapting and may find their lives enhanced by an earlier peak in nurturing activities, as there is more room for and need for fathering. Hochschild (1989) notes: "The 'female culture' has shifted more rapidly than the 'male culture'; the image of the go-get-'em woman has yet to be fully matched by the image of the let's-take-care-of-the-kids-together man" (p. 205). Although men may welcome women in the workplace, they have not necessarily altered their view that the home duties are "women's business," producing conflicts between roles and uncertainty of what is expected within a role. Women's roles cannot change in isolation. Men are still supposed to be the upwardly mobile heroes of the world of work and their involvement in the home will inevitably alter those priorities (O'Neil et al. 1987). Each couple must carry out an open and ongoing examination of their shared gender-role value system in this time of role transition.

LESSONS FROM THEORY

A key concept in the dual-career relationship is that of *equity*, that the two individuals are receiving equal relative gains based on the overall balance of rewards and costs in the relationship (Walster et al. 1978). "Equity introduces a sense of fairness, rather than a condition of equality, as the essential component for evaluation of a relationship by its participants" (Rapoport and Rapoport 1975, p. 422). Inherent in this concept is that the sense of equity will allow each partner to tolerate some transient inequality or even a longer-term imbalance in the relationship if they feel that ultimately both individuals and the family will flourish. This is contrasted with an *egalitarian* relationship in which the focus is on equal and often carefully measured distribution of the various roles, responsibilities, and obligations.

As any couples therapist knows, the focus on measured equality often can lead to a competitive struggle. The woman may set non-negotiable quality standards for household task completion or the husband may focus on income disparity as his measure of fairness. Hochschild (1989) describes this uneasy alliance in a couple for whom all bills are split down the middle, banking accounts are separate, and home tasks are meted out, but the husband states, "Since I earn more, I demand that she make dinner every night." Partners who share the concept that the good of the couple's unit at any given time outweighs the individual good usually have a less stressful relationship (Rachlin and Hansen 1985). It is less effective to legislate tasks than to assess what each partner does best and then to divide up the less desirable choices.

As women increasingly have education and career prestige equal to that of their partners, there is often a shift toward more supportive behavior in both directions. Each can encourage the other to talk about work-related problems, to take advantage of professional opportunities, to understand extra time spent in the workplace, and to pitch in on extra household chores in a time of work crunch (Emmons et al. 1990). A more complex psychological issue is the appraisal of equity: in several studies married women professionals tended to overvalue the amount the husband "helped" at home and to apply harsher standards to their own performance in the marital and parental roles than to that of their husbands (Wortman et al. 1991). A 1993 survey by the Family and Work Institute (*New York Times* 1996) reports that working women still do 87 percent of the shopping, 81 percent of the cooking, 78 percent of the cleaning, and 63 percent of the family bill paying. Men tend to contribute more to the family income and thus perceive their lower level of domestic work as fair. Women may accept this accounting principle for the same reason, but by doing so decrease the likelihood that they will ever increase their own income potential. Wives' dissatisfaction with the domestic and child-care load is more related to the amount of their husbands' contribution than to the load personally carried (Lewis and Cooper 1988). In Wortman (1988) and her colleagues' study of domestic chore distribution, they found that for all household tasks except for repair and maintenance, women to a far greater extent than their husbands felt it was their responsibility to see that the task was accomplished. Women often report that they feel lucky if their husband "helps," and hesitate to precipitate conflict by asking him to assume primary responsibility.

Despite shared roles, the difference in gender socialization discussed in Chapters 1 and 2 means that there is often a lack of emotional empathy by each partner for how the other experiences the world. In their study in 1984, Thomas and colleagues noted that the more the positive regard between the spouses, the greater was the marital quality. Positive regard for spouse meant perceived similarities, consensus in values, and validation of the self by the other. In the low-quality marriages, 75 percent of the husbands underestimated their wife's stress level significantly, while in high-quality marriages most husbands

126

either accurately estimated or overestimated the amount of stress experienced by the wife.

The concept of *role strain* (Davidson and Cooper 1983, French et al. 1982) includes both the appraisal of conflicting demands within and between roles and the ambiguity of each role based upon the uncertainty of others' expectations. It appears that role ambiguity is a more potent source of work–family conflict for men than for women (Greenhaus and Parasuraman 1989). *Role overload* simply implies that the demands of the role exceed the resources regardless of whether it is the domestic role or the work role (French et al. 1982). Lewis and Cooper (1988) note that employed women are more likely than men to experience domestic overload. The period of peak stress for women in dual-career relationships has consistently been shown to occur when there are preschool-aged children in the home, which increases women's domestic management tasks even when they are at work (Bryson et al. 1978). Although overload in the workplace is experienced by both men and women, it seems to have more of a stressful impact on the dual-earner husband (Pleck and Staines 1985). Professional-level careers also bring up the concept of role overflow in which work tasks leak into the home environment as boundaries are poorly defined. Women report a reduced perception of stress at work even when the hours are long and inconvenient as long as they feel that they have the autonomy to modify their schedule for family reasons (Lewis and Cooper 1988). No matter what level of career success they attain, women tend to differentially make more accommodations than do their partners in their daily schedules. Even when they are at work, women maintain the "domestic executive" expectation of feeling responsible that home issues are covered competently (Apter 1993), a role overflow in the other direction.

A related concept is that of *role underload* (Lewis 1986), in which a partner decreases involvement at work or home but finds that accommodation to be a source of stress. For some women cutting back is experienced as a defeat, like the supermarket shopper poignantly described by Hochschild (1989) who wants to run down the aisle screaming, "I'm an MBA, I'm an MBA!" (p. 196). Working mothers tend to feel both superior to housewives and envious of them. The high-powered woman who returns to work part-time and is given less demanding projects may not perceive that the lack of challenge at work is compensated for by her increased opportunities for domestic involvement.

The "role underload" experience may also be about mothering, as detailed in Chapter 4, where Amy Tyson describes how maternity leave often ends just as the developmental period of greatest mother–infant attachment peaks; the return to work may leave the new mother feeling bereft and preoccupied. Moreover, the reentry into the workplace after maternity leave may reveal a virtual demotion as others have seamlessly taken over important tasks. Often there is a poor fit between the needs of the individual and the needs of the workplace; even the feminist campaigner for liberal parental leave policies may be taken aback when she becomes the supervisor scrambling to find replacement coverage.

Given the complexity of the role shifts, what would a marriage look like that could successfully balance both intimacy and autonomy for each partner? As Wallerstein and Blakeslee (1995) describe, "A companionate marriage is founded on the couple's shared belief that men and women are equal partners in all spheres of life and that their roles, including those of marriage, are completely interchangeable. Both husband and wife lead important parts of their lives outside of the home. While one partner, usually the wife, may take time from her career to devote to young children, she remains committed to both work and family" (p. 155). The love for each other includes a respect for the partner's profession. There is a profoundly mutual engagement in the task at hand that holds the marriage together and allows personal needs to be placed on the back burner at high-stress times.

The rewards of a dual-career relationship are substantial but so are the sacrifices. The man gives up the power of the exclusive breadwinner role but gets to be closer to the kids. The woman gives up the protection of reliance on her husband's financial support but she gains fiscal autonomy instead of her mother's financial dependency, and the freedom to pursue work she loves. What's exciting about the new companionate marriage is that everything represents a choice. There are no foregone conclusions and all role decisions are on the negotiation table.

LESSONS FROM LIFE

Joan, age 39, is a vice president and manager at a large urban accounting firm. She supervises twenty-five employees and commands a salary well over $150,000 a year. Her job entails forty hours-plus a week as well as many business dinners, breakfast meetings, and some travel.

Her husband, Brian, age 41, is a headhunter working forty hours a week in a small office near their home. He grosses between $80,000 and $100,000 a year and has some flexibility to coach soccer and baseball teams after school. He attends one major business meeting a year lasting for a week.

The children are Sam, age 8, and Becky, age 4. Becky is in a daycare/preschool program from 8:30 A.M. until 5:30 P.M. Sam goes to school and an aftercare program at his elementary school.

A typical weekday schedule is that Brian takes the kids to school in the morning and Joan either drives or takes a bus to work in the city. Brian picks up the kids and takes them home. Joan arrives home at 6:30 to 7:00 P.M. and fixes dinner. While Brian does the dishes, she gets the kids bathed. They both put the kids to sleep and then watch TV, make phone calls, talk a bit, read, do the laundry, pay bills, or simply go to sleep.

On the weekend, the first priority is child-focused activities that both Joan and Brian try to participate in fully: soccer/baseball games, birthday parties, play dates, visits to the park or pool, family outings. Joan typically does the laundry, which Brian helps to fold, and the majority of the grocery shopping, which Brian puts away. During the week, Brian or Joan will often stop and pick up some needed foodstuffs at the local market. On weekends, evenings are generally spent at home, with occasional spontaneous dinners with other families with young children. A few times a year, Joan and Brian will exchange babysitting with another family or hire a babysitter in order to go out for special occasions.

Each feels that the quality of their marriage is eroding and they jointly decide to enter couples therapy.

Joan has the following concerns and complaints:

- Feels constant pressure from work
- Feels that she handles too many of the family chores
- Has no time for self
- Is jealous that Brian gets time with the kids in the afternoon if he is able to get away from work early

- Feels she is too much of a mother and not enough of a woman

    Brian protests about the following:

- Does not feel appreciated for what he does
- Has no time to play tennis with friends
- Wants to plan a weekend away with Joan but feels she is uninterested in spending time alone with him
- Feels their sex life is practically dead because they are always tired
- Feels Joan does not take his financial suggestions seriously
- Secretly worries that he is drinking too much

The Joan/Brian story is not the stuff of novels or even sitcoms. They are looking for help to bring meaning back to their relationship rather than justification for leaving it. Neither is carrying on a clandestine affair: How would they find the time? Yet contained within their description are many of the patterns of miscommunication, clashes of values, and burnout that haunt dual-career marriages.

Developmental Asynchrony

Perhaps one of the most synchronistic days in a couple's life is the day of their marriage. On that day, presumably, each person is focused primarily on the other, the marriage, and shared priorities. After that day, however, each individual in the couple ebbs and flows with being in and out of sync with the other person. Perhaps some of the asynchrony is attributable to the major differences in male and female adult development discussed in Chapter 1. For example, Uma Sekaran (1985) showed that irrespective of their level of self-esteem and sense of competence, women derived lower levels of job satisfaction when they spent more of their discretionary time at work as compared to men, who had the opposite reaction. These differences in perception can lead to misunderstanding of each other. Joan is jealous of Brian's more flexible access to the children and Brian resents her more absorbing and prestigious career path. Most couples do not do a lot of conscious decision making and coordination of their career paths. The more common story is that the woman sets aside or consciously alters her career aspirations to support her husband's career or to carry out child-care obligations. Even this choice of the wavy path by many career women usually has an unarticulated plan of "your turn, then my turn," which can lead to unexpected resentment when the husband wants to transfer job locations in mid-life or a child has urgent needs in adolescence or adulthood.

Fatigue

More than ten years ago, two of us (Kaltreider and Gracie) did an unpublished interview study of both partners in dual-doctor relationships in the San Francisco Bay area. We found that women more often than their male partners complained of emotional depletion and fatigue. Women physicians often felt guilty, especially when it came to their own critical performance assessment of their mothering or other nurturing roles. The sick or frightened child still usually called out for "Mommy," and there was no way not to respond. Male physicians in the study did not take into consideration as consistently the effect of their working hours and habits on their wives and children and did not generally experience the need to modify their own career plans to support family needs. Chronic fatigue has a particularly debilitating effect upon the ability of the couple to communicate effectively.

Time

The shared authorship of this chapter represents the reality that the first two people who had planned to write it (Gracie, Sirulnick) made valiant attempts that crashed and burned in the daily pressures of their lives. "Perhaps if I had had more time to ruminate and reorganize the precious time I have to work at my computer . . . perhaps if I had been more willing not to go to swim meets every weekend or to family outings or showers and . . . ," wrote Carole Sirulnick. Lyn Gracie described how she sat in the backseat of the car working on the literature review while her husband drove the family toward their ski-week destination, then holed up by the ski lift with her papers as family members came and went. But creativity and focus can't emerge in twenty-minute aliquots interrupted by urgent family or patient needs; the final writing of the chapter fell to the author in mid-life (Kaltreider) whose children are safely out of the nest, giving me the glorious freedom of unstructured time.

Time is of the essence in a dual-career relationship and much of the communication is about the endless managerial planning needed to order the tasks and events. Joan and Brian had effectively figured out how to get food on the table and the clothes cleaned and the car serviced. What was lost was the companionship of the early relationship as they now became like two ships that pass in the night. Others describe the "relay race marriage" in which the kids are efficiently handed off from one partner to the other but the runners can never stop to connect. But blocks of time do not magically appear, one's professional obligations are never really finished, and both partners in a good marriage long for the sense of validation and connection that they dimly remember from the past.

Intimacy and Sexuality

The glue in good dual-career marriages is often sexual satisfaction (Thomas et al. 1984), perhaps achieved by scheduling intimate moments with as much priority as other competing events. One of our husbands presented a gift of a "To Do Today" tablet with number one on each page being an evocative line drawing of a couple making love. When this priority is not set, the loss of sexual drive may be as simple as time and fatigue, but on another level it may have much to do with individual feelings of anger, loneliness, and a perceived lack of volunteered intimacy by the other. Much as with Brian and Joan, if the relationship is shaky, there may be underground resistance to scheduling time to be close because of the fear of confronting the painful reality of falling out of love. The reciprocity necessary to intimate connection may be harder to achieve in dual-career relationships because the partners tend to have a high achievement orientation and to set perfectionistic standards for their marriage and partner (Rice 1979). Effective partnerships in which there is positive regard between the spouses seem to be more easily achieved with partners who are engaged in similar career pursuits so the understanding built by "work talk" feels like an intimate connection (Thomas et al. 1984).

132

Children

It is clear and understandable that two-earner partners with children experience more stress than nonparents and that the stressors are especially great for parents of preschool-age children (Lewis and Cooper 1983, Pleck et al. 1978). The stress may increase with the number of children (Keith and Shafer 1980). A crucial factor in predicting marital quality is the husband's assistance with child rearing (Thomas et al. 1984). Men report more psychosomatic symptoms and lower levels of happiness when there are children in the home (Benin and Niemstedt 1985, Lewis 1986) than do their dual-earner wives. In our interviews with dual-doctor couples, the current perceived adequacy of child-care arrangements seemed to be the most powerful predictor of the stress level experienced.

Husbands are more likely to participate in the fun aspects of child care (like Brian coaching the soccer team) and less likely to volunteer for the more burdensome tasks like getting up in the middle of the night or staying home when the child is sick (Wortman et al. 1991). Wives often seem reluctant to confront these issues of inequity and instead try to subtly manipulate their spouses into participating in child care. For example, one mother described how she would try to ignore her 2-year-old son's urgent requests for "more juice" several times, hoping that the repetition would catch her husband's attention. Aside from passive manipulation, a woman may actively discourage her husband's participation by sending signals that "all is well" either because of her anticipation that the husband would be inept on the domestic front or from a deep-rooted value system that the mother's role is one of omnipotent responsibility. Although the major issues of schooling and religious upbringing are usually discussed by couples ahead of time, there is generally little planning ahead about how the day-to-day juggling act will be handled, often leaving new parents caught unprepared by the array of tasks.

When dual-career couples share both ambition and pleasure in each other's company, it is understandable why the choice is increasingly made not to include children in the package (as described in Chapter 6) or why the baby decision is postponed so often that the right time never does come (as described in Chapter 5). When birth control was variably effective and society spoke of "marriage and children" as if it were one word, the wish not to bear children could not be spoken aloud without censure so many couples feigned infertility; now children are a choice and couples on the fast track may find it a less attractive one than previous generations did or else they may opt to have a single child who can be fit more easily into their adult world.

Eldercare

With the aging of the baby-boomer generation, the issue of eldercare is becoming an increasingly important factor in the lives and time commitments of mid-life adults, particularly the time-deprived dual-career couples. Often the aging parents' needs increase before the tasks of dealing with one's children have been phased down. Even when the children have left the nest, the relative postponement of retirement savings goals for immediate educational expenses makes the dual-career couple reluctant to take on financial responsibility for aging parents or to give up work commitments that they have waited so long to savor. The needs of senior citizens vary and can change without warning; their impact is multiplied when the dual-career family is geographically distant and there is no low-key way to interact. Couples now should be factoring these needs into the juggling equation and discussing their values in this area with each other and with their parents. At any one time, one of the partners will need to keep some kind of career flexibility to handle cross-generational emergencies and transitions. Working out geographical proximity and involving one's maturing children in the process may be a part of the solution.

Competition

It is unlikely that women who are increasingly welcomed into the workplace as full partners will not bring home that model, including a newfound pleasure at being successful and powerful. Over and over, studies have shown that the greater the salience of the woman's work role and the more obvious her prestige, the more at risk is the marital relationship. Brian's sense of not being appreciated or taken seriously by Joan is at least partially a reflection of his being threatened by her more committed and remunerated work role. Moen (1985) suggests that the "absorptiveness" of one's emotional involvement in career is a po-

134

tential predictor of its intrusion into the home domain. A woman's work–family conflict appears to be more dependent on her own job involvement than on the intensity of her partner's work, while men seem to feel most at jeopardy when each person regards his or her own career as having greater priority (Greenhaus and Parasuraman 1989). Even when a woman has a conscious plan to sequence her family and work priorities, it can be painful to see a spouse moving rapidly ahead on a path of opportunity that seems potentially lost to her. In these days of political correctness, a man may give overt support to the acceptance of her increasing career responsibilities but rail about why dinner is late or do an about-face when the choice collides with his own career ambitions. In a social setting the man with a powerful wife is often met with quizzical looks and comments like "she must be a handful." The derogatory intensity of the term *pussy-whipped* makes it clear that this discomfort with feminine power in a marital relationship is a societal prejudice and not just a personal conflict.

Employer Inflexibility

Dual-career parenting cannot become the normative mode for young professionals without accommodations occurring in the workplace. Recognizing that the male partner is no longer likely to be the only breadwinner requires important shifts in order for companies to recoup their investment in rising male and female managerial talent and to avoid absenteeism triggered by work–family conflicts. Companies and professions are now experimenting with offering child care on site, flexible work hours, telecommuting, and hotlines to assist with child and eldercare snafus. Based on the economics of losing a highly skilled employee's time, some firms even wrap and send out Christmas presents or run summer day camp programs. Family-friendly legislation is moving forward and maternity is no longer regarded as an unpredictable event.

Such programs tend to have positive effects on employee morale and may have the hidden benefit of decreasing both partners' stress level by encouraging the maintenance of crucial relationship ties. Less anticipated but speaking to the power of social imperatives, the job flexibility is often used by women to pick up more of the home responsibilities or to try to accomplish a full-time job for a half-time salary. In this country and abroad, companies that offer paternity leave as an option find that it is rarely utilized because of the implied stigma of the man not being a serious contender in the workplace.

Professional Stress

So many people who carry a professional level of job commitment complain about a syndrome of chronic fatigue, anger, and cynicism that floods into the relationship (Gardner and Hall 1987, McCue 1982). Maladaptive efforts to deal with this stress include passive-aggressive behavior with colleagues and spouses, social isolation, denial, exaggeration of obsessive-compulsive character traits, and substance abuse. Partners who recognize these inevitable internalized stressors and do not try to displace them into the relationship have less interpersonal conflict. In our dual-doctor study, respondents described themselves as being tired either "usually" or "always." A workplace environment in which the number or hours at the desk is equated with competence and dedication can be particularly troubling. One female physician noted "most of my concerns about my professional competence are neurotic, and I realize that my anger at the training system has nothing to do with my husband." She recognized through her own psychotherapy that her frequent perception of her husband as unsupportive was really about her male-oriented work environment and that her own needs for control often led to blocking of her husband's frequent attempts to be helpful. Several of the physicians in our study were in their second marriages and ruefully noted that, in retrospect, they could see how much their own professional stress symptoms exacerbated the problems in their first marriages. In the case example, both Brian and Joan may be confusing work and family stressors and attributing too much of their dissatisfaction to relationship issues.

Gender Norms

In this time of societal reorganization of long-held value systems, most couples have not talked about the profound impact of gender-role expectations on their own conceptualizations. Recall that Joan was vaguely uneasy about whether she was enough of a woman and that

Brian was hurt that his male expertise in finance was not taken seriously enough. The issues leak out in unanticipated ways: a woman's sense of panic when she signs their first mortgage and realizes that her salary is crucial to the contract and not just "play money," a husband's assumption that his wife will be the social planner for all the special occasions of their extended family, or even the shared expectation that the husband will "know" how to parent and do domestic chores intuitively although he has had no adequate parental role model.

As detailed in Chapter 1, men and women have different aims in communication and may experience the same event with very different meaning structures. Two of us did a study of health professionals' responses after the 1989 Loma Prieta earthquake rocked the Bay area (Kaltreider et al. 1992). Most men tended to go back to work and get on with the business of life as soon as they reassured themselves that no damage to the home had been sustained. The women found themselves preoccupied by the potential threat to their families and torn by the question of whether in a future crisis (a possibility reinforced by the recurring aftershocks) they belonged at home taking care of the family or at work taking care of their patients. Each partner was puzzled and often critical of the other's response to the traumatic event. The lack of intuitive empathy for how the other experiences and reacts to life can take a toll on the interpersonal validation so necessary to maintain a marriage. Marital satisfaction should greatly increase if couples take time to reevaluate gender-role concepts together and share their own perceptions of what it means to be a man or a woman.

COPING STRATEGIES

There is no tradition or societal support mechanism in place for dual-career marriages. Thus the principles for survival described in this chapter are mostly anecdotal in nature and still in process. Both partners need strong positive regard for the other and must affirm the importance of career achievement for each of them. Even though each is obviously competent and attractive, each needs validation from the other that that is the case. A dual-career couple needs excellent communication skills and a sense that the family is a shared enterprise with a flexible willingness to negotiate roles. Moving from being a couple to a family should be a choice made with eyes wide open; the changing responsibilities should be discussed ahead of time. Most of all, a dual-career couple needs to take pleasure in the richness of their variegated lives, which will allow them to move through obligations sequentially without having to enter the burnout zone.

Communication between partners about career development, family coordination, and the maintenance of intimacy is essential. Couples who anticipate the conflicts that arise from divergent developmental paths are better prepared to hit the issues head-on and make compromises that feel equitable to both. Ongoing discussions will serve to reduce stress even when agreement is not complete, and daily time to check in with each other should be a predictable part of the routine. There are some basic guidelines: all criticism should be constructive, think before you speak, ask for time out if you feel flooded with emotion while you figure out what is going on, watch for the "window of opportunity" for change. The time initially spent on communication in the relationship will be time saved later on.

Set aside, even schedule, time for adult interaction—sex, fun, and relaxation. Share books and movies by discussing them. Consider yourselves as social revolutionaries and talk together about what shifts there are in your perception of gender roles and what choices still make you feel guilty. Acknowledge that the task distribution will never seem quite equal but figure out how to make it seem more equitable. Discuss values openly, describing the differences between how you feel and how you think you should feel. Evaluate what models you carry from your parents' marriage, both positive and negative. Plan regular evenings out alone with each other and an occasional weekend away. Even though you feel that you hardly see the kids, your intimacy is a good investment for them as well. When the nest is finally empty, you don't want to be facing a stranger across the table.

Most dual-career parents set aside personal interests and hobbies because that appears to be the area of most flex in the system. The inevitable question on the high school reunion questionnaire about "How do you spend your leisure time?" usually evokes guffaws from working parents followed by answers like "pay the bills" or "fall asleep." Yet each member of the couple should make a significant effort toward maintaining his or her own physical and emotional health. Going for a short run before the babysitter leaves can be the most soothing time of the day and obviates the need for a predinner drink just to let down. Give your partner a surprise present of a day at the spa or two tickets to the ball game. Taking care of the self is ultimately taking care of the marriage because it is impossible to be supportive unless you are feeling whole. As the children's need for you becomes less all-consuming, begin involvement in community-based activities that will link you to other couples in similar situations. Two of us (Gracie, Kaltreider) have been part of a dinner group of women psychiatrists that has met monthly for more than ten years. Together the group has moved through infertility, pregnancy, starting a practice, building a university career, coping with parental death, setting limits for adolescents, and now the first hot flashes. The answers shared were not profound but each new developmental issue had usually been faced by others in the group, now lovingly characterized as the "psychochickens" by our adolescent children. The developing of a sense of generativity and rootedness is an antidote for the frequent loss of meaning that can occur in mid-life.

In the discussion groups in the symposium that generated this book, the sections on dual-career relationships were packed. The topics brought up for discussion were far ranging and it soon became clear to everyone that there were no obvious solutions and that no one was doing it perfectly. That knowledge alone somehow seemed therapeutic. The women encouraged each other to let go of the driven need to be superwoman, to accept a more modest level of cleanliness as civilized, and to identify what tasks could better be done by others for pay. They talked about how to maintain flexibility, self-esteem, and intimacy without waiting for the world to change first. The older women in the groups suggested that not all things are possible or even necessary and urged investment in the couples' relationships as paying the best long-term dividends. Being in a good marriage in which the capacity "to love and to work" is valued by both can be transformative. After the academic accolades are forgotten and the promotion to partnership is remembered as a mixed blessing, it is the loving connection to each other and to the next generation that can give life meaning.

8

Career and Parenting: Women Make It Work

Lynn E. Ponton

L Y N N   E .   P O N T O N

What they had in mind was not complicated. . . . Somebody, a "nurturing" woman with no threatening presumptions, would look after the kids each day while Mom and Dad worked at their important jobs. Nights and weekends, Mom and Dad would divide the labor fifty-fifty. Dad would be a New Man, and Mom would be a Fulfilled Woman. . . . What they hadn't specifically foreseen: that the baby would start calling the sitter Mama; that the pipe would burst, the roof would leak, the train would stall; that the dry cleaner could never get out the spit-up stains; that the indelible bags would materialize under the eyes; that the stay-at-home moms would invoke the No Nannies rule for play dates; that the Entenmann's cake sent to school for the bake sale would become an object of brutal gossip; that the fifty-five minute session locked inside the conference room with the breast pump would end with everything spilled all over the final draft of the Armbuster agreement; that Dad's secret motto would become, "Thank God it's Monday."

[Singer 1996, p. 65]

The working mother gives her children a clearer picture of what life is about. In order to do both, she needs things to work for her, too, which usually means sufficient income and support at home and work. It is a true challenge, yet women make it work every day.

—My mother, Elizabeth Ponton, who raised
three children and was a teacher for more than 30 years

INTRODUCTION

Women have always adopted multiple roles and used creative solutions to fit all the pieces of their lives together, so today's interweaving of parenting and career for women is actually an old story with a new twist.

Mothers are now working outside the home at a steadily increasing rate. This chapter begins with a focus on what we could learn from research studies about the impact of working mothers on their children and on themselves. These sections are followed by an examination of changes as they are expressed by different cohorts—recent generational groups of women—focusing on how one generation prepares the next, and the adoption of innovative solutions. This is followed by an examination of working mothers worldwide, looking at how this transition is taking place in other cultures. Three women's lives in our own culture are discussed in some detail to better understand specific problems and possible solutions. The chapter ends with a discussion of desirable traits for working mothers today, based on a consolidation of what we have been able to learn from these different avenues of study, and suggests paths for future exploration.

Examining the Child of the Working Mother

An overview of the health and well-being of the children of working mothers was completed by Arlie Hochschild (1989) in *The Second Shift* and by Terri Apter (1993) in *Working Women Don't Have Wives*. Their descriptions of harried career mothers also carrying a disproportionate share of domestic chores encouraged me to think about creative solutions. Each of these authors makes the point that if a mother is successfully able to delegate some of her caregiving responsibility to another responsible person or persons, she is providing adequately for her child. Both underscore the detrimental effects of the common misconception that children of working mothers suffer from neglect. It is true that, without planning, children can miss out. In at least one study, children of working mothers are reported to lose eight to twelve hours of weekly time spent with adults (Fuchs 1988). Terri Apter (1993) highlights that what children need is for someone to be delegated to be with them during those hours; Apter understands this as a larger social question that needs to be addressed as such, noting that meanwhile the burden currently falls on individual mothers to find their own solutions.

There are also some small but significant findings (Bogenschneider and Steinberg 1994) indicating that full-time maternal employment is associated with slightly lower grades among middle- and upper-middle-class boys; among the latter group, maternal employment during preschool was also associated with lower grades in later school. The authors report that full-time employment throughout the boys' lives had greater negative impact on grades than did progressively increasing maternal employment over time. In contrast, for girls, contemporaneous full-time maternal employment had no impact on grades in elementary, middle, or high school, but full-time maternal employment during preschool did have a negative impact, largely in reported behavioral symptoms. Why sons of working mothers have lower grades is a question still unanswered. One might speculate about a loss of contact and support from mothers for sons, balanced by the benefits for girls of a more complete role model.

The literature also addresses two other groups of children at risk related to maternal employment: adolescents and latch-key children. Overall, neither of these groups has fared as badly as predicted. Richards and Duckett (1994) found that, depending on how much time their mothers spent working, the daily experience of adolescents with working mothers differed in the following ways: full-time maternal employment was associated with more time spent doing homework with mothers and less time spent in general leisure with them, while part-time maternal employment was associated with more time engaged in sports activities with both parents. Compared to those with nonemployed mothers, adolescents with part-time employed mothers reported more positive daily moods and higher self-esteem, while youth with mothers employed full-time were reported to be the friendliest. Unhealthy adolescent risk-taking, a frequent sign of neglect and overall difficulties among adolescents, is not higher among adolescents whose mothers are working full-time (Hillman et al. 1993).

Dr. Hyman Rodman (1990) has examined the widespread phenomena of latch-key children, a group defined as 6- to 13-year-olds left at home alone or with younger siblings on a daily basis and estimated to number more than 1.8 million. This is a serious concern, but Dr. Rodman believes that the media has exaggerated the negative effects of this experience by highlighting and generalizing from a few unfortunate cases. He notes that most working mothers provide supervision for their child even if it is by telephone. Dr. Preuss-Lausitz (1992) highlights how schools in Germany are now open longer hours because both parents are working and no one is available to take care of the children. This is a concept that should be examined carefully for use in other countries.

The welfare of children of working mothers remains an area of concern, but the initial findings do not suggest a cause for alarm. On a societal level, changes such as the extended school day in Germany are promising; on an individual level, single working mothers or parents in a two-career family still need to provide for the care of their children when they are employed.

An Examination of Working Mothers

In the United States alone, women currently represent nearly half of the work force (Apter 1993). Many of these working women are mothers. This is a very large group, worthy of significant study. Yet in reviewing the literature, I found only studies that presented negative effects, such as increased psychological and physiological stress and role strain on these women. I did not find studies that looked at positive effects, although sociologists (Valdez and Gutek 1987) have suggested a theory of "role accumulation" in which losses are overridden by the benefits of having multiple roles that can protect against failure by broadening the sources of self-esteem. The customary omission of any focus on the positive effects of employment on mothers is a curious oversight. Does society see working mothers as an inherently problem-ridden group? Is it assumed that the impact of working on their lives would be necessarily negative? I will review the negative aspects as reported in the literature, but I encourage the reader to remember that little in human experience is without more complexity that these data suggest.

In general, working mothers report significantly greater "role strain" and both physical and psychological health symptoms than do men with children and working adults of either sex without children (Greenberger et al. 1989). Role strain is defined in Chapter 1 as encompassing both conflict and ambiguity; it is a self-reported assessment of measured discomfort about juggling two or more roles. This can be counterbalanced. Supports—in the forms of paid help and/or assistance from friends or family—decreased both symptoms and role strain for this group of working mothers. Barnett and Marshall (1992), as part of the Center for Research on Women at Wellesley College, found that a stratified group of more than 400 employed mothers were more distressed than working women without children. They noted that there was both positive and negative spillover from one role to another, and that negative spillover contributed to psychological distress. Having a good relationship with one's children is associated with lower levels of distress both at home and at work. The authors raise the question of how much more "distressed" working mothers actually are, and suggest that however more symptomatic they may be, whether they have a greater number of actual psychological conditions or dysfunction is currently unknown. Assistance with child care from either the husband or hired caregivers that has decreased over time is associated with an increase in reported depressive symptoms by the mother (Lennon et al. 1991).

A review of studies that looks at the status of the working mother reveals that even current research remains one-sided in its focusing on negative outcome and overall distress. In an effort to balance this, a later section of this chapter—Valuable Traits for the Working Mother—will draw on the positive experiences shared among members of a discussion group on career and parenting at a recent symposium on developmental issues for professional women.

Changing Attitudes and Cohorts over Time

During the past sixty years, each generation of new mothers has had to struggle with issues of career and family. Confounding generational learning are the ways in which the rules change over time, leaving these women adrift, confused about their choices, and searching for role models.

A more extensive examination of this topic offers us some understanding of the lack of clear guidelines. The individual components of work and family are complicated endeavors subject to unremitting social change. The interface between these two intricate and important areas is even more complicated. There is no obvious solution regarding the balance and integration of these spheres, so it is no surprise that individual women experience a personal victory when they are able to successfully combine the two for themselves.

Even with a rapidly shifting landscape, individual cohorts of generational groupings of women have shared similar problems and choices in this ongoing process of learning to manage multiple roles. Expectations about fertility and time taken out of work to rear children are two of the factors that have varied by cohort (Kingsbury and Greenwood 1992). A historical examination underscores the unique problems that each cohort of women has faced. The 1940s saw mothers enter the labor force in large numbers supported by a social mandate to serve the country. Consistent with this mandate, rules barring married women from employment were dropped (Apter 1993). During the 1950s, at a time when many of us grew up, the social pendulum shifted back again, nearly mandating women to return to home and raise children, emphasizing the benefits of women's commitment to home and family for children and society at large. The turbulent '60s, a period of social upheaval and change, saw the role that women had taken in the recent past criticized, and encouraged women to seek and develop new solutions. One of the outcomes of this movement was crystallized in the '70s with the advent of the "career woman," who focused largely on developing and shaping her career, putting aside fertility issues during her twenties and thirties and perhaps even permanently so that she could fully devote herself to her work. The '80s recognized that many women wanted to have children, including the large group of women who had delayed child bearing in favor of their careers, but now women were being encouraged to have it all—career, home, children, and partner— if they could do it all. Again, it is important to underscore that this was not an entirely new notion, though it was complicated by work now being quite geographically separate from home. Women throughout history have performed multiple roles, for example, managing the home at the same time that they raised children and ran a business. In pre-industrial England women were successfully running cottage industries, managing their homes, and raising children, albeit in a culture that supported and even encouraged this arrangement.

The '90s have seen the solutions of recent decades reworked. The "superwoman" ideal of managing to have it all, and in many ways managing it all, has been attacked as being not only impossible but life-threatening to many of the women who attempted it. Tailoring career and parenting solutions to each woman's needs has been highlighted. Acceptance of this more individualized approach offers a certain amount of freedom, but it has also been accompanied by changes in the workplace—increased hours, pace, and competition—that work against flexibility for the mother attempting to combine several roles. And as women grapple with similar issues as they struggle to combine work and managing home and relationships with children and partners, their choices are modified by parameters of social class and cultural background. This will be discussed further in the case vignettes below, which describe the stories of working mothers from various cultural and socioeconomic backgrounds.

Women often start out with one set of expectations for managing children and career, and are forced to modify these expectations and develop strategies once the endeavor is under way. Kingsbury and Greenwood surveyed a cohort of mothers in 1992, a largely baby-boom group, and compared them with a future cohort of potential mothers destined for the 2000s. Contrasted with the boomer mothers, the mothers of the future envisioned themselves with a larger number of children and taking time off from work for both maternity leave and later child-related activities. The study supports the long-standing reality that many young women do not realize what they're in for in taking on these dual roles, and that the daily work requirements of mothering are minimized. When Kingsbury and Greenwood surveyed the boomer mothers, they found that among these women the confrontation with reality had hit hard. Most of these mothers described being shocked by the amount of work they had to do as mothers, forcing them to re-evaluate their choices and priorities and make shifts accordingly.

One Generation Prepares the Next

In spite of the fact that each generation of women has had to redesign the solutions of those that preceded them, there has also been a gradual accumulation of knowledge suggesting that successive generations of women have helped to prepare those who followed. One example of this type of exchange was recounted by Westerbeek and Brinkgreve (1994), who studied a sample of university-educated working mothers and their daughters. They reported that the daughters described learning from their mothers that they should go to college and prepare for their future jobs irrespective of whether they expected to have children. A large-scale study that examined eleven cohorts beginning in 1920 indicated that maternal occupational status has a strong effect on the education and occupation choice of the next generation, independent of the father's education and occupation (Kalmijn 1994). This particular study found the benefits were as marked for sons as for daughters.

Although studies have indicated the importance of a mother's occupation and education on the level of education and the career choice of her children, the working mother's role is not always viewed positively by her children. One example of this can be seen in a study conducted by Judith Bridges and Ann Marie Orza (1992) that examined a population of college students and found that approval ratings for working mothers were higher if the mothers were working for economic necessity rather than for personal fulfillment. One can speculate about the reasons for this. Culturally, mothers are still expected to fulfill a fairly narrow role. This type of study hints at one of the major problems that the working mother confronts, that is, the powerful myth of the generic good mother. The mass entrance of mothers into the work force in the 1970s and 1980s has created conflict for families. The working mother violates the icon of the all-nurturing and all-available mother, especially in the middle classes. In lower classes, mothers have always had to work and raise children. Women from upper socioeconomic classes have often worked, but they have received and/or purchased more assistance. The myth promotes the ideal of the loving, available woman who does not work outside the home but who exclusively cares for the home and the children while her breadwinning husband is at work (Keller 1992). The myth provides some allowance for mothers who are forced to work to provide for their children as long as they continue to fulfill their designated role of nurturer. The myth also suggests that raising children is easier for women than it actually is; the biological mother's capacity for responsive attentiveness arrives with the baby, and then the rest is supposed to be easy (Apter 1993). This myth has been passed from generation to generation of mothers and continues to surprise women who find that not only is motherhood itself not easy, but that combining work and motherhood may be one of the hardest things that they have ever done; beyond that, the assumed stability and adequacy of the husband as breadwinner is uncertain.

Another factor complicating the passing of information from one generation of mothers to the next is that mothers themselves do not fall into neat cohorts. A mother can become the parent of a baby at 15, 25, 35, 45, and, today, even 55. Now more than ever, all of these ages are reflected among mothers nationwide. Important issues shift depending upon the age of the mother, but this wide age range also makes transmission of information from one generation to the next difficult, if not impossible. The result is that information is transmitted piecemeal, and to some degree women must search it out personally rather than relying on the culture at large to provide it.

Last, the process of parenting is not only complex, but also lengthy, often ending only at the time of death for parent or child. As emphasized in Chapter 1, a life-cycle perspective is essential for making wise choices. There are many phases to this process—parenting preschoolers calls for skills very different from those required to parent adolescents or adults in their twenties. The stressors vary too; getting ready for work can be impeded by the baby who spits up on your clothes or by the adolescent daughter who has "borrowed" them. Women have to understand the dynamic nature of this role, and then be able to adapt and change accordingly, flexibly modifying parenting styles they may have used at an earlier point (Ponton 1997).

Learning the skills of mothering is difficult. Hampered by myth, by a diverse peer group, and by the actual complexity and changing nature of the task, it is no wonder that imparting knowledge from generation to generation becomes difficult. The addition of another, simultaneous job only increases the complexity of the process.

Cross-Cultural Models

American women are not alone in this, and we can learn from others' experience with aspects of this problem in order to expand our thinking about potential solutions. One of the most consistent findings worldwide across studies that have examined the multiple roles of the working mother is that these mothers still undertake disproportionate shares of domestic labor compared to their spouses. A recent study (Xuewen et al. 1992) examined a large group of employed mothers in three cultures chosen because of presumed differences in approach regarding their treatment of working mothers—the People's Republic of China, Great Britain, and Japan. Yet in each of these countries the working mother bore a disproportionate amount of the housework. China was most distinctive in that women there uniformly combine full-time paid work with domestic work and their spouses play an increased, although still secondary, role in housework. Among these countries, gender-role segregation is greatest in Japan, where the housewife role is heavily endorsed. Consistent with societal expectations, working mothers in Japan report the highest level of personal satisfaction when they are employed in a more limited capacity either on a "Mommy track" with a more limited role or strictly part-time. The situation for

British working mothers lies somewhere between the Japanese and the Chinese, with most of the young working mothers there involved in part-time work, which is associated with more gender segregation than full-time work. This study also examines women's reactions to gender injustice in the work arena—a commonly reported finding in this particular study, perhaps not surprisingly. Chinese working mothers, who are more active in the work sphere than their Japanese and British counterparts, report the highest degree of dissatisfaction with injustice at work. This study is particularly interesting not only because it examines three very different cultural approaches to combining work and mothering, but because it also highlights what appear to be culturally widespread issues for the working mother—disproportionate domestic work load and gender injustice at work. The study also demonstrates how patterns are affected by the societal values and economics of individual countries.

It is not surprising that in countries where women's roles have rigidly been assigned to child care, there is a significant struggle as women attempt to integrate careers. What is surprising is that women are fighting as hard as they are to incorporate careers outside the home into their lives. This is noteworthy in a region like the Middle East, an area that has been influenced by the progress of the women's movement in the past twenty years. For Middle Eastern women, a part of this struggle has been waged in the home, and has been about choices and long-standing values about women's roles. The children in these homes have watched their mothers' struggles, and are reportedly aware of the efforts their mothers are making in this direction (Adams et al. 1984). This region of the world will be an important one to watch in the future.

Countries that are more progressive in terms of reforms for women face different types of problems. Sweden, known for having some of the best parental legislation and programs in the world, still has significant problems for the working mother. Dr. Karin Widerberg (1991) interviewed a large cross-section of working women in Sweden and found that except for staying at home with their newborn children, women hardly used their legally mandated rights designed to accommodate motherhood in the workplace. In fact, women reported that when they did use their legally mandated rights, their working conditions worsened. Dr. Widerberg noted that the women seldom protested this, believing instead that it was their fault, a view held by both employers and labor union representatives. The Swedish law that mandates rights for individual women actually supports the employer's position by not accompanying these mandates with laws addressing corresponding obligations of the employer. The legislation in this "advanced" country points out the importance of writing laws that include built-in obligations for the employer. A clear recommendation of this study and others is that there has to be a socially and legally sanctioned atmosphere for women to feel comfortable using the opportunities available to them in order to make their dual duties of mother and worker easier. Even in Sweden, where parental supports have existed for decades, this atmosphere does not yet exist (Moen and Forest 1990, Widerberg 1991).

Working mothers in the Middle Eastern and Scandinavian countries tend to represent opposite ends of the spectrum, but there are important similarities. Laws supporting parental activity and combating discrimination in the workplace, along with equitable distribution of home tasks, may be more favorable toward women in Scandinavian countries, but significant problems still exist wherever women try to combine the two roles. A second important finding from cross-cultural studies during the past twenty years is that women in all parts of the world are searching for solutions to this challenge, and continue to struggle for answers that will work within the parameters of their own culture. The imperfect nature of the solutions illustrates how difficult a task this is.

Dr. Ruth Katz (1989) studied a population of 1,500 married couples in Israel and found that the burden (measured in hours and role strain) on working women with children is significantly larger than the comparable burden on working fathers or homemaker mothers with children. This finding is no surprise, and is consistent with what has been found in studies worldwide. Trial solutions used by women in Israel to make their lives easier include reducing tasks in both home and work arenas to a minimum, family planning for fewer children, working part-time and reducing work hours whenever possible, recruiting hired help, especially in the home arena but also in the work arena, and maintaining work continuity (i.e., avoiding frequent moves). (These solutions are explored in more depth in Chapter 9.) Mothers who are rich in resources (income, education, or occupational prestige) are better able to develop solutions. It is noteworthy that the Israeli working mothers did not find that greater assistance from their husbands was one of their available solutions (Katz 1989).

Countries where working mothers are lacking in resources illustrate how difficult it can be for mothers to find solutions to the challenge of combining work and parenting. A study of married couples conducted in Yugoslavia, where more than 90 percent of parents with children under the age of 15 years are fully employed, provides such an example (Cernigoj–Sadar 1989). Yugoslavian parents have almost no choice concerning matters related to employment status. Consistent with Dr. Katz's (1989) study, working mothers in Yugoslavia report that they are significantly more burdened with household and other "informal" work (i.e., income sources in addition to their main employment) than are their husbands. Working mothers report that they lessen their burden by seeking help from friends and relatives, engaging in informal work that adds extra income to the household but increases their overall work load, and limiting their own personal time watching television or other entertainments. Here again, it is noteworthy that they do not report shifting some of this burden to husbands.

In summary, a cross-cultural examination of the lives of working mothers reveals some worldwide commonalities. First, more and more frequently, women around the world are finding themselves in the position of trying to combine parenting and career, and also find themselves burdened with a disproportionate amount of household tasks in contrast to their husbands, who have more leisure time. Second, even in countries such as the Scandinavian nations, which have a long-standing reputation of respecting parenting and career and have passed favorable legislation, these laws have not been foolproof. Third, working mothers worldwide are searching for solutions to lessen both their role strain and the large number of hours engaged in formal or informal tasks.

Working on legal solutions that can be enforced and utilized by the working mother without fear of reprisal is crucial. And negotiating the shared distribution of labor with partners before a child is born (as discussed in Chapter 1) as well as changing societal expectations for fathers is an important task for future mothers. The role strain of working mothers is a worldwide problem without clear answers at this point. It deserves further attention both in political circles and on a personal level.

INTERWEAVING PARENTING AND CAREER: THREE WOMEN'S LIVES

Large-scale studies are extremely valuable in outlining the scope of the problems and providing valuable information about solutions that working mothers have found to be particularly effective. But the struggle of mothers to fit into multiple roles is a dilemma that has to be solved on many levels—politically, socially, and personally. In this part of the chapter three women's lives are discussed in some detail to provide a better understanding of personal problems and solutions.

I have chosen women from three age brackets—30s, 40s, and 50s—and three different ethnic groups, Caucasian, Asian-American, and African-American. They have different levels of education and economic resources. There are significant similarities, however: all of these women live in the greater Bay area in northern California, and I came to know all of them as a psychiatrist working with them in a therapeutic situation. With the women in the first two vignettes, Alena and Samantha, I was their therapist. I came to know Angelina, the woman in the third vignette, while I was working with her daughter in therapy. All three—Alena, Samantha, and Angelina—were working mothers struggling with questions about how to fit these two aspects of their lives together. The stories of their struggles remind us that combining parenting and career is an intensely personal struggle in which, at least for now, each woman has to ask and answer her own unique questions.

Alena—"The Planner"

Alena , a 39-year-old married Caucasian psychotherapist with two children (ages 1 and 3), initially came to see me at the age of 35 when she was several months pregnant with her first child. She was thinking about how to space her children and career. She reported to me that her own mother had worked full-time as an attorney, and had had only limited contact with Alena and her siblings. Alena did not want to repeat this pattern with her children, nor did she want to give up her career as a practicing psychotherapist, and thought that it was best to do some planning to avoid this. I strongly supported her thoughtful concerns and agreed that it certainly was a topic best addressed by thinking ahead.

Additional concerns for Alena included balancing her career with that of her husband, who was both an attorney and a writer, and had a moderate commute to his office. When he worked full-time as an attorney, he had a significant income, but he wanted to work part-time as a writer, and under those circumstances would likely make considerably less income. When Alena first contacted me, she had an office that was several miles from her home and required a half-hour commute.

Our work together took place intermittently over a four-year period during which Alena had two children, spaced two years apart. She stopped work for a six-month period following the birth of her first child and for a three-month period after the second. She then made the decision to return to work part-time, compressing her therapy hours with her patients into more compacted time periods. The reduction in her total salary was only 25 percent using this schedule. Alena also decided to develop a home office so that she could be in closer contact with her children and with her in-home child-care employee. This gave her the feeling that she was even more available than her actual thirty hours/week work schedule indicated. One of the discussions we had in therapy focused on the benefits of working in her home. She had been concerned that her children's cries would be heard by patients, and that the patients would interfere with her home life. Despite her fears, careful soundproofing was effective and her patients commented that they liked the pleasant home environment.

The resolution of Alena's conflicts and difficulties around balancing work and home was relatively easy for several reasons. First, she had a career based on a high level of education. Many studies indicate that women with good educational backgrounds are more successfully able to balance career and family (Katz 1989). Second, she had a career with moderate to high earning potential. Last, she had a career that offered flexible hours in this self-employed mode. All of these were of benefit to her, combined with her decision to plan and discuss her career and family issues relatively early on.

One problem that surfaced in the context of our work together was that after Alena had made a decision to develop a home office, her husband decided that he too would like to write at home and to share some of the benefits that he saw his wife having. He was able to adjust his hours, and he and Alena are currently located in different parts of their home working during the week. He too has echoed the benefits of a home office when one is working and raising a family. Additional conflicts included division of household tasks between Alena and her husband. This required that she develop good negotiation skills and accurately portray the amount of housekeeping and child-care work that was needed in their home.

Alena was particularly fortunate because she was able to work out a solution in which her children were close by. Studies (Barton 1991) have reported that the morale of the working parent is enhanced when they have the security of knowing that their children are cared for in close proximity. In Alena's situation she could visit her children on breaks, and reported that both she and her children enjoyed the frequent, brief contact. We discussed how this particularly pleasant aspect of her work situation probably encouraged her husband to follow her example.

Samantha—Considering a Change

Samantha came to see me as a 42-year-old Asian-American attorney with a 9-year-old child. She was working full-time as a partner in her law practice, but reported problems and unhappiness with her long work hours, and told me that she and her husband were planning to divorce in the next few months. She had concerns about the impact of the divorce on her child and on her own career. At that time, Samantha was commuting more than an hour a day each way to work.

Our discussion of her issues consisted of looking at some very hard facts. Currently Samantha was spending only a limited amount of time with her daughter. Her daughter was asking for more contact with Samantha, and although she and her daughter shared a close relationship it was extremely difficult that Samantha worked so far from the family home; she had to take off whole days of work to attend her daughter's functions, and was not able to participate in most of her daughter's school activities.

157

Samantha's husband also worked as a full-time professional, and Samantha was concerned that he would be even
less available to their daughter after the divorce. Her own law
practice was also quite busy and demanded more than sixty
hours per week in the office. In her current place of residence,
she had only limited family and neighborhood support, but
several members of her extended family lived a half-hour away.

Divorce—a fact of life for 50 percent of American families, and one
that often raises issues related to career as well as family—presented as
a significant stressor to Samantha, her husband, and their daughter.
Planning was crucial in determining the favorable outcome they were
able to achieve.

Upon discussion, Samantha recognized that her goals at this point
in her life were complex. She wanted to provide the most secure environment for her child, maintain at least a minimal income, and survive the divorce. After much soul-searching, she made a decision to leave
her job as law partner and set up her own practice in the small town
where her family members resided. She involved her husband in discussions of these decisions, pointing out that she would be much more
available to her child during the period of the divorce. She also limited
her lifestyle based on the planned drop in income that would occur as
a result of both her divorce and leaving the well-paid practice where
she had been a partner. All of this resulted in considerable compromise
for Samantha, including the loss of her original home and the prestige
of partnership in a well-recognized firm. Factors working in her favor
included the fact that she and her husband had planned their divorce
together and considered the needs of their child. An additional positive
factor was her potentially well-paid career, which, like Alena's, had been
the result of a high level of education. Yet a third positive factor was
the strong extended-family support available to her when she moved
closer to her relatives.

Angelina—Intergenerational Concerns

Angelina initially came to see me when I was working with
her 15-year-old daughter, who already had one child, was
considering having another, and was seeing me around this

and future child-planning decisions. Angelina was a 54-year-old single African-American entrepreneur with a self-developed, successful hat-making business she operated out of her home. Angelina had three children living at home: the above-mentioned 15-year-old girl and two boys, 17 and 19 years old. Angelina also provided a home and residence for her one-year-old grandchild and for a friend of one of her sons. At the time she saw me, she worked approximately fifty hours per week at her business, but had a flexible schedule.

I often meet with the parents of adolescent patients when there are issues around the family situation that need to be addressed. In addition to focusing on some family dynamics, Angelina and I spent some time considering how her work was affecting her parenting, and together came up with some ideas that would benefit Angelina herself as well as her children. One of the difficulties Angelina was experiencing was providing housing for her children and managing expenses for her business simultaneously. Historically, she had had very limited support from the fathers of her five children (two were older and lived outside the family home at the time I knew Angelina) and her own extended family, but she was considerably enterprising. When she and I spoke, we worked out a way that she could leave the community housing that was proving to be quite risk-provoking for her three adolescent children, and get into an assisted housing program where she could purchase, with financial support, a small home.

One of the other issues that Angelina discussed with me were multiple ways to pursue loans to assist her with her business. This proved relatively easy because her business had grown and was achieving a certain success. Advantages that Angelina presented with included a flexible work schedule that she had designed to accommodate her parenting responsibilities and the fact that she was a savvy parent who was knowledgeable about risk taking, a special benefit when raising teenagers. She was also enterprising, and cared well for her children as a single parent.

Still, Angelina's story differs from Alena's and Samantha's in some important ways. Angelina, like most working mothers in America, did not have a high level of education, a high level of social or professional status, or a high income. She represents the majority of working mothers in our culture who are struggling to cope with less opportunity and financial reimbursement than men of comparable experience and education. Often such women are relegated to the "pink ghetto," characteristically low-paying jobs into which women are differentially tracked and from which they ultimately can't escape. A majority of women work while they are on welfare and over two-thirds of the women who exit from welfare exit via employment (Harris 1993). Angelina's story illustrates some of the strategies that have encouraged such women to become self-sufficient.

Assisting Angelina with housing was a vital step in her path to success as a working mother. Angelina was most worried that her adolescent children would become involved in unhealthy risk-taking activity (substance abuse, gang activity, and unprotected sexual intercourse). From the perspective of being a working mother, she need not have worried. Dr. Hillman and his colleagues (1993) have looked at the effect of maternal employment on adolescent risk-taking behaviors and their results show no significant effects of maternal employment on adolescent risk-taking. But realistically, Angelina had reason for concern. The urban neighborhood where she and her adolescent children resided prior to their move was a well-known site for gang activity, and gangs frequently forced adolescent males in the neighborhood to join up. It is in this context of looking at the total picture of Angelina's life and her primary concern that one can see how valuable the move to the assisted housing program in a new, safer neighborhood was to her and her children.

Angelina's story is also important because as sole parent and breadwinner, she represents a large number of mothers. Fifty percent of all African-American children under 18 live with single mothers as the sole head of household (Maison 1986). In addition to poverty and problems with housing, two other factors—lack of education beyond high school (Jackson 1992) and raising a son (Jackson 1992, 1993)—have been shown to be risk factors related to higher levels of stress for this group of women. Four of Angelina's five children were sons, and she had completed high school only by obtaining her General Equivalency Degree (GED). But Angelina also exhibited one of the major protective factors: she was in a self-chosen type of employment that supported both her creativity and her entrepreneurial skills. Choice in work has been shown to be important; finding a preferred type of employment has resulted in lower role strain and greater life satisfaction for single African-American mothers (Jackson 1992). On the other hand, Angelina did not have extended family support in raising her children, a protective factor for many African-American mothers compared with their Anglo-American counterparts (Benin and Keith 1995). In fact, Angelina was providing extended family support in the form of housing and child care for her 15-year-old daughter, who was already a mother raising her own daughter.

Finally, maternal employment in low-income families reportedly predicts higher scores in English and mathematics for the children of working mothers, even after controlling for income (Vandell and Ramanan 1992). Angelina's sons were performing well in school and she was assisting her daughter to ensure a return to school after the daughter had dropped out to have her baby.

I believe that there is another lesson to learn from Angelina's story. She was not only raising her five children, she was also performing a vital role in helping her daughter raise her child. She was providing the intergenerational support she had never had, and demonstrating that parenting for women is often a lifetime work, extending long after a child is 18 years old, even into playing a role in the lives of one's great-grandchildren. Dr. Brunetta Wolfman (1984) believes that the lives of African-American women specifically have much to teach us about working and parenting. Having a long-standing history of working outside the home, African-American women have evolved coping strategies and attitudes toward work that might well be learned by others. Wolfman underscores the fact that as women enter the workplace, there are many pressures on them to imitate men. Angelina and women like her demonstrate that women can find their own paths despite numerous obstacles.

Valuable Traits for Working Mothers

Although I plan to use some findings from the cross-cultural studies for this section, many of the ideas and strategies for success offered here come from the members of a group I led on career and parenting (in the 1996 Symposium on Developmental Issues for Professional Women) and from the many working mothers whom I have seen in my practice. This is an area in which women can learn a great deal from each other. The frequent warm laughter of recognition in the group suggested that a support group for working mothers could prove an important resource. The enthusiasm these women demonstrated for jug-gling these two important roles in their lives and being able to enjoy most of it is infectious. On balance, most of the working mothers I have had contact with say they would not make other choices. One woman in the group commented, "Being a parent is the most difficult and re-warding thing I've ever done."

Several different coping strategies appeared in the group. Some women tried to integrate their home and work lives as much as pos-sible; others preferred to compartmentalize, choosing career directions such as emergency room medicine, where there was no after-hours spillover. The reduction of roles and more important, of role expecta-tions was seen as essential. One woman commented, "I can't do it the way my mother did." However much these women hoped for shared responsibility with partners, each generally found herself to be the so-cial organizer for her entire family.

Life choices were under constant revision as the women reevalu-ated priorities. Once clear on what was important and what they were willing to give up, the women could then become effective negotiators in the family. Especially stressful areas were making a patchwork of summer activities for the children and parenting in divorced or blended families. Caring for the self by buying services and protecting time was seen as essential. However, even with increased assistance, the woman remained the responsible manager of the system, overseeing and remem-bering the needs of each family member.

For these highly organized women, giving up control was quite difficult, and sometimes a focus on content overwhelmed process. One woman perceptively commented, "If my son doesn't take a shower or has popcorn for dinner, he'll survive. I have to survive too. My son was becoming just another chore on my list. Now I realize that the quality of time with my kids is more important than fixing the perfect dinner."

It became clear in the group that each person was searching for an individual solution in part because government or society had created so few supports. This deficit, combined with the lack of generational models, made decision making a daunting process. There was general agreement that "we have to fix the world too"—ironic, perhaps, in that this gives us all yet another task.

Again, not surprisingly, Katz (1989) found that working mothers with more resources—education, status, income, a more desirable oc-cupation—do better. Worldwide, however, most women do not have these resources available to them. In light of this fact, it is particularly important for all women to be aware of the importance of planning and education for themselves and their future children. In most cultures women have been seen as resources to be added to men's lives. As women today struggle to combine career and parenting, helping them reconceptualize their lives is crucial. After education and planning, knowing one's choices and learning how to make decisions for themselves is most important. In many ways this point interfaces with education; many women are not aware of what their choices actually are. Some have children at 13 or 14, long before the opportunities for choices in their lives can even be visualized or understood. Others, even in their fifties, still don't know what their choices are. One can argue that women have fewer choices, and thus knowledge of these limits would be disheartening, but one could also argue that it becomes even more important to know exactly the available choices to make decisions most effectively about what is important to them.

Women trying to balance career and family also benefit from acquiring specific skills outside the realm of a formal education. Two of the most important skills are the abilities to prioritize and to negotiate. Learning how to prioritize was articulated very well by one member of our career and parenting group who said that she had had to learn that "not every job is a job worth doing well," and described how she has had to learn to lower her expectations as she struggled to do both her work and parenting. Negotiation skills are needed in both work and home arenas, and appear to be particularly vital when attempting to balance two such important areas (Chapter 11 explores these strategies in more depth).

In addition, the arenas of work and home each appear to have their unique problems. Recognizing those problems early on and working out the best solution for everyone involved is important. At home, child care is particularly complex, both hard to find and a dynamic necessity whose requirements shift as children grow older. They also need to recognize that this important work is minimized on a cultural level and is much more demanding and complicated than it first appears (Apter 1993). Expectant parents who anticipate needing child care should explore various options, looking at both in- and out-of-home care; one versus multiple providers; and the age, experience, child-care education, and skills that the provider can offer them. It is important to obtain recommendations from others who have worked with the provider; it is also vital to spend enough time with the provider to discover whether there is a good fit between the provider and the parents as well as the child.

Women need to be able to organize and develop a support system among their partners, hired help, friends, relatives, and colleagues to make this juggling act work. Often the support people in a woman's life have to function in both arenas, like the woman herself; the type of double duty that surrounds the life of the working mother spills over into the lives of those nearby. For example, an assistant at work might have to field calls from a child's school, and a child's caregiver might have to assist the working mother with some of her business or academic life. A flexible support system provides the backup that a working mother needs. The women in our symposium discussion group echoed this over and over again. Flexibility was the overall characteristic that they felt was necessary for the working mother, allowing her to creatively develop new solutions for problems as they arose.

It is important for the working mother to care for herself, to address her own physical, psychological, and social needs. It is one of the greatest challenges in negotiating the multiple roles of a working mother, but one that can't be neglected without risking a loss of meaning and pleasure that defeats the purpose of the entire process.

SUMMARY

During the past fifteen years, I have worked as a psychiatrist helping many women to figure out their own choices and to find a balance around the issues of parenting and career. I myself have struggled with these issues as I work and raise two daughters. In writing this chapter, I was made even more aware of how difficult and necessary it is for women following these paths to endeavor to find their own unique solutions for traversing the difficult terrain. Although women have varying degrees of choices in a world still limited by discrimination, they do have choices, and it is increasingly important that they know what those choices are so that they can make the best decisions for themselves.

Once women recognize that they have to become educated about their options in this struggle, the material presented here becomes more valuable. There are many secrets to making such a life work. Role models, mentors, and support groups offer important ways to share them. Hopefully, this chapter serves as a companion to these other methods.

164

9

Part-Time Career, Full-Time Life

PAMELA MARTIN

INTRODUCTION

This chapter is for those women who decide that "having it all" has a unique personal definition rather than that prescribed by the culture or by what some women expect of themselves. Women who choose to be part-time professionals may "want it all" in a different way—they want a balanced life, time for other pursuits, more time for intimacy with family and friends. Their values and priorities may be different. They may, as suggested in Chapter 1, be less driven by the need to excel by following the expectations of the full-time workplace—but not necessarily less driven by the need to excel by their own personal standards. The difference is that they set their own standards. The evidence from recent studies is compelling that the choice of part-time work is one that creates a high degree of job satisfaction and less tendency for depression than either the choice to work full-time or to be a full-time mother. There are many external and internal changes that need to take place for a part-time career to be a viable option for most women.

The external changes that need to take place are discussed by Felice Schwartz (1989):

> Part-time employment is the single greatest inducement to getting women back on the job expeditiously and the provision women themselves most desire. A part-time return to work enables them to maintain responsibility for critical aspects of their jobs, keeps them in touch with the changes constantly occurring at the workplace and in the job itself, reduces stress and fatigue . . . and, not least, can greatly enhance company loyalty. [p. 73]

Schwartz (1989) describes the changes needed in organizations to acknowledge women's worth in the workplace and to make the necessary changes to accommodate the needed flexibility:

> The greater cost of employing women is not a function of inescapable gender differences. Women *are* different from men, but what

increases their cost to the corporation is principally the clash of their perceptions, attitudes, and behavior with those of . . . the policies and practices of male-led corporations. What we need to learn is how to reduce that expense, how to stop throwing away the investments we make in talented women, how to become more responsive to the needs of the women that corporations *must* employ if they are to have the best and the brightest of all those now entering the work force. [p. 66]

The internal changes that need to take place for a woman to make the choice of part-time work will also be reviewed. Individual attributes of women that influence these choices will be discussed as well as the practicalities of this decision, including how to reach a decision about a part-time career, how to change a full-time career into a part-time one, what the personal/family benefits and challenges are to a part-time career, and the potential gains and losses for one's professional development. In addition, I will share vignettes from women who have used this option as well as examples of their full-time lives.

Why would a professional woman who has devoted five to ten years to graduate training for career preparation consider working part-time?
Many developments may have occurred in a professional woman's life to bring her to this decision. She may have found her life priorities have changed, that her life is either unexpectedly pleasurable or unexpectedly difficult. At the stage when most women are training for their profession, they are in their twenties or thirties. Given the rigors of their training, they may have put off finding a life partner, having children, or developing other interests in their lives. As women get older, they may go through different developmental phases. They may experience intense attachment and pleasure with their children or they may discover that their marriage quality has changed for the worse as their available time is taken with work, travel, and children. They may have realized their personal limits, developed a health problem that requires time for self-care and rest, or had a personal stressor such as a divorce. Women may have older children and adolescents with clear needs for a parental presence in the house. Career women may find other important sources of meaning and creativity in life, or they may be winding down toward retirement and want to develop other parts of their life. As a woman's professional life meanders through its undulating course, her relationship to the amount of time she wants to dedicate to her work

will vary. At these times of change, part-time professional work becomes an attractive and viable option to consider.

*What are the cultural and workplace influences on professional women's
decisions to work part-time?*

For many generations our culture has valued the work of men—
the role of going to a workplace for many hours a day and making
money—while the appropriate work role of women was clear—to take
care of the children, the aging parents, the household. This "women's
work" was not necessarily valued, or even recognized as an essential
contribution to the culture. As a result of these expectations in the
culture, women developed some dependent traits that tended to keep
them in these roles. They became experts on taking care of others, fighting for the underdog, second-guessing others' needs, and becoming
reliant on others' opinions of them. As Karen Horney's (1950) work
illustrates, this emphasis created a neurotically dependent pattern for
women. They were not as good at intuiting their own needs or in getting them met. As women have moved into the professions, they have
expanded into the work world and broken from the old models of
"women's work"; but as Alexandra Symonds (1974) suggests, women
have not changed their habits of not speaking up for themselves, being
dependent on other people's opinions of them, and not asking for help
when they need it. There is currently pressure on women to be able to
do it all—to work full-time, have children, raise the children well, be a
spouse, and be able to identify their own needs and get them met. The
decision to work part-time can be one that makes a statement that it is
part of women's needs to have time for themselves or for the activities
they choose. A part-time career choice can be an affirmation that the
traditional feminine qualities and skills are important and personally
valued. This can be a courageous and self-supportive move.

When women first began making such decisions, the issue of the
"Mommy track" came up. Schwartz's (1989) article in the *Harvard
Business Review* began an intense debate about whether or not women
really wanted to be in the workplace, make money, and earn the same
privileges men have had in this society. Table 9–1 (Krener 1994) details the attitudinal difference between women seeking traditional or
"Mommy track" careers. Many respondents to this article made it clear
that employers should not assume that all working mothers would be
willing to trade career advancement for more time off.

169

Table 9–1. Professional choices of women[1]

	Traditional Attitudes for Success	"The Mommy Track"
Definition	Doing "a man's job" the way a man would do it; having the same career goals, etc.	Combining career and family (accepting responsibility for child care and maintenance of the home, physically and psychologically)
Attitude about work	Goal-oriented	Experience-oriented
Attitude about money	A symbol of success or a vehicle for success (e.g., getting a grant, if not the first time, then on reapplication)	Money is traded for time (e.g., writing a grant and not getting it might be seen as "wasted time")
Attitude about time	Focus on future: 10-year plan of full-time employment (or more) assumed; same time-line as men for career advancement, credential-gathering (long-term)	Focus on present: "getting through this year"; part-time schedules an option, protection from pressure by choosing structured or less rigorous work situations
	Power lunch (short-term)	Skip lunch to finish in time to pick up child at day care
	(All time is money)	Time is divided between work time and home time
Self: measure of success	Self-promotion; competition, challenging when necessary, achieving recognition	Sharing, "fairness," seeking consensus, compromising, relatedness, feeling one has done a good job or tried hard
Self: use of	Organizing, delegating, producing a product	Accommodating, responding, or getting job done by oneself
Self: defense vs. discrimination	Various; may confront high price paid for this, or ignore. Likely to be vigilant, aware of discrimination, microinequities	Often ambivalent about success, participates in "auto-discrimination," may avoid or ignore discrimination gestures, and be unaware of microinequities
Attitude about travel, professional relationships	Important for making one's work known and for networking with colleagues at other institutions	Meetings seen as "stimulating" but feeling conflicted because of discomfort at leaving children, and imposing extra demands on colleagues

1. Reprinted from Krener 1994, copyright © 1994 by American Psychiatric Press, and used by permission of the publisher and author.

In a later chapter Schwartz (1992) says that she received angry responses from all groups of career women except for one—the married women with children who were not looking for high career achievement in this phase of their lives. She concludes:

> The career and family conflict is central to women, emotional, threatening, and both guilt and anxiety-provoking. It also raises issues of women's anger at men for what is perceived to be their easier or better life, their freedom from the second shift, their position of 'superiority' in the world, which implies the flip side, the potent feeling of women that they are still second class. [p. 123]

Professor Victor Fuchs of Stanford University (1988) says that the economic disparity between men and women stems from the conflict between work and family rather than from career investment patterns. He believes that this conflict is stronger for women than for men, and will remain so for the foreseeable future. For Fuchs, the key to female underutilization is the cost to women of combining work and family, a cost not borne equally by men.

What are the attributes of women that contribute to these choices?

The role of mothering is one of the most complex and demanding, yet satisfying and rewarding, jobs in our culture. Motherhood remains unsupported financially and unrecognized as a legitimate career, yet it is crucial for the future of our children and our society. Women, with their well-developed abilities to empathize with the needs of others, may be the ones that are the best at caring for children's needs, and may derive a great deal of pleasure from using those skills. They may also have a more difficult time tuning out the needs of their children or the needs of their immediate or extended family in order to travel or go to work. In Terri Apter's (1993) book she points out that even in Nordic countries where child care is abundant and free to the mothers, women still want part-time work, and they want it for family reasons.

How does a professional woman know if the decision to have a part-time career is a good decision for her?

The answer to this question is uniquely personal. You need to examine your values and goals in life at the present time. This requires defining success for yourself rather than let others define it by their standards. Often in our culture, what a person does for a living is equated with their identity. Redefining personal success requires time away from one's usual environments in order to gain a perspective. Take reflection time to look back over the last several weeks to see what has given you the most satisfaction and enjoyment. What have you felt the best about, what are your highest priorities, what do you want more of that you feel unable to get because of time pressures? If you find you might be happier with more time in your life, or more time with your children, or more time with an interest, but your career is still a source of satisfaction and enjoyment, you are a candidate for a part-time career.

> One woman internist who enjoyed her job a great deal also realized that she enjoyed gardening and had not enough time to spend on that healing activity for herself. She felt she spent long hours taking care of others competently but there was not enough energy left over at the end of the day for herself. She found an all-women practice where she began to work part-time. On her professional days she states she gets in her work clothes, cleans her fingernails, and gives her patients great care. On her days at home she stays in her overalls, gets as dirty and involved with her gardening as she would like, and enjoys those days thoroughly. She feels this is a great balance for her and for her patients since she feels she has much more to give to them since she is also taking care of herself.

In a paper published in the *Annals of Internal Medicine* (Levinson et al., 1993), 245 part-time faculty in academic medicine were surveyed. A high degree of career satisfaction existed despite the drawbacks of being part-time. On a 10-point scale their median rating for career satisfaction was 8.6. They found that most professional women do not initially plan to work part-time but begin to consider the option when they find themselves burned out or unable to be in multiple roles in a satisfying way. One obvious transition time is after the birth of a child. Another is upon learning about the onset of a health problem, or when a professional woman opens her own practice and has more flexible options. Yet another is after a woman has worked for ten or fifteen years and needs to consider a break to pursue other interests.

What adjustments are needed in changing from a full-time to a part-time professional with a full-time life?

The first adjustment is usually reduced income, although some women change from a full-time job to a higher hourly rate but without the former benefits or job security. For most women this means prorated health and retirement benefits as well as salary. This shift requires reassessment of the family priorities as well. Could the family live comfortably on less money? Are they open to changes in lifestyle in order to have more time together? How does the tax bracket change and how will that affect the amount of money brought in? What are the ongoing expenses such as health and child care and how would they be affected if a change is made to part-time? If the family has the financial choice and is open to a simplification of their lives, then the part-time option is a viable one. A resource book for this process is *Simple Living Investments* (Phillips and Campbell 1988), which states that the best investments one can make financially are in things that will make you a better person—happiness, health, well-being, ability to make friends, ability to adapt to change, ability to relate to many kinds of people—because they are the skills we all need to age successfully.

Another adjustment for part-time professionals is whether the possible alteration in how one is viewed at the workplace is worth the trade. Many companies will not give career status to part-time employees, that is, they will not let them take on supervisory positions or continue to progress in their profession. This may also bring up personal ambivalence about the career path. Does this mean you are not really a professional? This ambivalence about role may be based on accepting the judgment of the workplace rather than your own ideas of what is professional. These issues need to be sorted out to adjust well to a part-time career.

It is a confusing time to decide what it means to be a woman. Differences are common but not tolerated. This is quite obvious in observing women's choices about the roles of mothering and working. There are women who choose to take time off from their career until their children are raised, those who work part-time and mother part-time, and those who choose to work full-time and keep their children in day care. Often any one of these choices is judged by the women who've made either of the other two choices. Women are excluded from mothers' groups over these differences, and mothers are criticized through their children for their choices.

One woman physician who chose to take time off from her profession to get pregnant and have a child decided after the child's birth that she was not interested in juggling the multiple roles of working and raising an active child. Her choice to stay at home was easier because her husband is also a physician so there is adequate income for part-time child care to provide her some freedom. She feels this is the right decision for her, but was surprised to feel alienated from her neighborhood peers. Socially, she attempts to hide both her professional credentials and her child-care support, but when other mothers find out they are envious and distance themselves from her. This is a painful isolation at a time when she feels she needs a new peer group with which to have adult contact when her previous colleagues and her husband are still working full-time.

Eichenbaum and Orbach (1984) explain that in this time of changing opportunities for women envy and competition are common and healthy reactions to help a woman understand what she really wants for herself. Whatever she finds she is most envious about is what she most desires for herself. At the same time, people's actions when they are envious can be hurtful and unsupportive at a time when women need backing to find their own way in the maze of changing roles.

What if changing to a part-time career is not a choice but a necessity?
Some women are not making their careers into part-time careers by choice, but rather by necessity related to their health status. This is a very different situation, and can be seen as an unwelcome necessity rather than a proactive choice.

One woman in the field of marketing was diagnosed as having osteomyelitis of the skull. This is a rare but serious disease in which a chronic infection occurs deep in the bone where it is hard for antibiotics to reach. She experienced fatigue, but otherwise few symptoms. Her doctors prescribed as much bed rest as possible to prevent future problems. She did not feel "sick," and she had just reached a well-earned promotion that gave her great satisfaction. She could not accept the need to curtail her career goals due to future health risk. It took the input from a support group to help her reframe the situation. They encouraged her to view her cutting back to part-time as a way to listen to what her body needed rather than what someone else was telling her was needed, and to take good care of herself in order to enjoy a longer and more satisfying life.

How can one change a full-time profession into a part-time one?

This requires planning, negotiation, courage, and support. When planning to convert a full-time job into a part-time one, it is helpful to *establish oneself first as a valuable employee*—this could be because of unique skills, special contributions based on ethnic background or gender, seniority and experience, or many other reasons. Planning for eventual part-time work may mean attending additional training in an area that would be particularly useful to the organization.

In my own situation I had been at my job for four years as a half-time physician in the medical student education division while working the other half-time in private practice. When my son was born I kept the part-time job at the university and reduced my private practice. In that way I kept my commitments to the university and could even increase them because I had time to give to those pursuits on my days at home.

The second step is for the professional woman to *be clear with your superiors about the structure of what you are requesting.* Do you want to work fewer days or fewer hours per day? Which responsibilities would you like to keep and which delegate? How much salary do you need to make this a feasible option? Would you like to job share and with whom? Some women prefer to limit their job to a reduced number of days per week and find that structure sets a limit on how much work they can take on. Others prefer to leave early each day either to pick up children from school, or because their health cannot sustain a full day of work.

One woman physician decided to reduce her work after the birth of her second child. She agreed to work every weekday until 2:00 when she would leave to be with her children. She found, however, that it was too easy for her work to spill over the limits when she was present every day, when needs arose

175

to see an extra patient, to complete needed paperwork, and to interact with colleagues. She found she was taking the paper-work home every night and completing it after the children went to bed. When she reassessed her situation, she realized she was putting in full-time hours while getting paid for part-time work. She then switched her hours to three days/week. She felt this enabled her to devote herself completely to work on those days, and then to leave her work behind. In addition, she had some time to herself while her children were at school or day care.

An experienced woman attorney took eight months' leave when her first child was born. When she returned to work "part-time," which was thirty-five to forty hours/week, her office had been given away, her files had been stored in three inaccessible places, and they gave her the "leftover" work set aside for beginning attorneys. She requested a return to her previous supports and level of work. Over a three-month pe-riod, with persistent reminders, she was given these things and more. She then had to return to her supervisor, tell him she now had more clients than when she was full-time, and help him set clear expectations on how much she was now able to accomplish given her new schedule.

These cases illustrate the importance of setting a clear time frame-work and appropriate limits on work load, as well as the need for on-going discussion and negotiation about these issues. In the Levinson and colleagues (1993) survey of academic medicine part-time faculty, the women worked an average of thirty-five hours/week. Outside of the professions, such a schedule would be considered a full-time schedule.

The third step for part-time choices is to *develop effective negotia-tion skills* (covered in more depth in Chapter 11). Part of negotiating your new role means deciding whether you are willing to look else-where if you do not get support for a part-time position. This can be difficult in an uncertain employment market.

An experienced woman sales manager was tearful in our group discussion when she described feeling that she had been treated poorly by her employer. She had a significant outside interest that had potential for a second career but her employer was unwilling to accommodate her need for a part-time position. She left that job and had taken a much less satisfying one. She felt betrayed and bitter, but felt she had no recourse but to accept her employer's decision.

Another woman physician was offered a full-time position in an emergency room immediately after training. Knowing the work was particularly strenuous, she told the employer she would gladly accept the position if it were part-time, and the other part were given to a colleague she felt she could work well with. She felt confident during the two weeks of ensuing silence because she knew she could pursue other positions. After two weeks her employer agreed. She worked at the position twenty hours/week and the other twenty hours were given to an esteemed colleague. She and the colleague discussed the job frequently in order to maintain consistency in their work and kept detailed records of all transactions so as to function as one employee. The position worked out well for both of them.

The fourth step for establishing a part-time position is to *build a support system for making the change*. It is important to have someone willing to listen and help you sort out your thoughts and plan of action. You need people who will say, "This is a very sane decision to make." Finding supports now is important because your part-time decision may cut you off from work approval.

A professional woman who was working part-time was offered a prestigious full-time position by her supervisor and mentor, a man who dedicated seven days a week to his career while his wife was at home caring for their children. After careful thought and consideration, she acknowledged the vote of confidence from her mentor but said she needed to continue in a part-time career to pursue her involvement with her children. Her mentor left the room abruptly before she finished her sentence. He continued to avoid her and did not support a job advancement. She appraised the effect on her career and moved to another position where she could continue to advance.

177

Some women experience a cutting off of approval from their colleagues when they make the part-time decision, yet others who work in women-led organizations where the standard is to work part-time say they feel a tremendous amount of support. Many careers are more difficult or impossible to do part-time.

A woman scientist had worked full-time while her three children were small. Now that they were approaching teenage years she felt she needed to be home more with them. In part it was because she felt she had missed their childhoods, and in part because her children's needs were changing and they were at risk of exposure to drugs and alcohol without a stable place to go after school. She could not accommodate her research to a part-time position and made the decision to take a break from her career, which had potentially negative consequences for future grants and positions. Knowing the downside, she still felt clear that family was her priority now.

Some part-time professionals may feel isolated both at work and as a mother because they are not a part of the "stay-at-home-mother" group or the "full-time-career-woman" group. Others who choose part-time careers due to illness can also feel marginalized because of the stigma of chronic illness and how our society devalues taking time off for health concerns. Regardless of the reasons for choosing part-time careers, it is important to have validation for our choices.

The fifth step in negotiating a part time career is to *think about how to have a full-time presence at work* without a full-time commitment.

When I changed my hours from a half-day five days/week to three full days/week my supervisor expressed a concern that the responsiveness of the job required a full-time presence. This seemed reasonable so I requested a beeper and I call in for my messages on my days away from the office. I come in for special events, and I make it clear I can be called at home. As a result, most of my peers do not realize I work part-time and maintain my professional identity. When I am at my job I give it 100 percent of my attention because it is a refreshing break from my other career of mothering.

Many women I have spoken with who have taken this same approach have also found that they have more energy to give their job after enjoying the much needed time away.

What are the personal and family benefits to working part-time?

One of the women in our discussion group at the symposium was working full-time but said she was drawn to the group by the "full-time life" part of the title. She had spent the weekend hiking the trails of a nearby mountain and realized how nourishing that was for her, but that she had little time for it. She yearned for a full-time life and was reconsidering her options. The personal benefit of a part-time career is a *full-time life*. One's priorities can become everyday realities. Although most of the research has been done on women who choose part-time careers because of children, many women make a part-time choice for other reasons. Some of the women in the group spent time gardening, playing an instrument, writing a book unrelated to their profession, or becoming politically active in the community. Some spent time resting, being in nature, visiting friends, or managing the household. The key is that each woman remained aware of how precious the time was that she had regained from her career.

A woman physician, Dr. A., who had been full-time and chief of clinical services in her psychiatry department, changed to working a total of two days a week because her teenage children were getting into difficulty after school. She had experienced daily telephone struggles with one daughter over where she would be after school and eventually caught her in a lie about where she was. The physician questioned her decision because she had always felt that your children don't need you at home anymore after they start kindergarten. Her friends had also reported that as soon as their children were in kindergarten colleagues would ask them when they were coming back to work full-time. She was ambivalent because she had reached a prestigious position in her career, which was particularly meaningful to her as a minority woman. One day, while Dr. A. interrupted her work to argue with her daughter over the phone, a patient with a history of self-mutilating behavior approached her. The patient was covered with blood and said, "I just cut myself." Dr. A. realized at that moment that the two aspects of her life were too full to exist together and she chose to be home more with her daughters. Since then she reports great satisfaction in being able to spend time with them, cook with them, have time for discussions, and have her home be a central place for the teenagers to converge after school.

The myth about children not needing their mothers at home after kindergarten age is a pervasive one. Many sources refute this stance, and the teenage years are being seen as particularly difficult for girls in our culture today. Mary Pipher (1995, 1996) writes about how our fast-paced high-standards lifestyles are affecting adolescent children today. The popularity of her books suggests that many mothers are finding that it is especially important to be physically and emotionally present for your children at these turbulent times.

There is a different issue for women who have to choose to work part-time due to illness. However, many women have chosen a therapeutic and nourishing use of their free time so as to promote their health.

One woman with a long-standing health problem spent time away from her career taking a long walk each day, writing in her journal, connecting with a good friend with the same illness, setting weekly goals for herself, taking naps, and cooking nutritious meals that were consistent with the diet necessary for her treatment. As a result, she recovered completely and is now able to work-full time, but she continues to choose part-time work since she found the lifestyle so satisfying.

Overall, the main advantage to a part-time career is time for the feminine sides of our lives—time to slow down, to appreciate nature, to spend time with loved ones, to be creative in our own ways, to self-reflect, to pursue our spirituality, to regain physical or emotional health, or to catch up on unresolved issues that have been the shadow behind our fast-paced lives. As St. James (1996) states, "One of the reasons we keep our lives complicated is so we won't have to listen to our inner voice telling us what we need to do to make our lives work better (p. 73). We've been so busy being the good wife, the good mother, the good daughter, the outstanding employee, the successful entrepreneur, and everyone else's idea of what perfect is that we've lost touch with who we really are. . . . [A] benefit of having this newfound time will be the opportunity to begin to get reacquainted with yourself" (p. 219).

> I have continued to work part-time at the medical center despite a culture that reminds me that part-time employees are of less value and that full-time employees have better job security. I know that someone who works full-time would be in a better position to advance to head of my division. I make these choices because of my full-time life. I can work in my son's classroom; I can get to know his friends and have them be comfortable with me when they come to our house to help facilitate the building of community for our family. In addition, I get to have an uninterrupted lunch with my husband one day/week while my son is in school. This connection feels very important for keeping our relationship vital, romantic, and not burdened by things we have not had a chance to discuss. In addition, I take hikes with my friends when the trails are uncrowded, work on my computer, read books, and spend time reflecting on my priorities and ways to further simplify my life. I also have time to meet my physical needs for naps, doctor's appointments, exercise, and healthy food. I pay bills and get the overhead done so my weekends can be spent with family activities. This is a balanced and satisfying choice for me that enables me to be maximally creative in all areas of my life.

Terri Apter (1993) states:

The most recent studies of women and depression have found that though housewives are still more depressed than working wives, and working wives are still more depressed than working husbands, women who have children and who work part-time are significantly less prone to depression than are married women with children who work full-time. [p. 197] What women want most is good, challenging responsible jobs, but with reasonable work hours. Work hours for good, responsible, challenging full-time jobs are often, by any standards, unreasonable. They most certainly do not allow for a balanced life. [p. 252]

Are there personal and family disadvantages to a part-time career?
   One frequently discussed conflict is whether the professional woman now at home part-time will expect herself (or her partner will

expect her) to become the full-time "wife," the one who does the errands, grocery shopping, cleaning, repairs, and so on. The statistics support that women are still doing more domestic tasks than men whether or not they are working full-time (Apter 1993). The part-time career woman needs to give thought to how much she is willing to do, and whether, if she is working part-time, she feels comfortable having the family continue to divide up these tasks or to hire additional assistance.

> A woman physician who had reduced her work hours came into her psychotherapy hour tearfully describing that all her "free" time away from work was being spent taking care of the children, doing the grocery shopping, the cleaning, and going house hunting. She explained that her husband gets home so late and unpredictably from his job that she felt he needed his time protected to spend with the children. When she had a little extra child care, she spent it running to Costco, Trader Joe's, Target, and all the budget stores to stock up. She was angry and resentful that she had no time to herself. When we examined her options she realized that domestic management was her job now that she was not the primary money maker, and that she had no choices. Upon further reflection she gave her husband a list of some of the tasks to complete, and she spent her extra child-care time getting much needed rest from the children and her job duties.

Another issue that surfaces is that of the previously autonomous woman now needing to ask her spouse for money to buy groceries or clothing. In our society, money is often equated with power. The person bringing home the majority of the income often feels he should have more say in how things are done, or in how the money is spent. It is very difficult for the woman to value herself while having to ask for money each week.

> One woman chose to leave her high-powered marketing career when it became clear their daughter needed daily guidance as to socially acceptable behavior; her temperament was such that she was getting into difficulty with peers and teach-

ers. This decision was upsetting to her husband who is concerned about financial stability. He continues to pressure her to work full-time; failing that, he refuses to allow them to move out of the small rental unit they are in to a more comfortable place despite ample funds to do so. She feels she has made the right decision regarding the best interests of her child but says she "misses having money of my own" and dreads asking her husband for funds. In addition, her husband is now working late every evening attempting to make up the decline in their income.

Another common theme is spousal envy of the person working part-time.

One woman who had decided to leave a Wall Street job to pursue a doctoral degree in philosophy was still asleep when her husband left for work in the morning. Her spouse, an accountant, was so envious of her time to herself that he found himself making snide comments about her being lazy, sleeping in, or not doing anything with all her time. Through discussion he realized he was resentful of her "life of luxury" while he put in long hours. There ensued a couple's discussion in which he decided he also wanted to work part-time and they made a decision to change their lifestyles dramatically and move to a less expensive area where that life choice was possible for both of them.

Another issue that surfaced in our symposium discussion group was whether the woman's partner would have less respect for her as a part-time professional.

One of the women physicians who chose to go part-time asked her husband, a medical school classmate, whether he was disappointed in her since they had both always been very ambitious. She realized she no longer wished to pursue the goals that motivated her earlier and that although her career was important to her, climbing the ladder was not. Fortunately, her husband understood and supported her choices.

What are the professional advantages to a part-time career, full-time life?

Many women find that their career develops in different ways than anticipated after making the change to part-time. They specifically cited their creativity being enhanced and new directions emerging for them.

> The woman described above who had decided upon reflection to go part-time because she was not "ambitious" was pleasantly surprised. She found that she published her first two papers in the initial eight months of the change because she now had the energy and motivation to do it. She felt she was developing national recognition for the specific areas of interest to her.

Another source of career satisfaction is that women are forced to set clear priorities when time is limited. They often choose what is most satisfying for them and what they are best at. Others find new satisfaction from choosing a few things to do well rather than always having more tasks than they can complete.

One woman in the group felt her career was enhanced by the time she took to read philosophy and religion. Most women felt the part-time career choice was not just a holding pattern until full-time work status could be regained. Additionally, they felt that working part-time prevents burnout, which can allow one to stay in a job longer and to be healthier than full-time workers. There is evidence for this view in Lillian Cartwright and colleagues' (1995) longitudinal study of factors that predispose women physicians to good health in mid-life. She identified seven characteristics of intellectual efficiency that were shown to positively affect health outcomes in mid-life. One of these factors is setting goals for yourself and following through with them and a second is acknowledging limitations and living within them. Both of these are encompassed in the decision to be a part-time professional.

What can be the professional disadvantages to a part-time career, full-time life?

The professional disadvantages relate to how the individual's work environment responds to part-time careers. Many supervisors do not respect part-time employees or treat them fairly in promotion and advancement. In the Levinson et al. study (1993) of the 245 faculty surveyed, 86 percent were in nontenure track positions, and only 8 percent reported that existing institutional policies allowed part-time faculty additional years to meet promotion and tenure standards. In many places there is pressure to work full-time from peers as well as mentors. The other difficulty is that a woman professional may be losing skills in the areas where she has chosen to cut back. In some professions this changed skill set can mean that it is more difficult to find work in the future.

> One woman attorney who had been part of a large law firm chose to switch to hourly contract work when her daughter was born. She has been told this decision means she will never have the option to return to a large law firm or again command a large salary.

Another possible disadvantage was brought up by a full-time professional woman who has always had full-time help to care for her two children. She felt that part-time work meant you have two full-time jobs—parenting and career. She felt it is simpler to choose one than to feel continually conflicted about both. Curiously, the part-time career women did not feel this, but felt both roles gave them satisfaction. In general, despite some potential disadvantages, most part-time career women express great satisfaction with their choices.

SUMMARY

The decision to be a part-time professional is a personal one. It implies having the courage to prioritize one's values and to act on them. A part-time career necessitates adjustments at the workplace and in the family life. It requires having the internal conviction about the importance of one's values in order to combat external expectations that one should be a full-time mother or a full-time professional, or act invulnerable when one has an illness. It is likely that these part-time options in the workplace will increase in the future. Says Schwartz (1992), as gender roles change and the workplace becomes a more supportive place with greater flexibility, opportunities for part-time professions will increase for both sexes, allowing talented and dedicated men and women to make balanced decisions about their lives. As a result those who want it will have more time for connection with families and friends. Those who choose to live life at a slower pace or cut back for intervals in their lives may bring a different, useful perspective to a world caught up in an ever-accelerating pace.

10

WOMEN IN LEADERSHIP

ANNA M. SPIELVOGEL

More and more, women are entering the professions and business—but, unlike cream, they are not rising easily to the top. Within the changing managerial climate, the skills of creative thinking and team building are key, so women would appear to be temperamentally well suited to positions of power. Yet, as discussed in more depth in Chapters 13 and 14, women are still disproportionately absent from the top echelon. This chapter is a review of what is currently understood about the characteristics of leadership and how women have been shaped by their psychological development, societal role, and organizational barriers to fit uneasily into the traditional leadership format. Echoing the consistent theme of the book, viewing adult choices in a developmental context can help women enhance their unique leadership characteristics, know the unwritten rules of the game, and gain power in ways that can lead to institutional change.

The reasons for the lack of representation of women in top leadership positions in most organizations are complex. Stereotypical role expectations prevent women from learning "how to play hardball" (Heim 1993). Women are not afforded the same support and welcome as male leaders. Women with equal work achievements receive fewer promotions and financial rewards.

Adversarial relationships between women bosses and their subordinates, both women and men, are well publicized. Women bosses' expectations of their subordinates and vice versa are based on unattainable ideals of each other, influenced by early developmental models. Women set high standards for themselves and other women. They hope to be powerful and effective yet nurturant and equalitarian. Women's socialization to be relational and cooperative might account for the particular difficulty women leaders face when they have to be directive. In addition to overcoming their internal discomfort with giving orders, women bosses have difficulty winning the respect and trust of their female subordinates. Working out fair compromises regarding some women employees' wish to modify their work schedules or to take maternity or family leave may be particularly difficult for women leaders.

Many women's wish to combine child rearing with a career can diminish their internal drive to seek demanding leadership positions at crucial points in their family life. Different patterns emerge, contributing to the more wavy and varied career path of women. Women are called upon to design their own path by defining their special talents and priorities and coming to terms with contradictory internal and external demands. Women's preference for a flatter organization, their cooperative style and ability to sense and attend to the emotional aspects of people, can be major assets with the rapid changes occurring in organizational structures (Glaser and Steinberg 1995, Helgesen 1995, Rosener 1995, Scheidt 1994). The goal of this chapter is to weave together a number of perspectives on women's leadership and then to use an illustrative fable to demonstrate one woman's path to power. A woman's success in leadership requires that she clarify her goals, her passion, and her attitude toward power and assertion. Women need to learn about leadership styles appropriate for different situations and to deal effectively with internal and external barriers toward success.

LEADERSHIP: TRAITS AND STYLES

Leadership in the most general way can be defined as the ability to set goals and standards, exert influence on others to make things happen, and then be held accountable for the outcome. This requires a passionate vision of the future, an analysis of the situation, the development of a strategy, an ability to communicate the goal, and an approach to maximize cooperation. It necessitates significant personal resources to take appropriate risks, maintain a positive focus, and bear the responsibility for the task.

Characteristics frequently associated with leadership include:

- Strength
- Vision
- Intelligence
- Rationality
- Commitment

- Independence
- Competitiveness
- Charisma

Such characteristics are clearly distributed along a gender continuum, but they more closely approximate the stereotypic view of male rather than female traits.

Thus it is especially important for women leaders to have institutionally conferred authority, informally acquired power, and excellent interpersonal skills leading to the ability to influence people. An effective leader has to manage the external boundaries while obtaining resources, appropriately showcasing the products of the group, developing relationships with key people externally, and minimizing the impact of environmental stressors on the group. In addition, the leader needs to facilitate smooth internal functioning. Leadership takes many different talents and skills, and the list of requirements for excellence in leaderships seems to describe an almost superhuman being.

Women, in particular, might be daunted by the tasks of leadership. In general, women are less strongly driven to gain power and money, less comfortable with win/lose competition, and more strongly motivated by work orientation and contributing to their community (Lipman-Blumen 1992, Offerman and Beil 1992).

Add to this the burden of gender stereotyping and the path is even steeper. Rosener (1995) relates a telling anecdote in *America's Competitive Secret*.

> A friend of mine owns a large mergers and acquisitions firm that buys and sells companies. She was on her way from Los Angeles to New York for a business meeting when her plane was delayed. While she was waiting in an airport bar, a man approached her. "Hello, would you like a little company?" he asked. "Sure," she said. "Do you have one for sale?" She was thinking business, he was thinking female. This sort of misunderstanding is common today, now that women are in professions and managerial positions that have historically been all male. It's no wonder men are confused. [p. 70]

Rosener (1995) notes that women are not often seen in terms of leadership potential because they do not exhibit male attributes. Yet women will not attain leadership roles simply by imitating their male peers. The first step is for each woman to assess her own special talents and determine her goals and resources. It appears particularly important for women to feel passionate about their work and to enjoy their relationships with colleagues. The next step would be to look for the setting in which she is most comfortable and her style will be most effective.

Women and men do tend to prefer different leadership styles. As far back as the 1920s, Mary Parker Follett, the "mother of modern management theory" (Graham 1995), wrote about flat organizations, teamwork, participatory leadership, and cooperative conflict resolution. Rosener (1995) has focused on how women do it differently. She contrasts two leadership styles that tend to be gender congruent for men (command and control) or women (interactive).

Command-and-Control Leadership Style
- Top-down decision making
- Use of structural power
- Focus on self-interest of followers
- Control by reward for specific tasks
- Stress on individual contribution
- Emphasis on "rational" decision making

Interactive Leadership Style
- Shared decision making
- Use of personal power
- Focus on achievement of organizational goals
- Control by generating empowerment
- Stress on shared power and information
- Emphasis on nontraditional forms of decision making [p. 73]

Different leadership styles will be most effective in certain phases of organizational development or within organizations with particular primary values or objectives. For instance, the military is organized in a strictly hierarchical structure in which leaders have authority and are rewarded for skillful, decisive action and adhering to the standards of the organization. Most of the communications between superior and subordinate are unidirectional. Successful leadership styles here are skillfully directing others and picking competent subordinates for delegation of specific parts of the task. Both these leadership styles, directing and delegating, are often not as natural and comfortable for women as for men (Heim 1993). For women, who are a minority in hierarchical organizations, understanding the rules and playing by them is essential. Heim (1993) describes how to win in such organizations by understanding the rules of competition, never challenging the "coach," being useful as a team player, and drawing attention to oneself as a leader. Clearly, gender-stereotypic traits more strongly associated with men (Sargent 1983, Williams and Best 1990) are valued, such as strength, aggressiveness, independence, dominance, action-orientation; disorderliness, loudness, boastfulness, and coarseness would be tolerated as role-appropriate.

In male-oriented organizations like the military, surgery departments, or corporate law firms, women are more at risk for sexual discrimination and harassment since as an outgroup their preferred styles and norms for respectful interpersonal behavior will be seen as incongruent with the culture of the organization. Women successfully attaining leadership in such environments usually describe their love for their work and their pleasure in innovations or excellence in a highly valued skill and a willingness to work hard and persevere (Helgesen 1995, Picker 1996). These women have the ability to find the narrow balance between being feminine and authoritarian and have successfully managed devaluing and sexually provocative responses from their male peers. Successful strategies include early and persistent gentle corrections, such as using the word *women* in every response to references to women as *girls* (Heim 1993), pointing out the "inadvertent" negative effect of devaluing by team members, and seeking reasonable allies in bringing the general tenor of sexist talk to a superior's attention. (Chapter 13, "Strategies to Deal with Gender Discrimination and Harassment," explores these themes.)

On the other hand, certain institutions with long-term female leadership, a nonprofit status, or a primary advocacy focus may have a flatter organizational structure. Leaders might be specifically selected for their skill in cooperation and service to others and not for overtly promoting themselves or seeking status. Women who had been encouraged to develop relational skills would naturally fit the job descriptions and excel by using their preferred leadership styles of coaching and supporting (Heim 1993). Women leaders often like flatter organizations, receiving input and staying personally involved with their employees. They excel at praising and being sensitive to employees' personal needs.

Helgesen (1995) describes the leadership styles of four successful women. Their exceptional interpersonal skills allowed them to build organizations where the women leader positioned herself in the middle of a circle, sharing and receiving information directly from her employees and empowering work teams to find their own best solutions. In all cases, women's ability to know what services the customers wanted and providing them in a respectful and caring way gave these women the edge over the competitors. Ongoing relationships with the public, the customers, the competitors, and the employees were seen as key to success.

Lipman-Blumen (1992) describes an integrative leadership model, termed *connective leadership style*, which relies on women's favored achievement styles and fits emerging needs for global interdependence and cooperation. She describes three achievement styles: (1) the *relational style*, focused on joining forces, helping others and mentoring; (2) the *instrumental style*, which operates through empowering others, networking, and persuading; and (3) the *direct style*, which aims at excelling, outperforming, and taking charge. Women personally favor the first two, while in this country the direct style is glorified as the best leadership choice. Collaboration rather than self-focus is encouraged in business partners through initial cooperation, the expectation of long-term relationships, and past demonstrations of strength and toughness. Lipman-Blumen (1992) also notes that top executives are significantly more relational and less competitive than mid-level managers and suggests to women that learning how to play hardball by male rules is inappropriate because women should capitalize on their natural talents and use instrumental and relational leadership styles. However, the relative success of women who prefer cooperation and connection in organizations depends on the availability of a critical mass of individuals who endorse these strategies.

For both male and female employees, working for a woman is often depicted as problematic, a situation that will require coping. Two surveys (Sutton and Moore 1985) of *Harvard Business Review* subscribers done over a twenty-year period found that more women than men currently believe that women will never be accepted fully in the business world. The percentage of executives who felt that women would be uncomfortable working under a woman actually increased from 1965 to 1985. O'Leary (1988) suggests that a woman leader's actual performance is unlikely to be differentially evaluated by women but that women in general are less likely to be perceived as desirable leaders than men are. This may be related to their lower social status in the workplace or discomfort with the idea of a dominant women, the feared "Queen Bee."

DEVELOPMENT OF GENDER DIFFERENCES

How can we understand these gender differences in leadership style from a developmental perspective? From a psychological point of view, the role of the mother in children's early life is relevant to women's later experience in leadership, a theme introduced in Chapter 2. Girls and boys experience their mother as powerful in giving or withholding gratification and themselves as powerless infants. Girls recognize that they are like the mother and they mature by maintaining a close relationship with her. Unlike boys, their female core gender identity does not demand that they identify with the opposite sex parent and individuate by rejecting the relationship with mother. Women grow through relationships and develop increased ability for empathic connection (Gilligan 1982, Jordan et al. 1991, Miller 1976). They tend to exhibit less aggression and accept more caregiving responsibility than men (Nadelson et al. 1982). The girl incorporates characteristics of her father or other male role models, who traditionally provide encouragement for activities, intellectual pursuits, and risk taking. Her major concern is to maintain a close affectionate relationship with both mother and father (Tyson and Tyson 1990).

As elaborated in Chapter 2, problems can arise if the girl experiences a loss of affection from her mother when she increasingly asserts her own wishes, takes risks, and develops intellectually. She may respond by becoming more physically active and draw closer to her father. Because of the importance of relationships, subtle rejection by mother or father can create an internal conflict. A girl's self-esteem can be lowered and the expression of her full talents impeded. The girl can view her assertiveness as forbidden aggression, suppress it, and feel more depressed as a result (Nadelson et al. 1982, Tyson and Tyson 1990). The early fear of loss of relationships can inhibit women's future strivings for assertiveness and leadership.

Some of the most striking gender differences in young girls and boys are observable in their play. Boys show high activity and more rough and tumble play, and are more aggressive in getting toys. Girls play more peacefully, communicating with each other and sharing toys (Maccoby 1990, Tannen 1990). Interestingly, girls' style of play is influenced by the gender mix of their playmates (Maccoby 1990). In same-gender groups 3-year-old girls are active and independent, often sitting farther away from teachers than boys do in all male groups.

However, when girls play with boys, they usually are on the sidelines and do not have access to the toys unless an adult intervenes. Boys at about 4 years of age stop acceding to girls' requests and influence. They establish hierarchies and competitively vie for positions. These differences in play styles can be seen as antecedents to gender-role differences in achievement in adults (Beall and Sternberg 1993).

Social learning and gender schema theories offer powerful explanations of how these gender gaps widen and result in role differences that impact women's roles as leaders (Beall and Sternberg 1993, Fagot 1984). Parents reinforce gender-typed behavior for girls and boys (Hoffman 1991, Lytton and Romney 1991). Teachers call on boys more than girls. Most theorists agree that biological contributions are small compared to potent social and behavioral influences. Responding to adult and peer expectations and role modeling, children form asymmetric gender schema that associate more power and prestige with male categories (Hort et al. 1991). For instance, Williams and Best (1990) demonstrated that across many different cultures, attributes of strength, activity, adventurousness, independence, and dominance are associated with males, and attributes of weakness, softheartedness, gentleness, meekness, and emotionality with females. These gender stereotypes are seen beginning at age 3 and are fully developed by age 8, influenced both by home and community (Katz 1996). Stereotypes also extend to associating certain professions with men, others with women. Mother's employment, traditional or nontraditional, influence preschool children's occupational interests in the same direction.

As described in Beall and Sternberg (1993), the child not only learns gender-appropriate behaviors but starts to associate the presence or absence of power and self-esteem differentially with men and women, thereby reinforcing the patriarchal system. Gender schema then will color our perceptions about ourselves and the people we encounter. Occupations are gender stereotyped by children. When asked to draw a scientist, children draw a man (Beall and Sternberg 1993). Repeatedly, children encounter men in the role of leaders—president, preacher, headmaster, coach, surgeon, general. These stereotypes have not changed significantly in the last twenty years. They are learned early, but can be influenced by contradictory experiences—for instance, a mother working in a stereotypically male profession.

Unrecognized gender stereotypes held by women and men and their early experience with a powerful female figure, the mother, come into play when a woman is holding a leadership role. Unconscious attribution automatically and instantaneously ascribes activity, aggressiveness, instrumentality, and independence to males and evaluates them as appropriate and positive leaders while viewing the same characteristics in women as negative. These characteristics do not conform with desirable female stereotypical gender roles of being nurturant, supportive, and nonaggressive. In a Supreme Court case cited in Beall and Sternberg (1993) the defendant, Ann Hopkins, a corporate attorney, was not promoted. She was called "arrogant, self-centered, abrasive, and overbearing" (p. 63). These same characteristics in a man would be called outspoken, independent, self-confident, assertive, and courageous. The Supreme Court concluded: "An employer who objects to aggressiveness in women but whose position requires that trait places women in an intolerable Catch 22: out of job if they behave aggressively and out of job if they don't" (p. 63).

The intensity of negative reactions to "aggressive women leaders" and the personal attack on the woman leader can be explained by the activation of deep, unconscious fears of the bad mother, the witch archetype. Independent, nontraditional women who were seen as possessing power have run the risk of being labeled witches, hated, feared, and persecuted throughout the centuries (Prozan 1992). The witch constitutes the opposite of the nurturing, motherly woman who always puts the interest of others first. Even Hillary Clinton has had to package herself as the purveyor of cookie recipes and motherly concern after her initial attempt at a leadership role was met with scathing criticism.

Men successfully speak the language of the powerful (Heim 1993, Tannen 1990, 1994, Tavris 1992). Men interrupt more, express their opinions directly, speak for longer periods of time, focus on facts, and are less attuned to group members than women are. Tannen (1990) eloquently describes the cultural differences between men and women. Women use language to establish rapport and build connections, men to communicate facts and establish hierarchies. Tavris (1992) argues that these gender differences in language result from men holding more powerful positions in groups. She cites studies (Lakoff 1990) that show that these patterns can be altered by changing the gender mix of the group or the power status of members. However, women's "power talk" is not as successful as men's in influencing others. Carli (1990) reports that women who were tentative were often more successful in changing men's opinions.

Most experts agree that cultural, social, and situational more than biological or genetic differences account for the significant gender differences in leadership (Beall and Steinberg 1993). Across cultures women have less power, are minorities in prestigious, high-paying occupations, are paid less for equal work, and are underrepresented in leadership positions. Caution has to be exercised when describing differences in language, assertiveness, dominance, or connectedness observed in certain situations as potential male or female traits. Gilligan (1982), Jordan and colleagues (1991), and Miller (1976) changed the deficit model of women by emphasizing the positive aspects of women's psychological development-in-connection. Women's emphasis on care for others, harmony, and relationships has to be acknowledged as valuable. Yet these behaviors need to be understood not as inherent characteristics of women, but as skills developed in the social context of being less powerful. Perhaps their socialization process can help women to solve leadership problems in new ways that involve communication and empowerment.

BARRIERS FOR WOMEN'S ADVANCEMENT TO LEADERSHIP POSITIONS

External Barriers

The glass ceiling still exists for women in top corporate, academic, and political positions (as explored in Chapters 1 and 13). Earlier we discussed the development of gender-role stereotypes that equate male characteristics with desirable leadership qualities. Women with identical qualifications are hired less frequently for professional and managerial jobs, are paid less for identical work, and are less often considered for advancement. To achieve leadership positions, women have to deal with significant structural and psychological barriers; success in these roles requires strategic thinking, determination, and resilience.

Heim (1993) explains this phenomenon as due to the fact that women do not play by the same rules that allow men to be successful. Using the analogy of games, she describes step by step how women can succeed in a male-dominated environment by becoming knowledgeable about the rules of the game and playing it correctly. Her examples illustrate how women can inadvertently undermine their leadership potential by not supporting their male bosses' and colleagues' preference for hierarchical structure, power plays, and win/lose competition. Her advice is to learn the rules of the game and play by them until you are in a position to change them. A group currently in leadership will feel more comfortable and preferentially promote persons who are like them (Pfeffer 1981).

The importance of high-ranking mentors for women to achieve leadership positions has been amply demonstrated (Bickel 1995a, Jeruchim and Shapiro 1992). Women who are able to find mentors, male and female, who can guide them in work and family decisions clearly have an edge in career advancement, especially at the senior level of management (described in Chapter 14).

Women's competitiveness with each other has been widely described in the popular media. In some surveys women subordinates are particularly critical of women bosses (O'Leary 1988). In general, this is most pronounced when women leaders are new in their organizations. She also describes unrealistic expectations and demands as potential difficulties in the supervisor/supervisee dyad. However, employees with powerful, secure female bosses over time prefer their supervisory style characterized by frequent feedback and an interest in employees' personal life and career enhancement. Heim (1993) describes the resentment some women in service-oriented positions feel in cheerfully carrying out orders from females in authority.

Developmentally, theorists attribute some of these psychological difficulties to the mother–daughter relationship. Depending on the experience with the original woman in authority, there may be unrealistic expectations that the woman leader is going to be omnipotent, nurturant, and personally interested in each employee's welfare. Covert fears may also be activated that the woman leader is vulnerable, ineffective, overcontrolling, and threatened by the employee's success.

Combining childbearing and -rearing with a career is not only challenging for the woman employee but often difficult for a woman leader. While the law increasingly requires paid maternity leave and job guarantees for women who have children, many organizations do not allocate resources to replace these women, thereby increasing the workload of her peers. In addition, dealing with pregnancy arrangements often becomes a most hotly debated and divisive issue in the workplace with a woman leader.

VIGNETTE

Several years ago, as the unit chief of a psychiatric inpatient unit, I introduced the concept of developing a women's issues consultation team that would specialize in the treatment of pregnant psychiatric patients. When this idea was first introduced in the staff meeting, it was met with explosive objections and resistance. Fears were expressed that pregnant women with their emotional baggage would take over the whole unit, that staff not already competent in the care of psychotic pregnant women would be fired, and that the culture of firm limit-setting with psychiatric patients would be changed. As a leader, I had already secured the approval of my superiors and had some allies among some of the senior staff on the unit. I was not prepared for this intensity of response from a usually flexible, reasonable staff. Obviously, dealing with a female leader initiating change, especially about pregnancy, aroused very strong personal reactions. I thought that the staff's concern with the baggage metaphorically expressed their concern of being overwhelmed with "women's things." Staff discomfort was managed by gradually increasing their knowledge base and ease through individual meetings and the experience of successful treatment of some pregnant patients. Since I felt strongly motivated to pioneer the provision of expert and sensitive care to pregnant women with mental illness, it was possible to overcome the various obstacles and initial opposition.

Then a staff member became pregnant and the reaction of the predominantly female staff was again quite intense. When coverage was needed for her emergent absence and the potential candidates were polled as to who would be willing to fill in, they flatly refused, suggesting that I provide the coverage. Staff felt torn between wanting to be helpful and feeling extremely resentful about having to cover her duties. Lack of planning for the unpredictable absences during the pregnancy and after the woman's return from leave and a lack of alternatives for the group contributed to the escalation of an already hot topic. The pregnant supervisee is often expecting particular understanding and consideration from a female

200

boss, who as a senior woman is often involved in advocating for fair working conditions for female employees. However, a pregnant employee or leader can stimulate a painful awareness of differences. Clearly, each woman makes personal choices about her priorities regarding childbearing and career. Confronted with choices different from her own, a woman can respond by devaluation of her choice or the choice of the other woman; she is reminded of the impossibility of having it all. Women leaders are often in a particularly vulnerable position to negotiate a workable pregnancy and maternity plan and to deal with employees' strong negative reactions.

Internal Barriers

Discussing women's internal barriers to leadership requires caution in order not to reaffirm the old notion of women's deficits as cause for their lack of representation in top leadership positions. The internal barriers described are seen as a result of cultural conditions that relegate women to lower status positions. Nevertheless, identifying and overcoming personal internal barriers is essential to career success.

When recently facilitating a discussion group in the symposium on the topic of "Women in Leadership," the participants described to me how they were reluctant leaders, had stumbled on leadership by default, found personal satisfaction waning while in stressful leadership positions, missed meaningful connections with people, and were unsure how to combine leadership with caregiving responsibilities for family. Quietly, some of the women reported amazing achievements, yet quickly added that more could have been done or something was missing.

Women often start from a less certain position. Focusing intensely on long-term planning with specific goals and timelines (Heim 1993) is not as natural for many women and their career trajectory is often wavy rather than linear. Interestingly, many of the successful women leaders described in the literature noted that they were surprised to be where they were and had fallen into positions rather than competed for them (Glaser and Steinberg 1995, Helgesen 1995). Following a more intuitive approach is not inevitably a drawback, but enjoying strategic planning and the pursuit of a strongly desired goal can be potent motivators for successful leaders.

Women are often motivated by the wish to have meaningful, harmonious relationships with others. Several of my women psychotherapy clients described the profound feelings of betrayal they experienced in the workplace. Inevitably someone had made a decision that violated their own deeply held convictions about the importance of connections, loyalty, fairness, and care. When this happens, women are at risk for losing their job motivation and can withdraw and become depressed. While it is essential that they find a way of connecting with more appropriate partners such as friends, family, a special colleague, or therapists, work should not be expected to be a nurturing family and it requires analysis and a strategic response. To carry out this response the woman often has to mobilize her own assertive and competitive side.

Women in visible leadership positions must confront the feared affects of envy and competitiveness in themselves and others. Eichenbaum and Orbach (1988) suggest that women are uncomfortable with these feelings and seek to avoid them through inhibition of their success. Based on the mother–daughter relationship, many women expect that their success will threaten the other and will downplay it in conversation. Women are more comfortable competing about who is worst off, supporting weakness rather than strength. Other women's success evokes feelings of longing that they tend to evaluate negatively rather than using it as a signpost to their goals. The wish to be competitive is not familiar from earlier patterns and they expect disapproval and retribution for it.

My own most pleasurable leadership experience involved a coleadership position with another woman. We shared similar work ethics and a vision of excellence but complemented each other in our leadership talents. She has exceptional skills in coaching and supporting people, patiently negotiating with partners for a win/win solution, as well as excellent organizational and administrative skills. I contributed strong analytical and strategic planning abilities, comfort in sizing up situations and making decisions, good crisis management skills, and assertive negotiation skills to protect the service from avoidable stressors. Using joint decision making but with clearly delineated roles, we were able to set an example of effective collaboration and task-oriented leadership that resulted in innovations and smooth functioning of the service. One of the most important aspects of this coleadership relationship was our ability to support each other when we had lost a battle, had been criticized by superiors or staff, or felt temporarily discouraged by the workload. Our interactions always involved a combination of emotional support, fact processing, and strategic planning on how to recoup. With these strategies we managed our fear of envy from staff, and made explicit and handled envious feelings between us.

Women's relationship to success and power is more ambivalent than men's (Heim 1993, Offerman and Beil 1992). Socialized to be in subordinate positions, women become "relationship experts" and start to value the positive feedback derived from that (Tannen 1990, Tavris 1992). Women use language that indicates a willingness to yield their power. They speak in a tentative low voice, and present suggestions with qualifiers such as, "I don't know if it is a good idea, but. . . ." They tend to ask questions instead of making statements and are reluctant to speak up in a situation where the bottom line is the issue. For the sake of maintaining a relationship they might yield a point. Experiential research shows that when groups of women are given high status, they use powerful language and strategies just as men do, except that groups of men are less likely to give in and submit to the more powerful group of women (Carli 1990).

Women are less comfortable bragging about their achievements. Men attribute success to their innate abilities and failure to the difficulties of the task. Women attribute success to luck, effort, or ease of the task, but take responsibility for the failures (Bateson 1990). It appears that these attributions contribute to women's having lower self-esteem and feeling more burdened by their work. Women need to identify these attitudes within themselves, get a second opinion from a trusted friend, and then actively counteract self-defeating attitudes. It is essential for women leaders to have an advisory group of peers who can consult with them, assist with advertising the woman's achievement, and orchestrate adequate acknowledgment in group settings. This group of trusted peers can also be protective of women's sensitivity to failures and criticism. For instance, a group of prominent women psychiatrists on the East Coast have developed a telephone network to discuss specific political analyses and strategies for securing promotions, running for office in professional organizations, and dealing with setbacks. Resilience, perseverance, and support are particularly necessary for women to succeed.

A LEADERSHIP FABLE

The stories women tell about their successes are different from men's. Men's heroic tales often describe family obligations as transient impediments to heroic success (Lipman-Blumen 1992, Tavris 1992) while women present those issues as complex and interwoven. Following this tradition of storytelling, I present below the tale of one woman's path to power. It is important to note that there are many other paths, variations, and options for women. The story will serve to illustrate how old fables can come alive and speak to the psyche of the modern woman in a powerful way. This is a tale from the Uighar culture in China as retold and interpreted by Chinen (1992).

The Wife Who Became King

Long ago a poor but clever and gifted young woman married a good but poor man in her village. The woman sewed beautiful embroidered cloth, which came to the attention of the King. He had already many wives but sent his minister to fetch the woman to make her his wife. The woman refused, stating she was already married. The King was angered by her rejection and vowed to make her his wife sooner or later.

The young woman, tired of being poor, bought some silk and with hard work produced a beautiful quilt. She asked her husband to sell it. The King came by with his entourage and recognized the quilt as the work of the same woman who had rejected his marriage proposal. He took the cloth and instructed the man to have his wife prepare lunch for him at his house the following day.

The wife told her husband that she would hide and that he should tell the King that she was away visiting relatives. The King did not believe that message and he offered the husband strong wine until he fell asleep. Then the King found the wife and demanded she come back to the palace with him. The wife agreed but was able to leave signs for her husband to indicate what had happened.

When the wife arrived at the palace, she asked to have three days to prepare for the wedding. The King agreed. When

204

the husband awoke, he went to the palace, but could not get by the guards. He met an old woman who told him to buy combs and mirrors and offer them for sale at the palace. When the man appeared, his wife recognized him and met him at the gate. She instructed him to buy two horses and wait for her outside the palace wall in three days.

When darkness fell, the husband went to the palace with the horses and waited for his wife. Since he had been awake three nights worrying about their fate, he dropped off to sleep. As the wife climbed over the wall a bald-headed man, a murderer by trade, walked by. Mistaking him for her husband, the wife asked him to put her bag on the horse and follow her. The murderer did so.

When the wife recognized her error she told the villain that she would marry him under the condition that he accepted her cure for his baldness. She asked the villain to boil a huge pot of oil to cure his baldness. When the oil was hot she pushed his head into the pot, which killed him instantly.

Along the way, the beautiful woman was repeatedly propositioned by men but managed to elude them. Finally she decided to put on men's clothing to avoid further trouble and traveled to the next city. There was a big commotion and people were excitedly looking at the sky. The woman learned that their King had just died and the Bird of Happiness, released from its cage, would choose the new King by landing on a man's shoulder. The tension in the crowd built and finally the Bird of Happiness landed right on the woman's shoulder. According to tradition, she was crowned King and quickly learned her royal duties. She ruled as a fair and wise King and was well loved.

One day the wicked King who had previously abducted her came asking help to find his bride. To the horror of her ministers, the wife ordered the King put in prison. Finally a man appeared (whom the wife recognized as her husband) to ask if the King knew of the whereabouts of his wife. The woman who was King spoke to the man privately and revealed herself as his wife. They were overjoyed to find each other. She instructed him to be at a certain cafe in women's clothing the next day. When the woman who was King rode by the cafe

205

she pointed to her husband, dressed as a woman, and pro-claimed that she would marry this person.

For some time, the couple lived happily in disguise. Finally the woman who was King decided to tell her subjects the whole story. The subjects were moved by the woman's courage, wisdom, and great suffering and asked her to rule them as their Queen, appointing her husband as King to help her. They agreed to keep the wicked King in prison for his evil deeds. The royal pair reigned over the land for the rest of their lives.

LEADERSHIP LESSONS FROM THE FABLE

1. *Identify your strength and special skills.*
   The first step toward improving her unfavorable circumstances is the wife's recognition of her own talents and skills. She, un-like Cinderella or Snow White, does not wait to be rescued by the male hero. She takes responsibility for her own advancement.
2. *Decide you want to move ahead.*
   At the beginning of the story the power is held by an evil King. He has the means of bestowing rewards for the wife's skills, but only on the condition that she submits to him sexually. Realiz-ing the dangers, the woman still decides she should get an ap-propriate reward for her work and gets drawn into the King's realm. Women entering male-dominated professional areas face a similar situation. Being in a fairly powerless role, it is diffi-cult for them to have their talents valued without running the risk of having their bodies or minds captured by the power struc-ture and used for its purposes. It takes courage, cleverness, and desire for change to want to move ahead under these circum-stances. The woman needs to value her own skill and to be de-termined to improve her condition.
3. *Study the current power structure.*
   Being forcefully abducted and held prisoner by the powerful King, it would be futile to oppose him by force or to plead for mercy and fairness. The King can represent the male-dominated power structure in the external world or the woman's inter-nalized harsh, abusive voice that demands the forfeiting of her own interests in the service of family or society's demands. The

only remedy for this dilemma is to study the situation and devise plans to outwit the King. This is a difficult task. The woman has to master her fear, her anger, and her hopelessness and be quick on her feet to seize opportunities.

4. *Identify allies.*

   The wife's husband wants to help, has his heart in the right place, but is no match for the King and repeatedly falls asleep. Nevertheless, he provides some support for the wife. When starting out in leadership positions, women need to seek help from all available sources. To rally allies the wife has to buy herself time by flattering the King and pretending to go along with him. Many women aspiring to leadership will have to make decisions about what techniques they are comfortable with and what is unacceptable to them. However, drastic situations such as overt sexual harassment require drastic action. Women have to be able to pick the right time for their escape and often need to temporize so as not to put themselves in further danger. Befriending a variety of potential allies is an essential strategy. Sometimes they are found in unlikely places or can help only partially. Unbeknownst to the wife, her most powerful ally is the wise old woman who guides her husband in a strategy to connect with her. Wisdom and disguise provide solutions in this situation.

5. *Be astute about who is willing to help you and for what purpose.*

   In her attempt to escape from the powerful but evil King, the wife is in such a hurry that she does not notice that she has invited a murderer to ride along with her. The woman has escaped from the clutches of formal authority into the arms of a villain. Similar to the Bluebeard fairytale, the woman is careless about whom she relies on and encounters the darkest side of male energy, murderous aggression outside the law. Women's own aggression is often deeply repressed. Their lack of knowledge about aggression leaves them blind to its dangers.

6. *Be ready to use wit and decisive action to survive.*

   In this desperate situation the woman again sizes up the situation correctly. The murderer is vain and lustful and therefore not on his guard. She outwits him into participating in his own destruction by boiling the hot oil. Given the amount of unbridled, deadly aggression, only decisive action can free her from the murderer.

7. *To be chosen as a leader, you have to look like one.*

   Having learned about male strength, weakness, motivations, and actions by experience, she now actually takes on male clothing to avoid further trouble. In spite of the potential for women's strength, when she finds herself alone in unfamiliar territory among males, she has to adapt and fit in with the guys, even to "dress for success." She never loses track of her female core identity or her talents, cleverness, wisdom, fairness, and courage, but she puts on the appearance of maleness.

8. *Be in the right place at the right time.*

   The wife's experience of being chosen by accident is familiar to women in leadership positions. Often it seems as miraculous as the Happy Bird landing on their shoulder. But they are not giving themselves credit for their courage in persevering against all odds, having mastered the skill of accurately reading situations and acting decisively for their own self-protection.

9. *Once you are in a leadership position, you can use your skills to change the rules.*

   Being in leadership, women can change the rules to invest in the long-term payoff of collaboration, fairness, helpfulness, and respect for others. Initially the woman uses her talents, but pretends to be a man. The description of good leadership skills includes attributes that are often more associated with women, yet also found in top executives. A secure, successful male leader will have excellent relational skills, be fair, wise, and respectful and caring about his subordinates, peers, neighbors, and the environment. Women make excellent leaders if they obtain the opportunity and they can have a long-term beneficial effect on their work environment. However, even when in power, women need to firmly hold the abusive patriarchal power (here depicted as the evil King) captive so it does not cause further difficulties.

In summary, women leaders can call on numerous narratives to inspire them to find their own path to leadership. Endowed with many talents and beset by considerable obstacles, women are on their way to the top. It is important for them not to underestimate their personal strength and resources. They also need to connect with the strength that can come from combining forces and embrace the differences that have often divided women.

11

The Skill of Negotiation

CATHERINE L. GILLISS
NANCY B. KALTREIDER

Negotiation is not a sphere in which women feel at ease. It is more comforting to embrace the mythical perceptions that good behavior is justly rewarded, that the corporate or academic family will nurture all of its members, and that one's unique abilities will naturally lead to advancement. The more daunting reality is that the unwillingness to ask for the desired reward and then to negotiate to mutual agreement is a major reason why so many women come in second. When asked about the barriers they have experienced in the workplace, women consistently list blocks to career advancement, perceived lack of credibility, trivializing behavior, and stereotyping as the most serious problems (Agonito 1993); successful movement beyond each of these barriers depends on the skills of confrontation and negotiation. The essential strategies depend upon the core conviction that you are worth it.

Earlier chapters have set the context of feminine development with its conflicting loyalties to career and family. This chapter turns to skill building, learning to be strategic, to speak and be heard. It is not necessary to "do it like a man" but it is helpful to understand the expectations of the male-dominated hierarchy and to respond in an effective way leading to respect and power.

WHAT IS NEGOTIATION?

Each of us negotiates every day, throughout the day, at home and work. Some negotiations are simple, others more complex. Some outcomes are dear, others less valued. Nonetheless, the process of negotiation, the back-and-forth communication aimed at reaching agreement about shared and unshared interests (Ury 1991), is a fundamental aspect of daily life. The concept of interdependence and different goals inevitably means that there is some tension in the process. Women have learned the value of empathy in their relational development and this compe-

211

tence can be especially helpful in trying to anticipate the needs of the other party during the negotiation process. Less familiar to women is the systematic planning necessary to achieve a desired outcome; the concept evolved from the Greek *strategia*, originally applied to the planning of wars (Elgin 1995).

Building a repertoire of negotiation skills can greatly improve the outcomes of your negotiations and the quality of your experience during the process. One recent report provides specific examples. Stevens and colleagues (1993) examined gender differences in the acquisition of salary negotiation skills among MBA students. The results indicated that women can be taught the skills of salary negotiation, producing salary outcomes similar to those of their male counterparts. One significant outcome of the training reported by the women was their new sense of control in the negotiation process.

ARE YOU PREPARED TO NEGOTIATE?

Although most women would not go to a business or professional meeting unprepared, they may be less sure of how to get ready for a session in which they expect to ask for something they want. The first rule of negotiation is *Prepare, Prepare, Prepare*!

Begin by developing a sense of yourself as a key member of the team whether or not you are employed yet by the organization. Your sense of yourself must include the concept that you are an essential part of the group and that you and your supervisor are mutually interdependent. Many workers believe that management comes from the top down, overlooking the possibility that they can influence outcomes by "managing up."

Supervisors are dependent on those who work for them for productivity, and especially for information. Critical to success in negotiation is understanding the leader, including her/his goals, pressures, work style, strengths, and weaknesses. Gabarro and Kotter (1993) refer to this concept as "managing the boss" (p. 150). This knowledge will inform your ultimate understanding of the supervisor's interests as you enter a negotiation. Each of the steps of negotiation described below requires preparation. Some of the preparation is fact finding, some is soul searching.

UNDERSTANDING NEGOTIATION: TWO APPROACHES

While you are negotiating, two levels of process are developing. The first is the discussion of the substantive matter about which a decision must be made; the second is the development of a relationship with the person with whom you are negotiating (Fisher and Brown 1988). Each of these is important and the potential that they are related should be considered. Architects of the Harvard Negotiation Project believe that the people must stay separate from the problem, suggesting that relationship issues are less important or even detrimental (Fisher and Ury 1983). This can be difficult for professional women, especially those who place a high premium on relationships and building community in the workplace. In contrast, women will generally act to protect connection (Surrey 1991) and will anticipate that a disagreement over substance means that the other will no longer "like" them. More important than being liked is being respected, a force to contend with.

More recently, Greenhalgh and Chapman (1995) have proposed that relationships and negotiation are inseparable. Because negotiations typically do not occur with strangers or in a social vacuum, they indicate that the outcome of greatest importance is often the ongoing relationship rather than the issue under consideration.

These two models of negotiation provide contrasts that underscore the elements of the process of negotiation. Traditional negotiation models, based on game theory and economic assumptions, suggest that the motive for negotiation is to improve economic utility, without consideration of the needs of the other party. Self-interest predominates and knowledge of the other party is employed to improve one's own position. There is a bias toward confrontation and disclosure can be seen as a vulnerability in this *win/lose* situation.

Greenhalgh and Chapman's (1995) relationship-based model of joint decision making proposes that the negotiation process is set in motion by some occasion requiring the need to make a decision. Two (or more) parties define the situation under review and begin a process of negotiation intended to produce a joint decision leading to a desired outcome. The process of negotiation is concurrently influenced by each party's sense of identity, sense of responsibility, relationships, cognition, and feelings. Cooperation is the essential condition and the goal is for a *win/win* solution.

The primary difference between these two models is the assumption of the degree to which the negotiating parties are connected. Because professional women are likely to negotiate both at home with people who will continue to be a part of their daily lives and at work with colleagues with whom they will have enduring relationships, the relationship-based model of joint decision making appears particularly applicable. The traditional model does have the advantage of presenting a clear, crisp, contextual context that can provide important reminders of the steps to be considered in negotiation.

NEGOTIATION: THE METHOD

The faculty and researchers associated with the Harvard Negotiation Project have contributed significantly to the instructive literature on negotiation. In their now classic text *Getting to Yes*, Fisher and Ury (1983) propose four steps to include in the process of negotiation:

1. Separate the people from the problem
2. Focus on interests, not positions
3. Generate a variety of options
4. Clarify objective criteria for evaluation of alternatives

Separate the people from the problem. Most experts suggest that the problem can easily become the person unless the negotiating parties focus on the issue. Some suggest, "Be soft on the people, hard on the problem" (Fisher and Ury 1983, p. 13). Trust must be assumed and respect conveyed through the negotiation interactions.

Focus on interests, not positions. Essential to successful negotiation is understanding the defining interest of each of the parties. These interests suggest the alternatives that they will view as acceptable. Further, understanding what drives the other party through the application of your empathy may provide insights into alternatives not previously examined. Ask yourself what you are hoping to accomplish during this negotiation. Ask your opponent what she or he hopes to accomplish. What are her/his concerns and worries? Are there interests of unrepresented parties that must be considered? This inquiry solicits goals rather than the fixed terms of alternatives that both parties may have brought to the negotiation table.

Generate a variety of options. More often than not, the routes to a solution are numerous. Engage in brainstorming to generate options that you and others may not have thought of earlier. Work to assume that nothing is impossible, as so often things are impossible only because we will not allow ourselves to view them as options. No holds barred! This is an opportunity to be creative.

Fisher and Ury (1983) suggest that inventing options begins with identifying the problem in clear, concrete terms and contrasting it with a preferred solution. Careful analysis of the problem will focus on causes and barriers to solving the problem. The generation of options will begin to address the problem in specific ways by looking at causes and ways to avoid current barriers. Finally, a discussion of specific action ideas and steps should be developed.

Employ objective criteria. Principles should be identified and specific criteria generated to determine whether an alternative can be judged as acceptable. This stage of the negotiation involves reasoned persuasion. The work of identifying appropriate principles may be reasoned but the act of convincing the other party of their fit may involve persuasion.

KNOWING WHEN YOU HAVE A DEAL

One important aspect of preparing for negotiation involves developing your personal *Best Alternative to a Negotiated Agreement* (BATNA) or walk-away alternative. As explained by Ury (1991), "The purpose of negotiation is to explore whether you can satisfy your interests better through agreement than you could by pursuing your Best Alternative to a Negotiated Agreement. . . . BATNA is your best course of action for satisfying your interests without the other's agreement" (pp. 21–22).

The value of a no-agreement alternative cannot be underestimated as it is the key to your own negotiating power. For example, when negotiating for a higher salary in your current position, you may decide to take a new position in which such a salary has already been offered to you. Or when looking for a new position, the fact that you are satisfied with your current position and are willing to stay put represents another BATNA. Doing better than the BATNA in terms of each party's interests is a necessary condition for agreement. As these examples suggest, fully developing your BATNA is worth all the time and attention it will take.

215

THE NEGOTIATION SCRIPT

Moving from theory to practice, there are some clear do's and don't's in the actual application of the principles. Imagine that you want to ask your boss for a change in position with an associated pay raise. First, make a list of everything that needs to be negotiated. In this situation that could include such items as the position description, salary, office space, administrative support, responsibilities, benefits, protected time, travel, computer access, and many more. Don't forget to include quality of life on the list. Using this list, decide on your own interests, options, and BATNA. Then hypothesize what your boss may say and what her/his real motivation would be behind those statements. Prioritize your interests and consider the ideal package as well as the individual items. Think about whether you want to initiate the discussion with what you want or wish to begin by asking for a statement from your boss about the range of options. Decide if it would be strategic for your boss to get an outline of your agenda ahead of time.

This vignette of Dr. A. describes both the strategies and the pitfalls that can be encountered.

Dr. A. is the head of a major research laboratory in the medical school as well as a valued teacher and clinician. After consultation with several colleagues, she decided that it was time to ask for an accelerated promotion to full professor. She prepared her arguments carefully and scheduled a full hour with her chairman. Her strategy was to lead with some requests that would be easy for the chair to support to soften him up and then to move into her major priority. The chairman was running behind on his appointment schedule and warned her as they began that he might be interrupted for an important phone call from the dean. Feeling intimidated already, Dr. A. began by indicating how helpful it would be to have an upgrade of her personal computer system so she could model protein structures more effectively. He gave her a lengthy description of his plans for computer support in the department and then indicated that her request seemed timely based on his priorities. Dr. A. then mentioned her wish that she could work at home for one day a week while she was completing a crucial manuscript. The chair asked her for more information about that research project and she complied. Once again the chair agreed to support her. Heartened by her success, Dr. A. said that now she would like to talk about her wish for an accelerated promotion. The chairman checked his watch, said that "we don't have time to talk about that today," and laughingly suggested that she quit while she was ahead. Dr. A. found herself in the outer office before she knew what had happened.

Upon reflection, Dr. A. felt that she had been initially daunted by the power differential implied by being kept waiting and the pending phone call from the dean. Somewhat rattled, she stuck to her game plan of working up to the big item but found that the minor agenda got expanded and the chair felt that he had already met her needs before she got to the crucial area. She wondered if the session would have gone better if she had commented on the reduced time at the outset and asked the chair if they should reschedule a meeting to have time to give full consideration to her proposals. After consultation, Dr. A. decided on making her promotion the single agenda item, scheduled her next appointment at the beginning of the day, and sent a note ahead of time to the chairman indicating that her promotion was the reason for the meeting. She then met with a more experienced colleague to plan all the possible scenarios.

Some of the advice that Dr. A. received led her to take control at the beginning by entering the room with hand extended for a firm handshake and sitting in a strategic position where she could make direct eye contact. After a social pleasantry, she opened with a well-considered introductory sentence stating that she felt that she had been of great value to the department because of her nationally recognized research and therefore deserved an accelerated promotion. She indicated that two other colleagues in the department had recently been given early promotions based on merit, but chose not to say "two MALE colleagues," which could be construed as a veiled threat of gender discrimination litigation, a possibility about which most chairmen are painfully cognizant. She expanded on why she was an asset in the department and then described what the essential ingredients were in her upgrade. When the chair countered that her salary suggestion was out of range, she used her knowledge of the administrative structure to indicate that the impediment was that she had been given the responsibilities but not the job title of laboratory director, which had a different salary range. The chair suggested that she had limited professional opportunities because her husband and family were well settled in the area. Dr. A. remained silent for a minute, then said, "I would like to clarify that what you just said was that you assume I am not competitive for other positions because of my family responsibilities." The chairman quickly rephrased his statement to indicate how fortunate he felt that she was in the department and that he was prepared to take whatever action was needed to keep her there. The negotiations proceeded and Dr. A. received her promotion.

Embedded in this vignette are a number of important principles:

- Assume there is a solution.
- A single agenda item is always more compelling.
- Information is power.
- Don't lead with emotion.
- Don't be afraid of silence.
- Decide why you are an asset and present from strength.
- Reflect back if a statement seems threatening.
- Listen actively even when you disagree.
- Avoid the threat of legal confrontation.
- Don't be put off by firmness.
- If you sense you are losing, don't concede but indicate that you need time to think and to get consultation.

As a woman, it is important to use a negotiating style that suits you. However, it is also useful to have carefully observed the negotiating strategy of the other party over time and to think about her/his style. Typical strategies include staying poker-faced and not giving much credit to the other side. Once an offer is made, a good negotiator will not make a second offer if the first is turned down but wait for the other to make a counteroffer. Often the opposing negotiator will indicate that the cupboard is bare or that she or he has no authority to negotiate in this area. The boss may give in on a minor point to build leverage to get you to give in on the important, crucial point.

Once the negotiation is successfully concluded, mend any necessary bridges. Remember that your work colleagues do not disappear so don't go out of your way to rub in a victory. Credit others and yourself. Avoid gossip, bad mouthing, and recounting details of the negotiation inappropriately to others. Viewing the success as a joint victory, give credit to both parties for a job well done. Finally, enjoy the results.

PSYCHOLOGICAL BARRIERS FOR WOMEN IN NEGOTIATING

As described in Chapter 1, the socialization of women has poorly prepared us for the world of confrontation and negotiation. Boys generally learn to use language to negotiate status by challenging others and by self-display. Girls learn to downplay ways in which one is better than others (Tannen 1995). Doing a good job is insufficient unless the boss knows about your performance. Men see the work world as the playing field for a competitive team sport while women experience it as a series of separate personal encounters. For women, success means we all get along (Heim 1993). Learning to be an effective negotiator requires addressing a number of "feminine" issues head-on.

Self-Perception

Girls learn early that it is more important to be liked than anything else. This need poses an immediate problem because negotiation is not a popularity contest. It is absurd to expect that everyone will like everything that we do. Girls who tell others what to do are called "bossy" or aggressive and we are socialized to phrase ideas as suggestions rather than orders (Tannen 1994). The woman who may seem more likable is also seen as less competent and self-assertive than her more strident peer. Too often, being "nice" means giving in.

Similarly, girls who want too much are called "greedy" and they may fear attack from others. As women, we learn to self-denigrate ("What, this old rag . . .") to avoid envy and jealousy and then find that our less productive peers have gotten far better deals with the boss. Commonly, women report feeling empowered to negotiate for their colleagues but not for themselves, an extension of our programming to protect our children even at the cost of our own lives.

Women are usually quite uncomfortable with the open expression of anger whereas men are more willing to enter into a ritual fighting pose to push their agenda. Men can disagree intensely and then go out together for a beer; women are more likely to experience work opposition as harmful to a friendship (Tannen 1994).

Emotional Expression

Many women are unpracticed in using their anger as a positive motivator in negotiation and tend to express their anger indirectly, often by withdrawing and then complaining to others. You may have a right to be angry, but learn how to use it strategically—don't scowl, pout, or verbally erupt, but do let your anger show sufficiently to force conflict resolution (Heim 1993). It is helpful to disagree with a point, not with a person. Excessive anger can be contained by having a safe place to vent and then returning to face your challenger with new clarity. It is exhilarating to stare hostility in the face and remain unmoved.

For women, anger and tears are often closely linked and this confusion may be one reason that women avoid confrontational situations. It is important not to flog the opponent with your tears, a particularly dreaded situation for most men. If you feel tears welling, it may be useful to identify the underlying anger and express it. If that isn't helpful, consider trying to gain control by a strong stimulus like digging your nails into your palm; alternately, excuse yourself, regroup, and return with new composure and focus. Worst-case scenario: just blow your nose and announce that you will be ready to continue the discussion in a moment.

Women may find themselves feeling quite intimidated in the face of a power display, a reaction that Dr. A. described in her vignette. Here it helps to plan ahead, thinking about the most troubling scenarios and preparing a response. Otherwise you are playing out another version of the "battered woman syndrome" in which you feel helplessly trapped. Often such reactions are precipitated by your own transference reactions in which you experience the other as if she or he were a parent or powerful figure from the past.

Power Talk and Power Actions

Women have learned a style of communication that often relies on the conditional tense and the use of modifiers and hedges rather than positive assertions. Observe carefully as your friends go through the litany of "maybe, sort of, a little problem, perhaps you could. . . ." signaling tentativeness and indecision to the male listener. Women have learned to downplay certainty and men to minimize doubts in communication. Heim (1993) points out that we are schooled early and gives a graphic example:

> Boy Scout oath: "On my honor I will do my duty . . ."
> Girl Scout oath: "On my honor I will *try* to do my duty . . ."

Briles (1996) shows how women often follow up an assertive statement with a disqualifier ("This needs to be completed by four o'clock. Is that OK with you?"). We also automatically say "I'm sorry" as an acknowledgment of another's distress but it can be misinterpreted as an admission of responsibility. Women often invite disagreement by prefacing a negotiating point with "You may not like what I am going to say, but . . ." Briles suggests a three-part approach to more assertive communication modeled on the style of "When you [do x], I feel . . . , because. . . . I prefer . . ." Clear communication of the problem is essential to successful negotiation.

While proceeding with a negotiation in a reasonable manner, you may start to realize that the other person is reacting on the basis of stereotypes. For example, your boss may feel that as a woman you would not be willing to travel, to work overtime, or to supervise male colleagues. Bringing this distortion into the open is useful because your boss may not be conscious of his assumptions that led him to decide that you were not appropriate for the job (Agonito 1993).

In this changing social climate, behavioral choices can also be interpreted as hierarchical.

> A woman psychotherapist described that she customarily steps aside to let a patient enter her office first after greeting her/him in the waiting room. This implies both a welcome and the therapist's ownership of the space and power. A male pa-

tient, CEO of a major corporation, could not tolerate that and always motioned her to go first, after which he would enter and pull the door shut. When she inquired about his motivation, he said it felt "unmanly" to precede her.

In negotiation situations, be aware if you are giving off unnecessarily deferential signals nonverbally by seat selection, lack of eye contact, or movements that imply powerlessness.

Those who speak up quickly or don't wait to be called on are more likely to be heard in a group setting. During a negotiation session it is common to be interrupted. The assertive woman who is confident of her point does not fall silent but continues speaking or firmly says, "I haven't finished yet," and continues. This is not a common life experience for most women.

All these responses suggest why confrontation is not easy or natural for many women. It is possible to take responsibility and to hold the other accountable without being seen as "bitch." Each time you hold your own, it gets a little less stressful.

ENJOYING RESPECT AND POWER

The successful acquisition of negotiation skills can mean that you will assume more visible positions, more crucial roles. It is important to have a clearly articulated career plan so you can seek more challenge and authority in your present position. When you do well, ask for feedback and request that it be put in writing if it could be of major import to your future. Always actively support other women who have come along on the same bumpy road that you have traveled. In the negotiation process, as in life, if you treat the other with fairness, respect, and dignity, it will be reflected back upon you.

Our colleagues Renee Binder, M.D., and Diane Wara, M.D., were especially helpful in the development of the ideas in this chapter.

12

Developing Entrepreneurial Skills

KIMBERLIE L. CERRONE

INTRODUCTION

This chapter is written with the view that understanding and developing entrepreneurial skills can be helpful to women who are balancing commitments to both work and family. As an attorney specializing in rapidly growing, technology-driven companies, I have observed that, although there is a considerable range of attitudes and abilities in both men and women, women generally seem less comfortable with self-promotion and less adept than men at attracting the human and financial resources needed to execute their entrepreneurial plans. As a wife and the mother of four young children, I am well aware of the relationship costs of a major commitment to a career. This chapter suggests that a partial remedy to the dilemmas of a double life for some women may be the application of certain attributes and skills that are traditionally seen as "feminine" in nature to entrepreneurial situations.

How do you define *entrepreneur*? It may strike you initially as a masculine-sounding term associated with a person who leads, organizes, manages, and assumes the risks inherent in the creation and development of a project or business. Yet entrepreneurial success can be obtained only if one's "feminine" nature is accessed as well. Nurturing a new project or business along the path from conception to fruition requires many characteristics traditionally thought of as feminine, including the capacity for long-term planning, the ability to delay gratification, the building of sustained relationships, and a willingness to share and collaborate.

The number of American women who are choosing to be entrepreneurs is increasing at a dramatic rate. During the 1980s there was a 76 percent increase in the number of women entrepreneurs in the United States compared to only a 13 percent increase in the number of male entrepreneurs during the same period (U.S. Small Business Administration 1989). In 1992 there were an estimated 6.5 million women-owned businesses in the United States (Rosener 1995), and today almost half of all new businesses are created by women (National Foundation for Women Business Owners 1992–1993).

The role of the entrepreneur is always to create new value in her project or business. She is working to develop new methods, to bring new goods and services to market, to create new jobs, and to establish new ways of doing business. The entrepreneur is exercising her ability to be imaginative, creative, generative, patient, and far-sighted. She also requires abilities that are often poorly developed in women, for example, the ability to promote oneself aggressively or to ask for money to support one's own project.

An entrepreneurial business idea is one that is able to attract the people, capital, and other resources needed to successfully bring a technology, product, or service to the market. Entrepreneurs succeed by engendering the cooperation and procuring the financing necessary for rapid and significant progress. Although women have no trouble generating entrepreneurial ideas, they have demonstrated little success in "Thinking Big." Recent surveys (Nelton 1994) show that the size and scope of women's projects and business are still generally quite small. Most women entrepreneurs are clustered in small businesses, often working as sole proprietors in sectors that are "traditional" enclaves for women, such as fashion, child care, catering, real estate, and travel agencies.

Interesting new entrepreneurial opportunities are now emerging for professional women. In the academic world, hallway conversations are now often about new inventions and start-up biotechnology, the Internet, or software companies. Entrepreneurs with medical training are forming physician networks and starting companies to offer innovative alternatives to the managed care model of practice. Women attorneys have led the way in designing and marketing services that consider the whole client, such as mediation services that coordinate social, career development, and financial counseling for clients who are dissolving their marriages. Women engineers and businesswomen are major contributors to the emerging Internet industry.

Women entrepreneurs are also beginning to establish themselves in many traditionally "male" fields. According to the U.S. Small Business Administration (1989), the percentage of sole proprietorships owned by women in the agriculture, forestry, and fishing industries rose from 10 to 17 percent between 1980 and 1990. While women owned 6 percent of the sole proprietorships in mining, construction, and manufacturing in 1980, they owned more than 9 percent ten years later. In 1990 women owned 14.6 percent of the sole proprietorships in the fields of transportation, communication, and public utilities, up from 6.3 percent in 1980.

However, very few women have senior positions in major entrepreneurial projects or businesses. They are still dramatically underrepresented in many traditionally male-dominated high-tech industries, where entrepreneurial success generally requires the accumulation of significant capital and other resources.

Women now constitute over 50 percent of the total work force in the United States, but they are still barely visible at the highest ranks of business. A survey by the Catalyst research organization released at the end of 1996 indicated that in Fortune 500 companies only 2.4 percent of the high-ranking positions, such as chief executive officer and chief financial officer, are held by women. More women hold vice-presidential level positions, but only 28 percent of women vice-presidents hold positions responsible for generating revenue and profits. A review of 1995 annual reports from Silicon Valley's fifteen largest companies (San José *Mercury News* 1996) found that only 5.4 percent of their corporate officers and directors are women. According to the International Network of Women in Technology (San José *Mercury News* 1996), in 1995 women accounted for only 2 percent of executives at the vice-president level or above among U.S. technology companies.

Enough time has now elapsed since women began to enter the professional work force in significant numbers to point out that we are not seeing a major shift of women up the corporate ladder despite their increased number. One poll of American women (Schwartz 1992) reported virtually no change between 1970 and 1987 in the number of women who responded "no" when asked if a woman with the same abilities as a man has as good a chance to become an executive of a company. In a 1989 survey of women attorneys (Schwartz 1992) 90 percent responded that they "believed that even if their firm offered part-time or flexible work schedules, women who used those arrangements would be slowed or blocked in their quest for partnership" (p. 183).

Women who demonstrate entrepreneurial talent within an organization often feel caught in a double bind that keeps them beneath the glass ceiling. If a woman strives to establish her own niche or domain within a company, she is criticized for being "selfish" and "unsupportive" by men who want her work to advance their own careers. But if the same woman continues to subordinate her own ambition in order to be "loyal" to her male superior, then she will be labeled as lacking the independence and initiative necessary to be promoted on her own. This common double bind has resulted in one professional woman I know receiving a performance evaluation from her male superiors that described her as "indispensable, but not promotable." This phenomenon has convinced many professional women that their only way to advance beyond the glass ceiling is to change companies every two to three years and to negotiate a higher position and increased autonomy with each new job.

Many women who have chosen to start their own businesses may also be voting with their feet. Feeling undervalued and stifled in traditional organizations, they often decide to seek out or design more female-friendly environments where they do not have to struggle to "fit in." Telling her own story, as well as that of other women entrepreneurs, Joline Godfrey (1992) quotes one respondent: "When I worked in a large corporation and wanted to see my son's softball game, I was called unprofessional, but now that I own the company no one ever calls me unprofessional" (p. 11).

Whatever a woman's motivation is for starting her own business, her comparative lack of relevant credentials, industry experience, and contacts, coupled with her inability to attract large amounts of financing because of fewer networking opportunities and negative societal attitudes, may limit her ability to succeed and advance in ambitious business projects. This chapter focuses on specific attributes and skills that will help women succeed as entrepreneurs. It also emphasizes strategies for increasing the size and scope of the projects available to women.

BACKGROUND: GENDER AND ENTREPRENEURSHIP

Several studies (Birley 1989, Bownen and Hisrich 1986, Chaganti 1986) have concluded that women who choose to become entrepreneurs report doing so for precisely the same reasons as men. They too are motivated by the opportunity for a challenging and successful career, a sense of contributing to the community, and the wish for affluence. Both men and women entrepreneurs desire independence, challenge, achievement, and the satisfaction of creating something of value.

The literature consistently concludes that there are no gender-specific personality traits that determine who does or does not succeed as an entrepreneur. In fact, numerous studies document that the particular personality traits exhibited by men and women entrepreneurs—including high achievement motivation, desire for autonomy, aggression, independence, goal orientation, tolerance for ambiguity, leadership skills, and desire for control—are indistinguishable. What most distinguishes entrepreneurs, both male and female, from everyone else are their very high levels of ambition and drive.

There are some acquired characteristics that correlate with entrepreneurial success that may be differentiated along gender lines. Men tend to have more relevant educational and work experience and greater access to capital. Male-centric business networks are generally larger and more influential. Many successful male entrepreneurs have supportive wives who function to relieve them of many of the responsibilities of daily living and family life that would otherwise distract them from their business pursuits. Men also commonly report feeling able to pursue their ambitions with less conflict about the cost of their career pursuits to their love relationships than do women. The joke, "What every professional woman needs is a wife!" is really no joke at all.

Studies of societal attitudes (Scherer et al. 1991) confirm that our society is generally more willing to identify a man as both a business leader and a good father than it is willing to accept that a woman can be both successful in business and a good mother. This double standard is added to another common double bind. If a woman takes extended time off to deliver and nurture her newborn baby, she is not serious about her career. If she returns too soon, she is criticized for being a bad mother. Women must therefore work harder than their male counterparts to be at peace with conflicting values when choosing both to raise a family and pursue an ambitious career.

Some surveys (Scherer et al. 1991) have reported that women often employ a broader, more inclusive definition of "success" than men. Success for women can include progress in careers while simultaneously raising children, caring for parents, and contributing at home and to their community. The researchers conclude that this phenomenon may cause some women to accept relatively modest professional goals for their careers and thus unwittingly contribute to the maintenance of the glass ceiling. This healthy attitude about the importance of a well-rounded life, while offering the prospect of genuine fulfillment, may nevertheless be a real limit on women's potential to achieve a board of directors' seat.

The literature also reports another gender difference that may be very significant to the development of entrepreneurs. Several studies suggest (Brown and Gilligan 1992, Scherer et al. 1991) that girls from prepubescence through adolescence have lower self-esteem and are less willing to take risks than boys. Although up to 86 percent of high school girls surveyed recently (San José *Mercury News* 1990) expressed the desire to own their own businesses, it appears that low self-esteem and significant risk aversion may preclude many of these young women from fulfilling their entrepreneurial ambitions.

CHARACTERISTICS OF AN ENTREPRENEUR

Entrepreneurs are particularly good at sharing. This is often a critical element of success because many, perhaps most, entrepreneurial ideas are larger than any one person. To the extent that woman entrepreneurs need to attract other highly qualified people to work with them, the feminine preference for cooperative efforts and our learned ability to share is a strong advantage.

Many commentators (Burch 1986) believe that men and women have differing attitudes toward failure. Women view failure as an opportunity to learn, and thus frequently describe a failure as a positive growth experience. Men often have less balance between career and family life with proportionately more of their self-identity invested in their careers than women have and therefore are more likely to be personally devastated by a business failure. While women are determined to learn from their mistakes, men are often busy blaming external factors outside their control, such as "a downturn in the economy" for their failure and thus may miss an opportunity for growth. The ability to ask for directions (Has anybody ever been lost with a male driver?) is seen as a related strength women entrepreneurs often exhibit.

The willingness to delay gratification (e.g., parenting a child through the sometimes trying stages to reach a successful adulthood) is a hallmark of the successful entrepreneur. The ability to bond, which in the entrepreneurial context simply means the ability to cooperatively organize around the effort to advance a project, is another important aspect of feminine socialization that can successfully translate into business.

Strategic planning skills are of paramount importance to the successful entrepreneur. Entrepreneurs usually exhibit the ability to multi-task, that is, to simultaneously consider multiple issues and perform multiple tasks. Many women clearly practice these skills daily by getting dressed, feeding the children, delivering one child to grade school and another to day care, and still getting themselves to their first meeting of the day by 8:30 in the morning. This "regular" schedule must also incorporate the adaptability and creativity needed to handle the minor mishaps that so often interrupt the normal routine. Women need to apply their highly developed skills when designing and executing their own career paths.

ENTREPRENEURS AND FEMININITY

Social attitudes that narrowly define "femininity" place female entrepreneurs in double binds and subject them to inappropriate standards. The fundamental entrepreneurial attributes of ambitiousness and drive are also viewed by society differentially along gender lines. When men exhibit these traits, it seems only to enhance their masculinity. Women who exhibit the identical traits are frequently viewed as lacking femininity. When men "think big" they are seen as visionaries; women with ideas of the same scope are often seen as simply unfocused. Many women report that they particularly enjoy "on-line" interchanges because their ability to communicate their ideas to a respectful and receptive audience is dramatically increased in the genderless environment of the World Wide Web. For women to succeed as entrepreneurs, it is important that *we* broaden our definitions of "femininity," acquire the requisite education and experiences, elicit active support from family and friends, and, most of all, take risks.

REVISITING THE GLASS CEILING

Often women at the mid- or senior levels of an organization begin to realize that they are unlikely to advance further. They may resign their positions and give management the explanation that the company is too male-oriented, or that they want more time with their family. However, women questioned by an independent interviewer (Strober and Jackman 1994) revealed that what they really want is the ability to reach their full career potential while enjoying a certain level of job flexibility and without being perceived as undercommitted. Many of these successful women report that they are choosing to leave the corporate world because they believe they are more likely to achieve these goals as entrepreneurs. Although these women report working more hours as entrepreneurs than they did in their corporate positions, they feel they have more control over their destinies. They also report enjoying their entrepreneurial roles far more than they did their former positions, and feeling that their ambitions and creativity are far less constrained after leaving the male-dominated organizational structure.

It is possible that women contribute, in part, to the perpetuation of the glass ceiling, or at least that we make decisions that do not force its quick demise. For example, women often make choices during the course of their education and careers that in effect ensure that they will not make it to the top of many professions. Most women entering business fail to earn the academic degrees in engineering, finance, accounting, business administration, the physical and chemical sciences, and other traditional "male" courses of study that are necessary to advance to the highest corporate ranks. According to the Federal Bureau of Labor, only 8 percent of the United States' electrical engineers are female. Women scientists have clustered in the fields of biology and biochemistry. The pool of women chemists, physicists, and mathematicians in this country remains very small.

The pipeline is widening, but it will take at least a generation before its effect reaches the boardroom. The number of undergraduate electrical engineering degrees being earned by women has increased by a factor of almost ten in the last decade. Women are almost equally represented in American law and medical schools today. This growth foretells the progress that the next generation of American women may achieve, but today's women still need to make hard choices in response to the current business environment.

Early career choices also affect the ability of women to reach the highest echelons of business. Most women do not train early in their careers as investment bankers, corporate and securities lawyers, chief technical officers, senior administrators, and other traditional paths to the executive suites. Of those women who have entered technology fields, most who are employed within the computer industry have gravitated toward software development. Hardware and electrical design fields are still almost exclusively male terrain.

Many younger women decide early that they are not willing to work the longer hours, participate in office politics, negotiate aggressively, or compete openly for rapid advancement. Women continue to cluster in disciplines that do not naturally lead to "core" or "line" executive positions. Our career choices may segregate us in jobs that are not revenue-generating or revenue-controlling positions, and therefore prevent us from gaining power. The glass ceiling is internal as well as external.

WOMEN LEARNING FROM WOMEN

During my years of representing women who have chosen to be entrepreneurial, I have found that there are some consistent patterns that seem to correlate with their success in the workplace.

1. Successful women entrepreneurs view the choices they make about their undergraduate, graduate, and continuing education as important strategic-planning decisions. They acquire relevant education, whether in technical disciplines, foreign languages, business, or other areas, that will later help them distinguish themselves. They also often acquire unusual combinations of credentials, for example, a degree in pharmacology and fluency in Japanese, or software programming skills coupled with an understanding of the complex and rapidly evolving medical services industry.
2. Successful women entrepreneurs think of their current job as an important means to the end they desire. They make strategic career decisions that allow them to develop the increasingly sophisticated experiences and skills that they will later use to justify the backing of their entrepreneurial projects.
3. Successful women entrepreneurs have mastered the fundamentals of their industry, its customers and technology, and the strategies and markets upon which it is built. They feel comfortable with openly advertising that mastery and making themselves visible to others.

4. Successful women entrepreneurs acquire superior verbal and written communication skills. They seek training in public speaking and interpersonal relationships. They master each new communications technology as soon as it begins to be employed by their companies and industries. For example, I was invited recently to join an exciting new project by an entrepreneur whom I actually had never met but who told me he had very much liked working with me in the past. He explained that he had really appreciated my contribution to an earlier project both for its intellectual content and because we had communicated back and forth entirely by e-mail.

5. Successful women entrepreneurs act proactively, aggressively, and effectively. They advertise the risks they take, the skills they acquire, and their accomplishments. They pursue every exciting opportunity to learn from other people in their field.

6. Successful women entrepreneurs make careful and strategic decisions about changing jobs. They manage their own careers and think of each position and assignment as an investment of their valuable time. If a position or project does not continuously "add value" to their resumes, they move on to the next opportunity.

7. Successful women entrepreneurs work out an evolving plan with their spouses and partners that enables them to work the demanding hours, travel as extensively as their career choice necessitates, relocate when necessary, and balance the many demands of the rest of their lives so they can be successful in both their career and their private lives.

8. Successful women entrepreneurs communicate their ambitions early, regularly, and articulately to both peers and superiors.

9. Successful women entrepreneurs base their entrepreneurial project or business on experiences, knowledge, and relationships they have acquired previously in their lives.

10. Successful women entrepreneurs screen out unpromising ideas as quickly as possible. They realistically assess their financial situation, personal preferences, and goals. They develop business plans that exploit their skills, their connections, and their values. Their business strategies complement their personalities, their levels of commitment, and resources as well as their ambitions.

11. Successful women entrepreneurs have the confidence to analyze situations quickly, make decisions, and act. They recognize undesired consequences of their decisions and immediately improvise to achieve the desired result.
12. Successful women entrepreneurs understand the value and mechanics of networking. They use it to widen both their horizons and their opportunities. They use their education and industry experience to break into male-dominated networks while establishing new networks of women. Successful women entrepreneurs develop formal and informal support groups of women with related interests and expertise.
13. Successful women entrepreneurs join state and nationwide professional organizations that address gender issues and attempt to modify the value structure (Rosener 1995).

CONCLUSIONS

Women entrepreneurs have been limited by their relative lack of relevant education and experience. Women have only recently begun to enter the "pipeline" to the top echelons of corporate power in significant numbers. They face many societal stereotypes and preconceptions that will have to be rejected and overcome. Women are often excluded from important and informal networks in ways that limit opportunities. They are still rarely present at the top ranks of corporate executives. Corporate cultures that are inhospitable to women are common.

Nevertheless, the rewards of an entrepreneurial life are great. The independence, the challenge, the sense of achievement, and the satisfaction one gets from growing a project to fruition are exhilarating. Women are increasingly choosing entrepreneurial paths as a way of reaching their full potential. They are discovering that many of their classically feminine qualities are definite assets in their quest.

13

Heads Up: Strategies to Deal with Gender Discrimination and Harassment

MARCIA CANNING
NANCY B. KALTREIDER

Why are these subjects important? We are living the experience. A high percentage of women report that they have had to deal with some type of both gender discrimination and harassment in their professional employment, and it is likely that a workplace environment composed of subtle microinequities has affected all of us at some time. M. Katz (1996) suggests that professional women tend to be exposed to a greater degree and range of gender bias, but also that they are willing to go through greater contortions to try to fit in. For professional women, the wish to be accepted into the "club" is increased by the high stakes of the many years invested in preparation, the substantial financial remuneration, and the jealous vigilance of those currently in control. Given the realities of this period of societal transition, we need to learn to deal with the issues—successfully.

THE LAW

The issues can be best understood within a historical context. In 1964 Title VII of the U.S. Civil Rights Act passed, containing specific prohibition about sexual discrimination but without mentioning sexual harassment. Eight years later Title IX of the Education Amendments of 1972 (Office of Education Amendments 1972) prohibited sex discrimination in institutions receiving federal funds, including many of the professional schools. Coming in parallel with the flowering of the feminist movement, the enactment of this legislation produced a dramatic increase in the percentage of women applying to medical school—from 9 percent of the pool in 1970 to 20 percent of the pool in 1975 (Bickel 1994). In 1976 sexual harassment was first recognized by the courts as a form of sexual discrimination, followed in 1980 by the Equal Employment Opportunity Commission (EEOC) issuing guidelines specifically naming sexual harassment as a form of gender discrimination.

Then, in 1986, the U.S. Supreme Court found that a woman employee who had a sexual relationship with her boss could sue even though her actions were "voluntary," if his advances were not welcome and she had gone along because she feared losing her job (*Meriter Savings Bank FSB v. Vinson*).

In 1991 the Ninth Circuit Court recognized that men's and women's responses about what is considered to be offensive conduct may differ and established the "reasonable woman standard," saying that:

> We realize that there is a broad range of viewpoints among women as a group, but we believe that many women share common concerns which men do not necessarily share. For example, because women are disproportionately victims of rape and sexual assault, women have a stronger incentive to be concerned with sexual behavior. Women who are victims of mild forms of sexual harassment may understandably worry whether a harasser's conduct is merely a prelude to violent sexual assault. Men, who are rarely victims of sexual assault, may view sexual conduct in a vacuum without a full appreciation of the social setting or the underlying threat of violence that a woman may perceive. [Footnotes omitted] [Ellison v. Brady 1991]

This concept was reinforced in the Komaromy and colleagues (1993) paper in the *New England Journal of Medicine* that surveyed students and residents in medicine and documented a harassment experience rate of 73 percent among women and 22 percent among men respondents. Most interesting was that the effect of the harassment differed between the sexes; more than 50 percent of the men alleging harassment felt that it had no negative effects as compared with only 13 percent of the women. The most likely explanation of this differential is the difference in power of the harasser; for men, nurses were the most frequent source of harassment, whereas for women, it most commonly was the attending physician. Also, in 1991, the Civil Rights Act was amended to increase the recompense due to victims of sexual harassment and discrimination. Initially, the law had provided only for back pay, attorneys' fees, and injunctive relief. There was no right to a jury trial. Now the law provides that punitive and compensatory damages could be awarded through trial by jury.

During these years of change, many states also moved toward specific prohibition of gender discrimination, including that of sexual orientation, and prohibition of sexual harassment. Gender discrimination in employment can include the areas of hiring, job assignment, job placement, promotion, layoff decisions, benefits, salary decisions, and terminations. The claim made is that the woman was treated less favorably because of her gender. These cases are often difficult to prove; later in the chapter we will address how to head off the conflict before it reaches the point of requiring a legal remedy. Successful cases have had a substantial impact in encouraging institutions to examine their practices to avoid costly litigation, but still many women (who in the past would not have dreamed of filing suit) have waged long dispiriting battles or left their profession because of gender disparities (Walsh 1995).

Sexual harassment cases have attracted more media attention lately. They are inherently sensitive, involving the areas of one's reputation, sense of worth, private life, and emotional stability. There are two types of cases in sexual harassment litigation. The first and often the most straightforward is the "quid pro quo" in which sexual advances or requests for sexual favors are unwelcome, but there is the express or implied statement that the exchange is a condition of employment and that refusal to cooperate will negatively affect one's job.

The second and more complex area is that of the workplace as a "hostile environment." In these situations the harassment is sexual in nature, unwelcome (neither solicited nor invited), and is pervasive and continuous such that it constitutes a term or condition of employment. Examples of such behaviors would include discussion of sexual activities, unnecessary touching, or commenting on physical attributes. Also included would be displaying sexually suggestive pictures in the workplace, using demeaning or inappropriate terms to an employee, or using unseemly gestures or crude or offensive language. Another aspect under the category of hostile environment is third-party claims that arise when the offensive behavior is the granting of job favors to some who engage in consensual sexual activity in a way that disadvantages others. These inappropriate behaviors are particularly likely to occur in an employment setting where sex ratios are unequal (Gutek 1985).

From this brief review, it is clear that changes in the law have been helpful in providing a context, but that they are only part of the answer. Public awareness and institutional policies would not be what they are today without the legal structures. However, it is clearly in your own best interest to avoid these painful legal confrontations of last resort by developing your own awareness and coping strategies for prevention and early intervention in the areas of gender discrimination and sexual harassment in the workplace.

SEXUAL HARASSMENT

There is a curious paradox in this area, because survey research repeatedly shows a high level of sexual harassment in all workplace environments, but rarely will individual women publicly disclose such experiences. Katz (1996) comments, "[V]irtually every woman that I called to interview for this book [*The Gender Bias Prevention Book*] commented that she would be delighted to discuss sexual harassment with me, but that she herself had not had any personal experience with it" (p. 15). The explanation may be in the need for professional women to deny in order to survive in the workplace or in grave concerns about the perception of being seen as a complainer.

Low-level sexual harassment in the professions is almost constant and more insidious when it remains unseen. Hallway banter, tone and comportment, and the differential treatment of female support staff all affect the work environment. However, when you work with men but do not act like one of the boys, you risk not being included or even being consciously excluded. When a woman reports sexual harassment on the job, she is often told that she shouldn't take it personally because the perpetrator is having a difficult emotional time right now. As a whistle blower, she may be regarded as being unable to handle difficult situations or clients, a "risk" for the organization. Women often perceive that more effort is made to "protect" the perpetrator because of the effect such accusations may have on his career and personal life without a like understanding of the effects of sexual harassment on her.

Given that a high percentage of sexual harassment does occur in the workplace, women should prepare themselves well in advance of an event to handle it effectively. Without having developed some strategies, you are left vulnerable to emotion, and it will be too difficult to represent yourself in the best way. First, as a practical matter, you need to maintain your part of the bargain by keeping business interactions direct and straightforward, without a hint that you would welcome an eroticizing of the relationship. It is also very important for you to join with other women to prepare and secure a commitment from the organization that you work for that it is willing to take action against harassment to ensure that the workplace serves both women and men.

In a workplace setting where harassment does occur, it is important that you know your rights ahead of time so you can make an accurate risk analysis about how you are going to respond. You need to be knowledgeable about the definitions of what constitutes harassment and what does not fall within that purview. You should be familiar with what internal resources your organization offers to provide support and mediation in this area. You need to think through the limits of what you are comfortable with. Compliments or requests for dates are not offensive to everyone. Being referred to as "honey" may be experienced as demeaning and unacceptable by one woman and within a normative cultural context by another. It is noteworthy that in a European study (Haavio-Mannila et al. 1988) a person's positive attitude toward flirting and high self-rated sex appeal were *not* related to experiencing sexual harassment. The likelihood of harassment was mainly dependent on an eroticized atmosphere in the workplace. Office romance is common and usually consensual, but if others feel unfairly treated because of special favors, then it too can become sexual harassment. Applying the "reasonable woman" standard to your evaluation of the situation is a good guideline.

When you feel that you are experiencing potential sexual harassment, address it as early and in as nonthreatening a manner as possible. Be clear and firm about what you don't like and that it is unwelcome. This is not a required step for legal action, but it is usually the best practice to ensure that the offensive conduct stops and that you don't have to pursue legal action. Try a low-key approach first. If that doesn't work, then it is time to take the next step of reporting the situation to someone in a supervisory capacity. Keep notes of all encounters and discussions that are pertinent. Remember that the point of the law is that you can do your job.

As you consider reporting the situation, think carefully about the effect on your career. This is not meant to discourage you against taking action in a wrongful situation but only to caution you to be sure that you have a good and well-documented claim. When you decide to make a complaint, it will be seen as a big deal. Others will be angry and threatened. The male fear of unjust accusation has led to an intense level of response within corporate and academic settings. This can be especially problematic when the cross-gender mentorship relation becomes sexually abusive (Katz 1996). Since thriving under the tutelage of a mentor is often the only path to professional advancement, a woman then faces the stark choice of putting up with the abuse and forfeiting her self-esteem or of publicly confronting it and dashing her career hopes.

Often the strongest steps that women can take involve joining with other women and men to have a more powerful voice and a source of support. Contact with the human resources staff can be particularly useful because they are familiar with internal work policies and collective bargaining agreements that may prohibit sexual harassment, and there may be mechanisms for pursuing claims through these avenues in addition to outside resources.

Professional organizations also have ethical codes that govern their members and may be used as a source of sanction. Reaching out to your local legislator will often institute a letter of inquiry to the employer that requires an official response. Knowing about this array of options is important in assessing your situation and developing a course of action. Most importantly, women who organize together in the workplace will have a strong collective voice, much like the effectiveness of labor unions.

GENDER DISCRIMINATION

Workplace discrimination based on gender is usually most apparent at three critical employment junctures: hiring, placement, and promotion. These are distinct but interdependent events on the career pathway. It is useful to think of all employment decisions over the course of your career as existing on a continuum influenced by your previous work history.

In addition to the effects of discrete actions, Rowe (1990) introduced the concept of levels of "microinequities." Least detrimental are the unconscious slights such as not being invited to work-related social events or not being mentioned as a likely candidate for a position. The next level involves invisibility, as exemplified in the classic boardroom cartoon caption, "That's an excellent suggestion, Ms. McCarthy. Perhaps one of the men would like to make it." Another level involves conscious slights such as scheduling a dinner meeting at a male-only club or planning a conference at the end of the day when a woman may have to pick up a child from day care. The fourth and most severe is

244

exploitation, such as differentially assigning women to dead-end positions or giving them such heavy clinical responsibilities that academic advancement is highly unlikely.

Even at the entry point, many professional women have been denied job access because of antinepotism laws (McGrayne 1990). Whether these are state laws or university regulations, antinepotism rules may prohibit the hiring of relatives of employees. The burden of these rules has fallen particularly heavily on women in science who often have poor job mobility because of family commitments. As an example of this vulnerability, almost 70 percent of the women physicists in the United States are married to other scientists, and almost half are married to other physicists. Exceptions to antinepotism rules are more commonly made for men. Women in professional partnerships with their spouse are often hired into informal positions without tenure or academic advancement potential.

What position you are hired into will have a determinative effect on where you are going. It is linked to your placement and status in the organization, the likelihood of your promotion—your future. It is important for you to recognize the importance of this initial step so that you can appropriately prepare yourself for negotiation. You will need to have information about the meanings of the job designations and their expectable future pathway. When interviewing for a job, if married, you may find yourself perceived as not really needing a position for economic reasons and unlikely to be geographically mobile. Recently a colleague revealed that in a discussion with her department head the chair said that he was offering a lower pay rate for a new woman joining the unit because he knew her husband held a well-paid executive position and that she "didn't need the money." At the same time she was hired, a less-qualified male colleague was hired at a higher rate. This is a recent event, not a dated anecdote. It may be advisable to specifically indicate that you expect salary negotiations to result in an amount that recognizes your worth and expected contribution and not to be based on other outside factors such as a working spouse. Inquiries about childbearing plans continue to occur and are far more common for women than men. You need to come to interviews prepared with well-thought-out answers for these queries, including turning the tables by asking the interviewer about company maternity policies that are of interest to you as factors in your decision about your future with the company. Most importantly, you should be prepared to negotiate, using some of the strategies discussed in Chapter 11 based on well-thought-out short- and long-term goals.

In our experience, professional women often seem uninformed about the career structure and rewards of their organization. Apparently grateful just to have been hired, they don't fully appreciate that salaries vary and that many jobs are not on the fast track toward tenure, partnership, or executive level. One colleague was hired as an assistant professor after an outstanding graduate school record. Later she was surprised to find that a male colleague with a less stellar record had been hired at the same time with the same appointment level and a higher salary. She asked him how he had accomplished this, and he replied simply, "I asked for it." In our experience this occurs as well with regard to professional needs such as access to equipment, space, computer support, and the like. Many women are reluctant to negotiate. They focus on the short-term plan of getting hired and then expect that choice assignments and promotions will come when they prove themselves. Cohort studies are now showing that the inequality of level and recompense experienced between women and men is early written in stone, because comparable male and female candidates enter the field at different levels.

If you are entering an organization and have a long-term goal of advancing in five years, then it is appropriate to ask questions like these: "In the past five years, how many employees have been promoted who held this position? How many were transferred to a promotable position? What are the expectations of the company about my future?" Questions like these are not unduly aggressive, but simply identify you as a serious contender. Your best chance at employment equity is often at the entry point. This same kind of focused inquiry should also be undertaken as you progress within a company. You need to keep your eyes open for opportunities and keep known to your employer your interest in doing interesting projects and in advancement.

It may seem to you that this emphasis is now unnecessary, since women have had such increased access to the professions and managerial positions in the last ten years. Women are entering these fields at an increased rate with more equitable pay, but this apparent statistical gain often represents relative decrements in male pay and women's jobs that are clustered at the bottom rung of the employment ladder. For example, a 1996 survey of women faculty and administrators conducted by the Association of American Medical Colleges found that women held 25 percent of the faculty positions, but only 10 percent of full professorships and 5 percent of the academic chairs.

In her review of gender bias in academia, West (1994) notes that women have steadily increased their share of the Ph.D.'s earned in the United States such that, in 1991, 56 percent were awarded to men and 44 percent to women; at the same time, the percentage of women ladder-faculty has also risen, but slowly. West notes that women faculty's salaries had not improved between 1982 and 1992. In 1982 women who were at the full professor rank earned 89 percent of male full professor salaries. In 1992 they earned 88.2 percent of their male counterparts' salaries. Comparable current data for law schools are that 28 percent of the faculty are women with 17 percent at the full professor level. Of the 178 law school deans, fifteen (8 percent) are women. At the fifty-four U.S. dental schools, 20 percent of the faculty are women, but represent only 5 percent of the professors. There are no women deans. Less than 5 percent of corporate CEOs are estimated to be women. Thus, although the pool is steadily increasing, the percentage of women at the top remains relatively stagnant, and these women are still in isolated positions without the social networks so important for continued success. A recent survey by Carr and colleagues (1993) of academic medical departments across the country debunks the "trickle-up" theory based on increasing numbers at the bottom by noting that women were as likely as comparable men to have tenure, but they had lower academic rank and received less compensation. They conclude, "Although women do similar professional tasks and achieve similar levels of academic productivity, they receive fewer rewards for their work, both in academic rank and monetary compensation" (p. 908). When considering the many variables that contribute to career development, it is useful to think about the concept of accumulated advantages and disadvantages (Zuckerman et al. 1991).

These conclusions were reinforced in a major study of academic pediatric faculty in the United States (Kaplan et al. 1996). They found that significantly fewer women than men achieved the rank of associate or higher. Academic productivity, the key to advancement, was inversely related to the amount of time spent in teaching and patient care, issues that need to be negotiated upon entry into the system. Similarly, the study found that institutional support of research (protected time, space, support staff) was substantially lower for women than for men. They concluded that greater representation alone will not eliminate sex differences in academic advancement over time.

Out of concern for the conditions that we are describing, the U.S. Department of Labor set up a commission to investigate the problems women have in being promoted to the higher levels. It looked at nine companies of mid to large size from a variety of industries. The commission found that, if not a glass ceiling, at least a discernible career plateau existed for women. In general, they found that monitoring for equal access and opportunity to progress up the corporate ladder was not considered to be an organizational responsibility. There was little oversight of gender balance in the total compensation system from mid to top levels. Out of the 147,179 employees in these firms, 32.3 percent were women. At the management level, out of 31,184 employees, 5.09 percent were women, and of the 4,491 employees at the executive level, some 6.6 percent were women. There was considerable variation in salary level by industry, but, in general, the commission found significant lags for women here as well.

What accounts for the continuing disparity in women's pay and advancement? Following the publication of the commission's most recent report wherein it was reported that only 5 percent of senior managers and only 10 percent of board members of firms reviewed are women, this question was posed to a number of industry leaders who were specifically asked to comment on whether in ten years these numbers would look different. As reported in the *San Francisco Chronicle* in January 1996, Robert Haas, chairman and CEO of Levi Strauss, said that after polling his top female managers, he found they had no expectation that their proportional representation would change. He indicated that the women believed that their major impediment to career progression was trying to balance work and the family. Also quoted in this same article was the chair and president of Hewlett Packard, who said that the most important step for a company to take to address this imbalance problem is to get their senior management to value diversity. He commented that many executives would like to have women in management positions, but that they want them to be just like the men.

Women are penalized in their career trajectory for time off due to pregnancy, moving because of the spouse's career, child-rearing responsibilities, and geographical inflexibility. However, it is also the case that women are steered into certain careers, are not showcased as widely as their male counterparts, and are often not considered for leadership positions.

In the AAMC (1996) report on *Increasing Women's Leadership in Academic Medicine*, they comment that, "As competition for patients and other resources mounts, institutions best able to manage their human resources and to tap the leadership potential of women as well as men will enjoy an edge" (p. 1). The committee goes on to recommend the addition of temporal flexibility to faculty hiring and promotion policies, provision of job search assistance to partners of candidates for major positions, and leadership development programs for women, including those at the senior trainee level.

Gender stereotyping often denies women and men the opportunity to be appraised on the balance of their unique traits. Gender bias may occur in relation to discrepant styles and communication characteristics, or it may come up when a woman's choice to take time off for family responsibilities is viewed as a lack of commitment (Bickel 1995). She cites Rosabeth Kanter (1977) who found in her work with corporate groups that in "skewed" groups (when 20 percent or less of the individuals are from another social "type") the "tokens" lack clout and any non-normative characteristics tend to receive undue attention.

Some of the findings of the Glass Ceiling Commission are instructive in considering useful intervention strategies. Hiring and recruiting at the mid to higher levels is generally done by word of mouth and employee referrals. Decisions are often left open to executive discretion. In a report on *The Executive Profile* done by Korn/Ferry International (1990) and the UCLA Anderson Graduate School of Management, they found that "comfort level" is an important factor in selecting for senior positions. If a culture's leadership is predominantly male, women who meet all the position criteria may still be viewed as a risk because they do not look or sound like their traditional executive. The hiring institution needs to become aware of your concern about this invisible bias and your conviction that diversity can be a boon to the business environment because of access to a greater pool of talent.

Once hired or promoted, women remain at risk because there is no monitoring system to assess whether there is equal distribution of the corporate "perks" of career-enhancing opportunities. When individuals are targeted as "high potential," they are given mentoring, high-profile assignments, and position rotation for exposure. Women need these opportunities as well in order to advance. These discrepancies need to be considered and assessed by the organization, but that is unlikely unless there is a "voice" in the organization speaking up on behalf of women's interests. This voice is best heard when it represents a collective interest.

Often search committees for high-level positions report that there are no appropriate women in the pool. Rather than accepting that observation, it is important for women's advocates to ask why. Many qualified women have had the repeated experience of having been the necessary EEOC token woman in a search process that was personally time-consuming and disappointing. Now they are hesitant to apply for another position unless they can discern that this search is a "real" opportunity.

Essential to change in gender bias is commitment at the highest level of management. For example, the Johns Hopkins School of Medicine Department of Internal Medicine made a pledge to institute a comprehensive and targeted approach to advancing women faculty (Stobo et al. 1993). After a survey that identified gender problems, a task force was appointed, and the survey results were discussed with departmental leaders. A consultant held workshops on eradicating gender bias, and an office of faculty development was established. The number of women associate professors was increased from four to twenty-six between 1990 and 1995 with no change in the promotion criteria. Under this program of targeted intervention, women faculty also had improved retention rates and more than two-thirds reported improvements in gender bias, social isolation, and salary equity (Fried et al. 1996). As noted in the AAMC (1996) report, "Concerns brought forward primarily by women faculty, e.g., need for better mentoring and temporal flexibility, are increasingly shared by men; such improvements stand to benefit both sexes and ultimately the quality of teaching and patient care" (p. 6).

In *America's Competitive Secret* (1995), Judy Rosener talks about four organizational stages of awareness and action about gender bias. She characterizes Stage One as, "We're staying out of trouble" (p. 142), in which organizations are driven to alter policies primarily to avoid legal action. "Women are viewed as a problem rather than a resource" (p. 142). In Stage Two organizations, managers are beginning to be aware of the high productivity costs of women's struggles in the workplace, but they still assume that qualified women will advance once they learn the ropes. In Stage Three, "It's a case of survival" (p. 142), organizations begin to realize that addressing gender problems is important, both for women and the organization as a whole. There are now a few women in positions of power, but they tend to exhibit male values and behavior. Women are appreciated for their capacity to contribute to the organization's economic survival. By Stage Four the organization has become proactive in addressing the underutilization of women and holds their corporate management responsible for recruiting and retaining women at all levels. Women are eager to work here because of the excellent career opportunities and family-sensitive benefits. Ultimately, in the ideal organization, no group of employees feels disadvantaged, and they are now truly gender-blind because they have been gender-conscious.

STRATEGIES

Women need to have an arsenal of tactics and approaches to combat the issues of gender bias. These include litigation, negotiation, and political pressure, both internal and external. Litigation may provide legal remedy and has been effective in leading to institutional change. However, in the litigation process the people involved often become defensive, and the plaintiff is seen as a troublemaker. It is a painful process that takes a great toll in money, time, energy, and emotion for all involved. The woman who pursues a strong case successfully often does a great favor for the women behind her in the institution at considerable personal cost. It may be possible that litigation becomes the only viable tactic but it should be assessed along with other options that may have more immediate results, such as negotiation and political pressure.

As discussed in Chapter 11, it is difficult for women to see themselves as effective negotiators, although the juggling required by their complex work–family responsibilities provides daily practice in this skill. Women may achieve as much as men, but they will not be equally rewarded if they are unable to negotiate. It is important to indicate to management when you feel you have done a great job and to ask for recognition. You need to be able to review with your boss the important projects on which you are working and the ways in which you see yourself contributing in the future. You should also understand that indicating at appropriate times, such as in the context of an annual salary discussion, that you have financial pressures that may cause you to go elsewhere can also be effective. Your point is to remind your employer that you really want to stay but that you too have obligations that need to be addressed through salary negotiations. Rest assured, others are making this point. When accurate, it never hurts to mention that you have had another job offer, but that you are loyal to the organization and would like to stay if something can be worked out. Discuss how your skills fit in with the organizational needs, and ask for what you need to prepare yourself for advancement. Think about a timetable, and talk about how this can work best for you and your organization. It will seldom be sufficient simply to work hard and expect to be rewarded.

Women banding together in formal and informal support organizations can be a powerful source for networking and internal political pressure. You probably cannot combat gender bias alone, and relative isolation is a major factor in women's frustrating struggle for workplace equity. Often, more senior women can serve as mentors both in understanding the informal politics of the organization and in the decision making necessary to balance family and career roles. You should also consider outside sources of support that can create political pressure.

SUMMARY

This chapter has been aimed at examining how you can increase your likelihood of success in the workplace. According to all the data, it is likely that gender discrimination and/or harassment will touch your work life in some way at some point. You can deal effectively with these issues by planning, setting your goals, knowing your rights, having a voice, and coming together with other women to work for change.

14

Senior Management: Can You Enjoy Another's Success?

DOROTHY FORD BAINTON

In the course of my life, during which I have evolved to become a senior administrator of a major health sciences campus, I have had numerous opportunities to reflect with other professional women. Some have felt that every day of their life has been a constant struggle and every interaction a battle. Others believe that they were born to be successful and that they personally have not encountered any problems. My experience falls between these two extremes; I have struggled, but more internally than with external forces. I am still learning, and I am eager to share my observations. I am going to cover what I believe to be the quintessence of becoming "a professional." I'll ask some questions that I think you should consider before seeking or accepting an administrative position. Once you make the commitment, you may find some helpful advice here based on my experience of first becoming a chair of a department, and subsequently Vice Chancellor of Academic Affairs at the University of California, San Francisco.

DEVELOPING A MATURE PROFESSIONAL IDENTITY

You don't have to be a chair, managing partner, dean, or president to be a leader in your chosen professional field. Indeed, many women are offered administrative positions and turn down the opportunity for excellent personal or professional reasons. However, if you have the privilege to be given the responsibility to enter senior management, there are several essential requisites to follow: (1) you must already be a true professional; (2) you must be willing to continue to master the subject by trial and failure, pain, and discomfort; (3) you must be at the stage in your life when you can enjoy other people's success more than your own.

What does this mean? First of all, it means you have to learn to do one thing very well. Over a period of years in your chosen profession, you learn to become competent, then consistently competent twenty-four hours a day. I have heard consistent competence compared to learning martial arts; like a karate chop, your immediate or reflex reaction should be "professional," that is, performed at the highest standards. You give priority, over a period of years, to becoming competent by deliberate planning and reassessing, setting goals and completing them. Finally, you have to be able to perform effortlessly at a high level *whether you feel like it or not*. A definite change has to occur when you once and for all master those deep internal reflexes of self-protection, yes, even self-indulgence, and are able to immediately focus on important external matters.

Agatha Christie (1977) discussed this shift to professionalism in her autobiography, describing when she was driven by financial necessity to write another book, and all the while having her young daughter standing by waiting for her attention.

> But Rosalind's eye upon me had the effect of a Medusa. I felt more strongly than ever that everything I was saying was idiotic! (Most of it was, too.) I faltered, stammered, hesitated, and repeated myself. Really, how that wretched book ever came to be written, I don't know!
>
> To begin with, I had no joy in writing, I had worked out the plot—a conventional plot, partly adapted from one of my other stories. I knew, as one might say, where I was going, but I could not see the scene in my mind's eye, and the people would not come alive. I was driven desperately on by the desire, indeed the necessity, to write another book and make some money.
>
> That was the moment when I changed from *an amateur to a professional*. I assumed the burden of a profession, which is to write even when you don't want to, don't much like what you are writing, and aren't writing particularly well. I have always hated *The Mystery of the Blue Train*, but I got it written, and sent off to the publishers. It sold just as well as my last book had done. So I had to content myself with that—though I cannot say I have ever been proud of it. [pp. 428–429]

Anne Morrow Lindbergh (1955) defines the condition even further. It is a very personal and more succinct statement of the state of mind she calls "grace," a kind of harmony with the self.

> In the first happy condition, one seems to carry all one's tasks before one lightly, as if borne along on a great tide; and in the oppo-

site state one can hardly tie a shoe-string. It is true that a large part of life consists in learning a technique of tying the shoe-string, whether one is in grace or not. [p. 24]

We can all recall grants, legal briefs, or business plans written under exactly these conditions. Eventually one becomes more realistic about the effort this takes, accepts the fact, plans ahead, and gets the job done in a less painful and even gratifying way.

UNDERSTANDING YOUR PERSONAL STYLE

Understanding yourself is a necessity if you are going to undertake the responsibility of directing the actions of others in carrying out the goals of an organization. If you don't understand yourself, there is no way you can size up other people accurately. There are many guides for this. The text that I read carefully, and still occasionally reread, was *Please Understand Me. Character and Temperament Types*, by Keirsey and Bates (1984). The basic premise is that people are different in different ways, and we all have an instinctive preference for how we ourselves function, a temperament, actually four temperaments or pairs of preference—extroversion versus introversion, sensation versus intuition, thinking versus feeling, and perceiving versus judging.

Let me give you a specific example that affects my ability to carry out administrative duties. I'm not particularly comfortable walking into a crowded room, such as a reception. I don't seem to know how to move successfully from one person to another. I either get deeply engrossed with one conversation and tie the person down too long or I say something superficial. Consequently I seldom look forward to these functions, unless I think I am accomplishing some specific goals for the University. But more than that, I come away from them drained and exhausted. My first memory of this is as a child attending a New Year's Eve party and standing aside watching people blowing horns and throwing streamers, just having a good time. Having had numerous experiences like this throughout my life, it was a great revelation to me after I was tested at age 54 that it was simply a matter of being a borderline introvert (a 5 on a scale of 1–10). My "battery" gets drained by such events, and I now know that I have to permit myself to "recharge" by scheduling some time in the garden early the next morning, or planning a refreshing nap before the event. Even better, take off for a base-ball game or a museum jaunt with a friend.

COMMITTEES AS THE TRAINING GROUND FOR LEADERSHIP SKILLS

Once you have analyzed your own style, consider what key experiences you will need to prepare for a leadership role. Committees have face-tiously been categorized into two groups by Parkinson (1961): those from which the individual member has something to gain, and those to which the individual member has something to contribute. I believe that experience on committees, particularly for an "academic," presents the best opportunity for continuing one's education after formal train-ing has ended, particularly in learning to understand and participate in the power structure around you. A leader has to be decisive and fair, and I will describe some concepts that I learned about decision making on numerous local and national committees.

Are you a good decision maker?
1. First of all, is it your decision to make (or "mind your own busi-ness")? Ask yourself, what is my role (responsibility) on this committee? What cap am I wearing? Am I here to represent my department, my gender, my professional interest? Remember, if you chair a committee, you should remain neutral.
2. Don't be pressured by the agendas of others or the need to be pleasing.
3. Think about whether you have all the data.
4. Keep an open mind and adjust your thinking as new informa-tion is presented.
5. Prove that you are willing to accept responsibility. Don't pro-crastinate or make excuses about not fulfilling your assignments.

Can you be objective?
1. What's right? What's wrong? Do you have insight into your own motivations? Are you being self-serving? What is the other person trying to achieve?
2. Strong self-discipline is essential. Work on being consistent and fair—"don't hit people" (Fulghum 1990).

3. Listen to the speaker's tone of voice and watch for other non-verbal clues that suggest that the issue is emotionally charged.
4. Avoid defensiveness and carefully consider the content of challenging remarks.
5. Recap what the other person has said to be sure your understanding is accurate. Listen for ideas and associations. Study other people. In a selfish way, you are trying to gain something from the time expended on a committee. It is not unusual to hear a solution to a problem that you are struggling with in a different area of your life.
6. Based on your observations, predict to yourself what will happen next. This will help, particularly if the meeting is boring, and will develop your understanding of group dynamics.
7. What are the alternatives? List all of the options. Be realistic.
8. Act—Implement—Don't delay, do it.
9. Have a follow-up plan in place.

Everyone makes mistakes.
1. Learn not to do negative things in public, like yelling, pointing fingers, and crying.
2. Consider whether you are doing something that is holding you back (Do you complain too much? Do you blame others?).
3. Be curious about "What did I do wrong?" Mistakes are not fatal. How can you improve? Since I have made all of the mistakes listed above and was still asked to serve on other committees, we can conclude that other professionals are very forgiving, or that they have very short memories.
4. Reestablish your priorities and try again.
5. Use the setback to consider if you have untapped skills. With experience, can you evolve into a more effective leader? If you really don't have the desire or capacity to continually evolve—stop here.

In summary, all of these interactions on committees have better prepared me for understanding and evaluating people and their motives and abilities. I believe Leo Tolstoy (1948) stated it best:

There are two methods of human activity—and according to which one of these two kinds of activity people mainly follow, there are two kinds of people: one use their reason to learn what is good and what is bad and they act according to this knowledge; the other act as they want to and then they use their reason to prove that that which they did was good and that which they didn't do was bad. [p. 9]

SHOULD I BECOME AN ADMINISTRATOR?
A PERSONAL DECISION PROCESS

In the summer of 1987, after it became clear that the search for a new Chair of Pathology was not going to yield a national candidate, I was requested by the Dean of the School of Medicine to consider applying for that position. This took me by surprise as I was not a traditional pathologist, and was deeply involved in a long-term research program, having just received a ten-year Merit Award from the National Institutes of Health. The real surprise to me, however, probably centered around the fact that in 1984, three years before, I had metastatic carcinoma of the breast diagnosed and had undergone six months of chemotherapy. I had not anticipated that the administration would be willing to take such a chance on me and my health.

Considering all of the above, why did the dean think of me? As described in Chapter 13, advancement often depends on key experiences that include new responsibilities and "showcasing." I believe that the dean was influenced by several past committee assignments I had carried out with dedication and fairness in his presence. At least ten years before I had served on a search for a chair of a clinical department led by the man who was now dean. I was the most junior member of the faculty on that committee, and perhaps the "token" woman. I was given the potentially tedious job of interviewing each member of the faculty of the clinical department and coming back to the committee with their impressions. My recollection is that I interviewed about twenty-seven people, going to their offices in the several hospitals that we operated and hearing their concerns for at least sixty- to ninety-minute appointments. This was an important process because the department needs to be assured that their individual opinions have been heard and taken into consideration when a search for a new chair is under way. This sounds obvious, but it is not always easy to achieve, and sometimes it is not even attempted. Later, the current dean served on the Committee on Academic Personnel, probably the most prestigious, laborious, and important committee of the Academic Senate as it judges faculty performance and makes decisive recommendations for merits and promotions. When he needed to be replaced, I believe he recommended that I take his place. On this committee I read the numerous files for merits and promotions, and participated in appointing the ad hoc committees and evaluating the final process before submission of the recommendation to the Academic Vice Chancellor, the position I now occupy. Nothing prepared me better for my current position.

In the research arena, another opportunity opened up by mentorship was developing. My department had a new Chair of Pathology, and one day he called me in and said that he wanted me to become active and visible in the experimental society of pathology. I began going to the national meetings, and, in particular, always attended the business meetings. As there was only a handful of people sitting around at these business meetings, and even fewer junior scientists, the council quickly noticed my interest, and before long I began to serve on several of their important committees. Within a few years I was nominated and elected President of the American Association of Pathologists. So, when young women assistant professors come to me and say, "How can I achieve more national visibility?" it is quite easy for me to tell them that the secret is going to the business meetings, showing interest, and, when given an assignment, performing it in a conscientious manner. By the time the national search for a Chair of Pathology had begun at UCSF, I was in line to become President of the American Association of Pathologists. This helped bolster my credentials in this area. Furthermore, when I met many of my counterparts throughout the country, I discovered that many chairs of pathology had backgrounds similar to mine. Their acceptance helped me learn to be an administrator. In fact, there are certain problems that you can discuss productively only with your national peers.

I would like to turn now to the decision-making process itself. I do have some very specific advice about this. You should very deliberately write down the pros and cons, advantages and disadvantages. I also think you should give yourself a limited period of time, about two weeks, to carefully consider and get back to the person who is offering your position with a definite answer. Being indecisive is not good preparation for being an administrator. After all, when you have gathered all of the relevant facts and considered the pros and cons, all you need to make a decision is courage. Listed below are my written process notes that I used to decide whether to become a Chair.

PROS	CONS
1. My national visibility in research and service would help the department.	1. Less time for research. When would I have time to work on grants and papers?
2. More women need to be administrators.	2. If I fail as a woman chair, it is bad for all women.
3. Family	3. Less time for family and social pleasures.
a) Our three children are all on their own now.	
b) Cedric (my husband) is an administrator and understands those pressures.	
4. Broad UCSF committee experience.	4. Not well known to local pathology community.
5. Be able to show gratitude to school of medicine, which sponsored my career.	5. Health—my disease could recur at any time.

I believe the single thing that made me decide to accept the position of Chair of Pathology—in fact, the first woman chair in 125 years at UCSF (soon to be followed by two other outstanding women as chairs)—was the fact that the University did not see me as disabled by my encounter with cancer. So why should I act disabled? I was so overwhelmed by this support that I decided to give it my all.

DOING IT: WHAT YOU NEED TO KNOW

First of all, *ask for advice*. When I first became chair, I made appointments to interview and get advice from certain chairs and administrators that I admired. I took notes, studied their comments, and I adopted and found useful many of their suggestions.

- You can't have close friends within your department.
- Put yourself in another's place before giving advice or criticism.
- Chew out in private—praise in public.
- Be appreciative of a job well done. Write thank you notes.
- Learn how to dismiss people: be calm, be prepared, know the personnel policy, try to put a positive spin on it by helping them to find another job. You *should* feel bad when you have to do this; the day you don't feel upset about giving someone bad news, you should resign.
- Ask your constituents for support—first noting, "I need your help."
- Look around for people with imagination. Give good people permission to do good things.
- Guard your time by making appointments. Most issues are too serious for making a decision in the hallway. Make appointments and go to their offices so you can leave when appropriate.
- Do something—appoint a committee. You will be forgiven for making a mistake but not for doing nothing. Try to eliminate misunderstandings and miscommunications by up-front contacts.
- Understand the political atmosphere and think about how to get people on your side. Here are my notes from my first pathology meeting after becoming chair:

  > I would like this faculty meeting to be the forum for discussion of the problems of the department. How we perceive ourselves and solve our problems is a big part of how our colleagues will perceive us. If we discuss our problems on a broader front, and do not solve them, it damages our ability to be influential in the university community. It helps if we have a good image of ourselves.

- How to get a lot of work done:
  Go in early.
  Then put on a disguise so you won't be recognized and can get to the ladies' room without delay.
  Stay late.
  Delegate, delegate, delegate. Put the most capable person in charge and back up their responsibility and authority (Roberts 1990).

RISKS AND BENEFITS IN SENIOR MANAGEMENT

In a leadership role you have immediate visibility and credibility, two advantages particularly valued by senior women. The role offers the individual an unusual degree of independence and autonomy not available in any junior administrative position. You can be a successful leader if you now can put other people's priorities ahead of your own. However, remember that your identity as a professional is important and still set aside time to pursue your own projects or scholarly work.

When you enter the zone of senior management, you will have line authority over more junior colleagues, women and men. Most of them have little previous experience in "reporting" to a woman and you can anticipate a range of responses. Based on her extensive interviews, Rosener (1995) suggests that men with a solid self-concept enjoy the freedom offered by a woman's interactive leadership style. She feels that men perceive women bosses to be less concerned about issues of power and status than male executives. Less secure men may be uneasy working for a woman because it makes them feel more inadequate, perhaps reminding them of the power their mother had over them. Women too may have maternal associations and can feel competitive or insufficiently nurtured by you. At the same time, they are excited and proud of your success and its possible implications for their own career futures. Since you are in an unfamiliar role for both sexes, you should anticipate that there will be repeated competency testing to be sure that you deserve your position and know how to be a good workplace parent.

One of the most interesting insights that I gained from reading Rosener's book, with which I agree completely, is the fact that women are accustomed to dealing with "chaos" every day and are relatively comfortable with it. In this context you should anticipate many frustrations and setbacks as you learn your new role. Chief among these are the constant interruptions, the sense that no day ever goes the way you had planned it. *Don't let the urgent always get in the way of the important.* It's best to try to solve problems, not cause them. When you are angry or confused, write out the pros and cons of the situation before acting. Beware of overly frank exchanges on e-mail that can easily be translated into a written and very public record.

Learn to listen and be able to see things from another person's point of view. All my life I have believed in the Golden Rule—treat others as you would like to be treated—but experience has taught me that not everyone thinks or reacts the way I do. George Bernard Shaw put this concept best when he warned, Don't do to another what you would like to be done by, because his taste may differ from yours (Eastman et al. 1984, p. 665).

Try to learn to be a good public speaker. Consider what personal traits may be holding you back; for example, Indira Gandhi (1993) described that when faced with hostility, "No matter how well-prepared I am, I get tongue-tied and withdraw" (p. 137). I personally don't like to be taken advantage of and I am still trying to find the appropriate reaction. Take ownership of problems; when things go wrong, don't look for someone else to blame.

One of the major roles of a senior administrator is recruitment of new people. My advice is to look for a unique person. Ask yourself, "Is this the right setting for this person?" rather than try to talk someone into coming. I heard a dean refer to certain faculty as high maintenance—those that you keep trying to satisfy. Look for good citizens. They do exist.

Being in a major administrative role will increase your effectiveness as a mentor but decrease the time you have available for that role. Thus it is particularly important to provide your mentee with some guidelines to prepare for your career conferences. It is not especially useful to suggest, "Let's get together to toss around some ideas about future directions for you," because that implies that the mentor will do much of the work and is able to give omniscient advice. Rather, suggest that the mentee come prepared with a clear statement of career goals and a written outline of her/his job accomplishments and responsibilities during the last year. An example is the outline of topics used in our academic medical center for the mandatory yearly career conference:

1. How to balance the required career components of teaching, research, clinical activities, and departmental and university service
2. Teaching: percent effort, level, evaluations by students and peers
3. Clinical activities: percent effort, congruence with research, collaborations
4. Research: percent effort, publications, collaborations, grant support, participation in professional meetings, national visibility, space and facilities

5. University and public service: percent effort, committee assignments, leadership training
6. Miscellaneous: what things may be getting in the way of academic advancement, nonacademic and personal issues, how to showcase one's work, how to "behave" in professional settings
7. Plan for the coming year: honest criticism and feedback about current year, suggestions regarding possible rearrangement of time allocation, comments on the likelihood that level of performance and balance of activities will lead to academic advancement

As I mentioned above, I found that it was very profitable to ask the junior faculty member to respond to these topics in writing so that we would have a framework for planning our discussion. I was frequently amazed at some of the conversations. For example, I asked one assistant professor of obvious potential where he wanted to be ten years in the future. He answered that he wanted to be chair of pathology, and yet he was not attending the national meetings that would allow him to network. We both made an effort to correct that.

In *Lifting a Ton of Feathers: A Woman's Guide for Surviving in the Academic World*, Paula Caplan (1993) suggests that as a woman at the top you play an important role in showing what is possible for other women. Through your administrative experience you will have a unique opportunity to learn the hidden rules and essentials of career success in your organization. You know the work of your senior colleagues well enough to be able to suggest collaborative relationships that will assist junior persons to enter the system more effectively.

Caplan also points out that, as a symbol of a successful "powerful" woman, you may find that your mentees bring a surprising set of psychological assumptions about you. Perhaps you will be seen as the woman who "has it all" or who has achieved success without effort or through favoritism. As a mother/mentor, you may be expected to be infinitely generous with your time and organizational resources. Since you have "made it," your mentee may be surprised and even resentful that you wish to protect your time for continuing creative work. Women mentees may be particularly convinced that it is your responsibility as a woman to be freely available to assist in the struggles of the women behind you on the career path. In fact, this is one of the great satisfactions of being a senior woman but it comes at a time when there are many constraints on your flexibility and time.

SUMMARY

As I look back on my administration, I feel that I have made gains in being better able to see things clearly and to make wise decisions. I am becoming more comfortable handling chaotic situations. It is satisfying having people recognize that you are doing a complex job well. I recall with pleasure having a faculty member at a national meeting take me over to meet his brother from another school because "I want to show you the type of person who goes into administration at UCSF." There is a real sense of personal growth in being of service to your organization. It is wonderful to work with such people and I have found that I really do enjoy other people's success.

Although I can think wondrous thoughts, I can't always express them. So I will end with a quotation from Rosalyn Yalow (1977), one of the few women Nobel Prize winners in medicine: "[W]e must match our aspirations with the competence, courage and determination to succeed, and must feel a personal responsibility to ease the path for those who come afterward" (p. 2).

AFTERWORD

Is It Worth It?

This book is written by women who love their careers and relationships. We are proud of using our intellect and skills in leadership roles that were rarely open to our mothers' generation. We delight in coming in from the outside to sit in the halls of power and speak in our own voices. We love our connections with family and feel that nurturing the next generation, by mothering and mentoring, is at the core of life's meaning. We rarely feel bored or empty because *The New England Journal of Medicine* and *Gourmet* equally stimulate our creativity.

This book is written by women who feel drained, frustrated, and guilty much of the time. Filling a complex array of roles, we feel that we have never reached our full potential in any area. No matter how shared the domestic tasks, we still track the family agenda in our heads while inside the boardroom and cringe when our kids ask why we don't serve hot dogs at the school like the other mothers. We have chosen partners who are stimulating and supportive but we are often so tired by evening that our interaction is cursory. We feel blocked on our career path by not knowing the rules of play or, worse yet, discover that the payoff in power and prestige that goes to the winner is not as intoxicating as we had dreamed.

Potentially, we are *all* of these women and that is the dilemma.

Writing and talking together, it was reassuring to learn that no one really knows the answer. The coping strategies were as various as the women themselves. However, the three-generation span of the authors helped us all to understand the importance of a developmental perspective and to realize that choices and paths taken could be reworked many times in the course of a lifetime. Understanding the psychosocial aspects of feminine development helped us honor our uniqueness rather than attempting to "do it like a man." There were many part-time and creative alternatives in our overly full lives and sequencing priorities seemed to be the key. Often the choices became a pattern only in retrospect; we longed for wise guides who had been on the road ahead of us.

Some of the chapter authors struggled with varying success to meet the writing deadlines—not out of laziness or lack of commitment but simply because there were so many conflicting choices. Still, it felt good and important to be designing this paper mentor because we had wished for it ourselves so often.

Guiding principles did emerge. Do what you love. Before making choices, think about the enduring sources of satisfaction in your life. Then work as hard as you can to gain the skill set needed to achieve your dream. Prioritize and sequence choices and hope that you don't die young. Nurture each other and also yourself. When you have climbed up the ladder, reach back to those who are still climbing.

Finding "the path with heart" can lead to an enduring sense of satisfaction based on meaning in both career and relationships. Multiple sources of self-esteem can buffer the fluctuations in any one area. It is crucial that the gains of feminism not just be translated into new and more elaborate traps of impossible lives. Honoring both the self and relationships is essential, and this book contains our collected thoughts about ways to accomplish that. Each generation will add new visions, but already the pattern of issues for women balancing careers and relationships is beginning to emerge.

Nancy B. Kaltreider

REFERENCES

Adams, L. D., Al-Rubaiy, A. A., and Lamonte, R. B. (1984). Implications for education and child-rearing: the role of women in the Middle East. *School Psychology International* 5(3):167–174.

Agonito, R. (1993). *No More "Nice Girl": Overcoming Day-to-Day Barriers to Personal Success*. Holbrook, MA: Adams Publishing.

Aldous, M., and Edmonson, M. (1993). Maternal age at first child birth and risk of low birth weight and preterm delivery in Washington State. *Journal of the American Medical Association* 270:2574–2577.

Altmann, J. (1987). Life span aspects of reproduction and parental care in anthropoid primates. In *Parenting Across the Life Span: Biosocial Dimensions*, ed. J. Lancaster, J. Altmann, A. Rossi, and L. Sherrod. New York: Aldine de Gruyter.

American Society for Reproductive Medicine (1995). *Guideline for Practice: Age Related Infertility*. Birmingham, AL: Practice Committee of ASRM.

Applegarth, A. (1986). Women and work. In *The Psychology of Today's Woman—New Psychoanalytic Visions*, ed. T. Bernay and E. W. Cantor, pp. 211–230. Hillsdale, NJ: Lawrence Erlbaum.

Apter, T. (1993). *Working Women Don't Have Wives: Professional Success in the 1990s*. New York: St. Martin's Press.

Arai, S. O., and Cates, W. (1983). The increasing concern with infertility—why now. *Journal of the American Medical Association* 250(17):2327–2331.

Association of American Medical Colleges (1996). *Increasing Women's Leadership in Academic Medicine*. Pamphlet. Washington, DC: AAMC.

Astin, H. (1984). The meaning of work in women's lives: a socio-psychological model of career choice and work behavior. *Counseling Psychologist* 12:117–126.

Auchincloss, E. L. (1982). Conflict among psychiatric residents in response to pregnancy. *American Journal of Psychiatry* 139(6):818–820.

Balint, E. (1973). Technical problems found in the analysis of women by a woman analyst: a contribution to the question "What does a woman want?" *International Journal of Psycho-Analysis* 58:289–300.

Ballou, J. (1978). The significance of reconciliative themes in the psychology of pregnancy. *Bulletin of the Menninger Clinic* 42(5):383–413.

Barnett, R. C., and Marshall, N. L. (1992). Worker and mother roles: spillover effects and psychological distress. *Women and Health* 18(2): 9–40.

Barton, L. (1991). Cross-cultural comparison of child care as an employer-provided benefit. *International Journal of Sociology and Social Psychology* 11(5):34–47.

Bateson, M. C. (1990). *Composing a Life*. New York: Penguin.

Beall, A. E., and Sternberg, R. E., eds. (1993). *The Psychology of Gender*. New York: Guilford.

Begg, E. (1984). *Myth and Today's Consciousness*. London: Coventure.

Belenky, M., Clinchy, B., Goldberger, N., et al. (1986). *Women's Ways of Knowing: The Development of Self, Voice and Mind*. New York: Basic Books.

Belsky, J., and Penshy, E. (1988). Marital change across the transition to parenthood. *Marriage and Family Review* 12:133–156.

Benin, M., and Keith, V. M. (1995). The social support of employed African American and Anglo mothers. *Journal of Family Issues* 16(3): 275–297.

Benin, M., and Niemstedt, B. (1985). Happiness in single and dual earner families: the effects of marital happiness, job satisfaction and life cycles. *Journal of Marriage and the Family* 47:975–984.

Berkowitz, G. S., Skovron, M., Lapinski, R., and Berkowitz, R., (1990). Delayed childbearing and the outcome of pregnancy. *New England Journal of Medicine* 322(10):659–664.

Bernay, T. (1982). Separation and the sense of competence-loss in women. *American Journal of Psychoanalysis* 42(4):293–305.

Bernstein, D. (1983). The female superego: a different perspective. *International Journal of Psycho-Analysis* 64:187–201.

Bickel, J. (1988). Women in medical education: a status report. *New England Journal of Medicine* 319:1579–1584.

——— (1995). Scenarios for success—enhancing women physicians' professional advancement. *Western Journal of Medicine* 162:165–169.

Bickel, J., et al. (1994). Women in U.S. Academic Medicine Statistics. Washington, DC: AAMC.

Bing, E., and Coleman, L. (1980). *Having a Baby after 30: Reassurance and Professional Guidance for Couples Who Waited*. New York: Bantam.

Birley, S. (1989). Female entrepreneurs: Are they really any different? *Journal of Small Business* 27:32–37.

Blum, H. (1976). Masochism, the ego ideal, and the psychology of women. *Journal of the American Psychoanalytic Association* 24(suppl.):157–191.

Bogenschneider, K., and Steinberg, L. (1994). Maternal employment and adolescents' academic achievement: a developmental analysis. *Sociology of Education* 67(1):66–77.

Bolen, J. S. (1984). *Goddesses in Everywoman: A New Psychology of Women*. San Francisco: Harper & Row.

Bownen, D. D., and Hisrich, R. D. (1986). The female entrepreneur: a career development perspective. *Academy of Management Review* 11:393–407.

Bram, S. (1984). Voluntarily childless woman: Traditional or nontraditional? *Sex Roles* 10:195–206.

———— (1986). Childlessness revisited: a longitudinal study of voluntarily childless couples, delayed parents, and parents. *Lifestyles: A Journal of Changing Patterns* 3:46–65.

Brauchey, L. (1983). Letters to the editor: pregnant residents in the 1960s. *American Journal of Psychiatry* 140:135–136.

Braun, D., and Susman, V. L. (1992). Pregnancy during psychiatry residence: a study of attitudes. *Academic Psychiatry* 16:178–185.

Bridges, J. S., and Orza, A. M. (1992). The effects of employment role and motive for employment on the perceptions of mothers. *Sex Roles* 27(7–8):331–343.

Briles, J. (1996). *Gender Traps: Conquering Confrontophobia, Toxic Bosses and Other Landmines at Work*. New York: McGraw-Hill.

Bronstein, P., Black, L., Pfennig, J. L., and White, A. (1989). Stepping onto the academic career ladder: How are women doing? In *Women's Career Development*, ed. B. Gutek and L. Larwood, pp. 110–128. Newbury Park, CA: Sage.

Brown, L., and Gilligan, C. (1992). *Meeting At the Crossroads*. New York: Ballantine.

Bryson, R., Bryson, J., and Johnson, M. (1978). Family size satisfaction and productivity in two-earner couples. *Psychology of Women Quarterly* 3(1):67–77.

Bunker, B. B., Zubeck, J. M., Vanderslice, V. J., and Rice, R. W. (1992). Quality of life in dual-career families: commuting versus single-residence couples. *Journal of Marriage and the Family* 54:399–407.

Burch, J. G. (1986). Profiling the entrepreneur. *Business Horizons*, September–October, pp. 13–17.

Burke, R. J., and McKeen, C. A. (1995). Work experiences, career development, and career success of managerial and professional women. In *Gender in the Workplace* [Special Issue]: *Journal of Social Behavior and Personality* 10(6):81–96.

Caplan, P. (1993). *Lifting a Ton of Feathers: A Woman's Guide for Surviving in the Academic World*. Toronto: University of Toronto Press.

Carli, L. L. (1990). Gender language and influence. *Journal of Personality and Social Psychology* 59:94–95.

Carlson, M. (1996). Washington diary. *Time*, March 11.

Carr, P. L., Friedman, M. D., Moskowitz, M. A., and Kazis, L. E. (1993). Comparing the status of women and men in academic medicine. *Annals of Internal Medicine* 119:908–913.

Cartwright, L. K., Wink, P., and Kmetz, C. (1995). What leads to good health in midlife women physicians? Some clues from a longitudinal study. *Psychosomatic Medicine* 57:284–292.

Cernigoj-Sadar, N. (1989). The other side of employed parents' life in Slovenia. *Marriage and Family Review* 14(1–2):69–80.

Chaganti, R. (1986). Management in women owned enterprises. *Journal of Small Business Management* 18–29.

Chan, C., and Margolin, G. (1994). The relationship between dual-earner couple's daily work mood and home affect. *Journal of Social and Personal Relationships* 11:573–586.

Chinen, A. B. (1992). *Once Upon a Midlife*. Los Angeles: J. P. Tarcher.

Chodorow, N. (1978). *The Reproduction of Mothering: Psychoanalysis and the Sociology of Gender*. Berkeley: University of California Press.

Christie, A. (1977). *Agatha Christie, An Autobiography*. New York: Ballantine.

Civil Rights Act (1991). 42 U.S.C.A.

Clay, R. (1996). Beating the "biological clock" with zest. *Monitor, Journal of the American Psychological Association*, vol. 37, February 6.

Cnattingius, S., Forman, M., Berendes, H., and Isotalo, L. (1992). Delayed childbearing and risk of adverse perinatal outcome—a population-based study. *Journal of the American Medical Association* 268(7): 886–890.

Cohen, J. (1985). *Parenthood after 30? A Guide to Personal Choice*. Lexington, KY: Lexington Books.

Cole, J. R., and Zuckerman, H. (1987). Marriage, motherhood and research performance in science. *Scientific American* 256:119–125.

Colman, L. L., and Colman, A. C. (1991). *Pregnancy: The Psychological Experience*. New York: Noonday Press.

Connidis, I., and McMullen, J. (1994). Social support in older age: assessing the impact of marital and parent status. *Canadian Journal on Aging* 13:510–527.

Cook, S. (1990). The childless executive. *Working Woman* 15:126–129, 172.

Crouter, A. (1984). Spillover from family to work: the neglected side of the work–family interface. *Human Relations* 37(6):425–442.

Daniels, P., and Weingarten, K. (1982). *Sooner or Later: The Timing of Parenthood in Adult Lives*. New York: Norton.

Davidson, M., and Cooper, C. (1983). *Stress and the Woman Manager*. Oxford: Martin Robertson.

DeCherney, A. H., and Berkowitz, G. (1982). Female fecundity and age. *New England Journal of Medicine* 307:424–426.

Denmark, F. L. (1992). The thirty-something woman: to career or not to career. *Gender Issues Across the Life Cycle*, ed. B. R. Wainrib, pp. 71–76. New York: Springer.

Eastman, A. M., ed. (1984). *The Norton Reader: An Anthology of Expository Prose*, 6th ed. New York: Norton.

Eichenbaum, L., and Orbach, S. (1984). *What Do Women Really Want: Exploding the Myth of Dependency*. New York: Berkley.

——— (1988). *Between Women: Love, Envy and Competition in Women's Friendships*. New York: Viking.

Elgin, S. (1995). *Business Speak*. New York: McGraw-Hill.

Ellison v. Brady (1991). Ninth Circuit Court 924 F.2d 872.

Emmons, C. A., Biernat, M., Tiedje, L.B., et al. (1990). Stress, support, and coping among women professionals with preschool children. In *Stress between Work and Family*, ed. J. Eckenrode and S. Gore. New York: Plenum.

Equal Employment Opportunity Commission (1980). *Guidelines on Discrimination Because of Sex*, 29 C.F.R., Section 1604.11.

Erikson, E. H. (1950). *Childhood and Society*, 2nd ed. New York: Norton.

Erlich, E. (1989). The mommy track. *Business Week*, March 20, pp. 126–129.

Fabe, M., and Wikler, N. (1979). *Up Against the Clock: Career Women Speak on the Choice to Have Children*. New York: Random House.

Fagot, B. I. (1984). Teacher and peer reactions to boys' and girls' play style. *Sex Roles* 11:691–702.

Fenster, S., Phillips, S., and Rapoport, E. (1986). *The Therapist's Pregnancy: Intrusion into the Analytic Space*. Hillsdale, NJ: Analytic Press.

Fisher, R., and Brown, S. (1988). *Getting Together: Building a Relationship That Gets to Yes*. Boston: Houghton Mifflin.

Fisher, R., and Ury, W. (1983). *Getting to Yes*. New York: Penguin.

Franzoso, N. (1992). *The pregnant therapist*. Psychiatry Grand Rounds, California Pacific Medical Center, unpublished.

French, J., Caplan, R., and Harrison, R. (1982). *The Mechanisms of Job Stress and Strain*. New York: Wiley.

Fried, L., Grancomano, C., MacDonald, S., et al. (1996). Career development for women in academic medicine. *Journal of the American Medical Association* 276:898–905.

Fuchs, V. (1988). *Women's Quest for Economic Equality*. Cambridge, MA: Harvard University Press.

Fulghum, R. (1990). *All I Really Need to Know I Learned in Kindergarten*. New York: Villard.

Gabarro, J., and Kotter, J. (1993). Managing your boss. *Harvard Business Review* 71(3):150–157.

Gandhi, I. (1993). *An Intimate Biography*. New York: Pantheon.

Gardner, E., and Hall, R. (1987). The professional stress syndrome. *Psychosomatics* 22:672–680.

Gerson, K. (1985). *Hard Choices: How Women Decide about Work, Career and Motherhood*. Berkeley: University of California Press.

Gerstel, N., and Gross, H. (1984). *Commuter Marriage*. New York: Guilford.

Gilligan, C. (1982). *In a Different Voice*. Cambridge, MA: Harvard University Press.

Glaser, C., and Steinberg, S. (1995). *Swim with the Dolphins*. New York: Warner.

Glass Ceiling Commission (1995). *A Solid Investment: Making Full Use of the Nation's Human Capital*. Pamphlet. Washington, DC: U.S. Department of Labor.

Godfrey, J. (1992). *Our Wildest Dreams*. New York: HarperCollins.

Godsen, R., and Rutherford, A. (1995). Delayed childbearing—fertility declines at 30 and is almost gone by 40. *British Medical Journal* 311(7020):1585–1586.

Graham, P., ed. (1995). *Mary Parker Follett—Prophet of Management. A Celebration of Writings from the 1920's*. Cambridge, MA: Harvard Business Press.

Greenberger, E., Goldberg, W., Hamill, S., et al. (1989). Contributions of a supportive work environment to parents' well-being and orientation to work. *American Journal of Community Psychology* 17(6):755–783.

Greenhalgh, L., and Chapman, D. (1995). Joint decision making: the inseparability of relationships and negotiation. In *Negotiation and Social Process*, ed. R. Kooner and D. Messick, pp. 166–185. Thousand Oaks, CA: Sage.

Greenhaus, J., and Parasuraman, S. (1989). Sources of work–family conflict among two-career couples. *Journal of Vocational Behavior* 34:133–153.

Greenson, R. R. (1954). The struggle against identification. *Journal of the American Psychoanalytic Association* 2:200–217.

Gutek, B., and Larwood, L., eds. (1987). *Women's Career Development*. Newbury Park, CA: Sage.

Gutek, B. A. (1985). *Sex and the Workplace*. San Francisco: Jossey Bass.

Haavio-Mannila, E., Kauppinen-Toropainen, K., and Kandolin, I. (1988). The effect of sex composition of the workplace on friendship, romance, and sex at work. In *Women and Work: An Annual Review*, ed. B. Gutek, A. Stromberg, and L. Larwood. Newbury Park, CA: Sage.

Harris, K. M. (1993). Work and welfare among single mothers in poverty. *American Journal of Sociology* 99(2):317–352.

Heim, P., with Golant, S. (1993). *Hardball for Women: Winning at the Game of Business*. New York: Plume.

Helgesen, S. (1995). *The Female Advantage: Women's Way of Leadership*. New York: Doubleday.

Hillman, S. B., Sawilowsky, S. S., and Becker, M. J. (1993). Effects of maternal employment patterns on adolescents' substance abuse and other risk-taking behaviors. *Journal of Child and Family Studies* 2(3):203–219.

Hochschild, A. (1989). *The Second Shift*. New York: Avon.

Hoffman, L. W. (1991). The influence of family environment on personality: accounting for sibling differences. *Psychological Bulletin* 110:187–203.

Hogan, D. (1987). Demographic trends in human fertility and parenting across the life span. In *Parenting Across the Life Span*, ed. J. Lancaster, J. Altmann, A. Rossi, and L. Sherrod, pp. 315–349. New York: Academic Press.

Horney, K. (1950). *Neurosis and Human Growth*. New York: Norton.

Hort, B. E., Leimbach, M. D., and Fagot, B. I. (1991). Is there coherence among the cognitive components of gender acquisition? *Sex Roles* 24:195–207.

Houseknecht, S. (1978). A social psychological model of voluntary childlessness. *Alternative Lifestyles* 1:379–402.

——— (1987). Voluntary childlessness. In *Handbook of Marriage and Family*, eds. M. B. Sussman and S. K. Steinmetz, pp.369–395. New York: Plenum.

Hurwitz, S. (1992). *Lilith: The First Eve*. Einsiedeln, Switzerland: Daimon Press.

Institute of Medicine (1995). *The Best Intentions: Unintended Pregnancy and the Well-being of Children and Families*, ed. S. S. Brown and L. Eisenberg. Committee on Unintended Pregnancies, Institute of Medicine, National Academy of Sciences. Washington, DC: National Academy Press.

Ireland, M. (1993). *Reconceiving Women: Separating Motherhood from Female Identity*. Scranton, PA: HarperCollins.

Jackson, A. P. (1992). Well-being among single, black, employed mothers. *Social Service Review* 66(3):399–409.

———— (1993). Black single working mothers in poverty: preferences for employment, well-being, and perceptions of preschool-age children. *Social Work* 38(1):26–34.

Jeruchim, J., and Shapiro, P. (1992). *Women, Mentors and Success.* New York: Ballantine.

Jong, E. (1994). *Fear of Fifty.* New York: HarperCollins.

Jordan, J., and Surrey, J. (1986). The self-in-relation: empathy and the mother–daughter relationship. In *The Psychology of Today's Woman: New Psychoanalytic Visions,* ed. T. Bernay and D. W. Cantor, pp. 81–104. Hillsdale, NJ: Analytic Press.

Jordan, J., Kaplan, A. G., and Miller, J. B., et al. (1991). *Women's Growth in Connection.* New York: Guilford.

Joseph, B. (1983). Letters to the editor: Another interpretation of residents' response to pregnancy. *American Journal of Psychiatry* 140:267.

Jung, C. G. (1933). *Modern Man in Search of a Soul.* New York: Harcourt, Brace.

Kalmijn, M. (1994). Mother's occupational status and children's schooling. *American Sociological Review* 59(2):257–275.

Kaltreider, N., Gracie, C., and LeBreck, D. (1992). The psychological impact of the Bay Area earthquake on health professionals. *Journal of the American Women's Medical Association* 47:21–24.

Kanter, R. (1977). *Men and Women of the Corporation.* New York: Basic Books.

Kaplan, S., Sullivan, L., Duke, K., et al. (1996). Sex differences in academic advancement. *New England Journal of Medicine* 335:1282–1289.

Kaslow, F. W. (1992). Thirty-plus and not married. In *Gender Issues Across the Life Cycle,* ed. B. R. Wainrib. New York: Springer.

Katz, M. (1996). *The Gender Bias Prevention Book: Helping Girls and Women to Have Satisfying Lives and Careers.* Northvale, NJ: Jason Aronson.

Katz, R. (1989). Strain and enrichment in the role of employed mothers in Israel. *Marriage and Family Review* 14(1–2):69–80.

Keirsey, D., and Bates, M. (1984). *Please Understand Me: Character and Temperament Types.* Del Mar, CA: Prometheus Nemesis.

Keith, P. M., and Shafer, R. (1980). Role strain and depression in two job families. *Family Relations* 29:483–488.

Keller, K. (1992). Nurture and work in the middle class: imagery from women's magazines. *International Journal of Politics, Culture, and Society* 5(4):577–600.

Kingsbury, N. M., and Greenwood, L. (1992). Fertility expectation and employment across three female cohorts. *Journal of Family and Economic Issues* 13(1):73–93.

Komaromy, M., Bindman, A. B., Haber, R. J., and Sande, M. A. (1993). Sexual harassment in medical training. *New England Journal of Medicine* 328:322–326.

Korn/Ferry International (1990). *The Executive Profile: A Decade of Change in Corporate Leadership.* Pamphlet. Los Angeles, CA: UCLA Anderson Graduate School of Management.

Kovacs, A. (1992). Helping men in midlife. In *Gender Issues Across the Life Cycle,* ed. B. R. Wainrib, pp. 137–156. New York: Springer.

Kraft, S. D., Palombo, J., Mitchell, D., et al. (1980). The psychological dimensions of infertility. *American Journal of OrthoPsychiatry* 50:618–628.

Krener, P. (1994). Gender differences in career paths in psychiatry. *Academic Psychiatry* 18:1–21.

Lakoff, R. T. (1990). *Talking Power: The Politics of Language.* New York: Basic Books.

Lampman, C., and Dowling-Guyer, S. (1995). Attitudes toward voluntary and involuntary childlessness. *Basic and Applied Social Psychology* 17:213–222.

Lansac, J. (1995). Is delayed childbearing a good thing? *Human Reproduction* 10(5):1033–1035.

Laurent, S. L., Thompson, S. J, Addy, C., et al. (1992). An epidemiologic study of smoking and primary infertility in women. *Fertility and Sterility* 57(3):565–572.

Lennon, M. C., Wasserman, G. A., and Allen, R. (1991). Infant care and wives' depressive symptoms. *Women and Health* 17(2):1–23.

Lester, P., and Notman, M. T. (1986). Pregnancy, developmental crisis and object relations: psychoanalytic considerations. *International Journal of Psycho-Analysis* 67:357–366.

Levinson, D. J., Darrow, C. N., Klein, E. B., et al. (1978). *The Seasons of a Man's Life.* New York: Ballantine.

Levinson, W., Kaufman, K., and Bickel, J. (1993). Part-time in academic medicine: present status and future challenges. *Annals of Internal Medicine,* August, pp. 220–225.

Levinson, W., Tolle, S. W., and Lewis, C. (1989). Women in academic medicine: combining career and family. *New England Journal of Medicine* 321:1511–1517.

Lewis, E. C. (1968). *Developing Women's Potential.* Ames, IA: Iowa State University Press.

Lewis, S. (1986). Occupational stress and two earner couples: a lifestyle approach. Unpublished doctoral disssertation, University of Manchester, Institute of Science and Technology.

Lewis, S., and Cooper, C. (1983). The stress of combining occupational and parental roles: a review of the literature. *Bulletin of the British Psychological Society* 36:341–345.

———— (1988). Stress in dual earner families. In *Women and Work: An Annual Review*, ed. B. Gutek, A. Stromberg, and L. Larwood, pp. 139–168. Newbury Park, CA: Sage.

Lindbergh, A. M. (1955). *Gift from the Sea*. New York: Random House, 1975.

Lindsey, K., Ehrensaft, D., Copper, B., et al. (1994). Valuing alternative families. In *Living with Contradictions*, ed. A. Jaggar, pp. 430–471. Boulder, CO: Westview.

Lipman-Blumen, J. (1992). Connective leadership: female leadership styles in the 21st century workplace. *Social Perspectives* 35:183–203.

Lisle, L. (1996). *Without Child: Challenging the Stigma of Childlessness*. New York: Ballantine.

Livson, F. (1981). Paths to psychological health in the middle years: sex differences. In *Present and Past in Middle Life*, ed. J. Eichorn, D. H. Clausen, N. Haan, et al., pp. 195–221. New York: Academic Press.

Lytton, H., and Romney, D. M. (1991). Parents' differential socialization of boys and girls, a meta analysis. *Psychological Bulletin* 109: 267–296.

Maccoby, E. E. (1990). Gender and relationships: a developmental account. *American Psychologist* 45:513.

Mahler, M. (1981). Aggression in the service of separation–individuation: a case study of a mother–daughter relationship. *Psychoanalytic Quarterly* 50:625–638.

Maison, M. (1986). *Understanding black single parent families: strengths and weaknesses*. Dissertation, Wellesley College, 25:1–22.

Maranto, G. (1995). Delayed childbearing. *Atlantic Monthly*, July, pp. 55–66.

Markham, W. T. (1987). Sex, relocation, and occupational advancement: the "real cruncher" for women. In *Women and Work: An Annual Review*, vol. 2, ed. A. H. Stromberg, L. Larwood, and B. A. Gutek, pp. 207–232. Newbury Park, CA: Sage.

Markus, H., and Nurius, P. (1986). Possible selves. *American Psychologist* 41:954–969.

Mayer, E. L. (1996). Erik H. Erikson on bodies, gender, and development. *Psychoanalysis and Contemporary Thought* 19(2):237–257.

Maynard, R. (1988). Falling off the corporate ladder. *World Press Review* May: 44–45.

McCue, T. (1982) The effects of stress on physicians and their medical practice. *New England Journal of Medicine* 306:458–463.

References

McEwan, K., Costello, C., and Taylor, P. (1987). Adjustment to infertility. *Journal of Abnormal Psychology* 96:108–116.

McGrayne, S. B. (1990). Why so few women? Bios of women scientists provide a partial answer. *American Physical Society News*, July 1994.

McWilliams, N. (1992). The worst of both worlds: dilemmas of contemporary young women. In *Gender Issues Across the Life Cycle*, ed. B. R. Wainrib, pp. 27–36. New York: Springer.

Mercer, R. (1986). First-Time Motherhood: Experiences from Teens to Forties. New York: Springer.

Meriter Savings Bank FSB v. Vinson (1986). 477 U.S. 57, 106 S.Ct. 2399, 91 L.Ed.2d 49.

Mikesell, S. G. (1992). Motherhood in the age of reproductive technology. In *Gender Issues Across the Life Cycle*, ed. B. R. Wainrib, pp. 95–102. New York: Springer.

Miller, J. B. (1976). *Toward a New Psychology of Women*. Boston: Beacon.
———— (1984). The development of women's sense of self. Work in Progress: Stone Center #12.

Moen, P. (1985). The two-provider family: problems and potentials. In *Family Studies Review Yearbook*, vol. 3, ed. B. B. Miller and D. H. Olson. Beverly Hills, CA: Sage.

Moen, P., and Forest, K. (1990). Working parents, workplace supports, and well-being: the Swedish experience. *Social Psychology Quarterly* 53(2):117–131.

Morris, M. B. (1988). *Last Chance Children*. New York: Columbia University Press.

Mosher, W. D. (1982). Fertility and family planning in the 1970's: national survey of family growth. *Family Planning Perspective* 14: 314–320.

Mosher, W. D., and Pratt, W. F. (1991). Fecundity and infertility in the United States. *Fertility and Sterility* 56(2):192–193.

Nachtigall, R., and Mehren, E. (1991). *Overcoming Infertility*. New York: Doubleday.

Nadelson, C. C., Notman, M. T., Miller, J. B., et al. (1982). Aggression in women: conceptual issues and clinical implication. In *The Woman Patient*, vol. 3, ed. C. C. Nadelson and M. T. Notman, pp. 17–28. New York: Plenum.

Nadelson, T., and Eisenberg, L. (1977). The successful professional woman: on being married to one. *The American Journal of Psychiatry* 134(10):1071–1076.

National Foundation for Women Business Owners (1992–1993). *Women Owned Businesses: The Economic Force*. Report.

Nelton, S. (1994). No longer for men only. Entrepreneurship. *Nation's Business* 82:64–66.

Neugarten, B. (1968). Adult personality: toward a psychology of the life cycle. In *Middle Age and Aging*, ed. B. Neugarten, pp. 137–147. Chicago: University of Chicago Press.

New York Times (1996). December 15.

Nieva, V. F. (1985). Work and family linkages. In *Women and Work: An Annual Review*, vol. 1, ed. L. Larwood, A. H. Stromberg, and B. A. Gutek, pp. 162–190. Beverly Hills, CA: Sage.

Notman, M., Klein, R., Jordan, J., and Zilbach, J. (1991). Women's unique developmental issues across the life cycle. In *Review of Psychiatry* 10:557–577. New York: American Psychiatric Press.

Offerman, L. R., and Beil, C. (1992). Achievement styles of women leaders and their peers. *Psychology of Women Quarterly* 16:37–56.

Office of Education Amendments (1972). Title IX, 42 U.S.C.A. Section 1681.

Office of the Actuary (1995). *Life Expectancy for Men and Women*, pp. 1920–2070. Washington, DC: Social Security Administration.

O'Neil, J. M., Fishman, D. M., and Kinsella-Shaw, M. (1987). Dual career couples' career transitions and normative dilemmas. *Counseling Psychologist* 15:50–96.

O' Leary, V. (1988). Women's relationships with women in the workplace. In *Women and Work: An Annual Review*, ed. B. Gutek, A. Stromberg, and L. Larwood, pp. 189–213. Newbury Park, CA: Sage.

Parkinson, C. N. (1961). Directors and councils or coefficient of inefficiency. In *Parkinson's Law or the Pursuit of Progress*. London: Butler and Tanner.

Pender, K. (1996). Management lacks women. *San Francisco Chronicle*, January 11, p. 202.

Perry, A. C., and Johnson, C. (1994). Families and support networks among African American oldest-old. *International Journal of Aging and Human Development* 38:41–50.

Perun, P., and Belby, D. (1981). Towards a model of female occupational behavior: a human development approach. *Psychology of Women Quarterly* 6:234–252.

Pfeffer, J. (1981). *Power in Organizations*. London: Pittman.

Phillips, M., and Campbell, C. (1988). *Simple Living Investments*. San Francisco: Clear Glass.

Picker, L. (1996). Lessons from some of America's most sucessful women. *San Francisco Sunday Examiner and Chronicle, Parade*. April 21, pp. 1, 4–5.

Pipher, M. (1995). *Reviving Ophelia*. New York: Ballantine.

——— (1996). *The Shelter of Each Other*. New York: Grosset/Putnam.

Pleck, J., and Staines, G. (1985). Work schedules and family life in two-earner couples. *Journal of Family Issues* 6(1):68–82.

Pleck, J., Staines, G., and Long, L. (1978). Work and family life: first reports on work–family interface and workers' formal child care arrangements. In Working Paper #11, *Quality of Employment Survey*. Cambridge, MA: Wellesley College Center for Research on Women.

Ponton, L. E. (1997). *The Romance of Risk: Understanding Adolescent Behavior*. New York: Basic Books.

Preuss-Lausitz, U. (1992). Should schools be open all day due to changes in childhood? *DISKURS* 1:6–11.

Prozan, C. K. (1992). *Feminist Psychoanalytic Theory*. Northvale, NJ: Jason Aronson.

Rachlin, V., and Hanson, J. (1985). The impact of equality or egalitarianism on dual-career couples. *Family Therapy* 12:151–164.

Rapoport, R., and Rapoport, R. N. (1975). Men, women and equity. *Family Coordinator* 24:421–432.

Redwine, D. B. (1987). The distribution of endometriosis in the pelvis by age groups and fertility. *Fertility and Sterility* 47:173–175.

Rice, D. (1979). Dual Career Marriage: Conflict and Treatment. New York: Free Press.

Richards, M. H., and Duckett, E. (1994). The relationship of maternal employment to early adolescent daily experience with and without parents. *Child Development* 65(1):225–236.

Richardson, D. (1993). *Women, Motherhood, and Childrearing*. New York: St. Martin's.

Roberts, W. (1990). *Leadership Secrets of Attila the Hun*. New York: Warner.

Robinson, G. E., Garner, D. M., Gare, D. J., and Crawford, B. (1987). Psychological adaptation to pregnancy in childless women more than 35 years of age. *American Journal of Obstetrics and Gynecology* 156(2):328–333.

Rodman, H. (1990). The social construction of the latchkey children problem. *Sociological Studies of Child Development* 3:163–174.

Rosener, J. B. (1995). *America's Competitive Secret: Utilizing Women as a Management Strategy*. New York: Oxford University Press.

Rosenthal, E. (1990). The therapist's pregnancy: impact on the treatment process. *Clinical Social Work Journal* 3:213–226.

Roskies, E., and Carrier, S. (1994). Marriage and children for professional women. In *Job Stress in a Changing Workforce*, ed. G. Keita and J. Hurrell, pp. 269–282. Washington, DC: American Psychological Press.

Rossi, A. (1980). Aging and Parenthood in the Middle Years. New York: Academic Press, pp.137–205.

——— (1987). Parenthood in transition: from lineage to child to self-orientation. In *Parenting across the Life Span*, ed. J. Altman, A. Rossi, and L. Sherrod, pp. 31–81. New York: Academic Press.

Rowe, M. (1990). Barriers to equality: the power of subtle discrimination to maintain unequal opportunity. *Employees' Responsibilities and Rights Journal* 3:153–163.

Rubin, S. P. (1980). *It's Not Too Late for a Baby: For Men and Women over 35*. Englewood Cliffs, NJ: Prentice Hall.

Safer, J. (1996). *Beyond Motherhood*. New York: Ballantine.

San Francisco Chronicle (1996). Management lacks women, January 11.

San José Mercury News (1990). June 8, San José, CA.

——— (1996). June 2, San José, CA.

Sargent, A. C. (1983). *The Androgynous Manager: Blending Male and Female Management Styles for Today's Organization*. New York: American Management Association.

Sarrel, P. (1991). Women, work and menopause. In *Women, Work and Health: Stress and Opportunities*, ed. M. Frankenhauser, U. Lundberg, and M. Chesney, pp. 225–237. New York: Plenum.

Scheidt, S. D. (1994). Great expectations: challenges for women as mental health administrators. *Journal of Mental Health Administration* 21:419–429.

Scherer, R., Brodzinski, J., Goryer, K., and Wiebe, F. (1991). Shaping the desire to become an entrepreneur: parent and gender influences. *Journal of Business and Entrepreneurship* 3:47–58.

Schwartz, F. N. (1989). Management, women and the new facts of life. *Harvard Business Review*, Jan–Feb:65–76.

——— (1992). *Breaking with Tradition: Women and Work, the New Facts of Life*. New York: Warner.

Schwartz, F. N., Schifter, M., and Gillotti, S. (1972). *How to Go to Work When Your Husband Is Against It, Your Children Aren't Old Enough, and There's Nothing You Can Do Anyhow*. New York: Simon & Schuster.

Sekaran, U. (1986). *Dual-Career Families*. San Francisco: Jossey-Bass.

Shakespeare, W. (1980). *Complete Works of William Shakespeare*: The Cambridge Text. London: Cambridge University Press.

Shaw, G. B. (1984). Quoted by E. H. Erikson in *The Norton Reader*, 6th ed., ed. A. M. Eastman et al. New York: Norton.

Sheehy, G. (1995). *New Passages: Mapping Your Life across Time*. New York: Ballantine, 1996.

Singer, M. (1996). Mom overboard! *The New Yorker*, February 26–March 4, pp. 65–74.

Spitz, R. A. (1965). The evolution of dialogue. In *Drives, Affects, Behavior*, vol. 2, ed. M. Schur, pp. 170–190. New York: International Universities Press.

St. James, E. (1996). *Simplify Your Life*. New York, NY: Hyperion.

Stevens, C., Bavetta, A., and Gist, M. (1993). Gender differences in the acquisition of salary negotiation skills. *Journal of Applied Psychology* 78:723–735.

Stobo, J., Fried, L. P., and Stokes E. J. (1993). Understanding and eradicating bias against women in medicine. *Academic Medicine* 68:249.

Stoller, R. J. (1968). The sense of femaleness. *Psychoanalytic Quarterly* 37:42–55.

——— (1985). *Observing the Erotic Imagination*. New Haven, CT: Yale University Press.

Strober, M., and Jackman, J. (1994). Some effects of occupational segregation and the glass ceiling on women and men in technical and managerial fields: retention of senior women. In *Human Factors in Organizational Design and Management IV*, ed. G. Bradley and H. W. Hendrick. New York: Elsevier Science.

Surrey, J. (1985). *The Self-in-Relation: A Theory of Women's Development*. Wellesley, MA: Wellesley College, Stone Center.

Sutton, S. D., and Moore, K. K. (1985). Probing opinions: executive women—20 years later. *Harvard Business Review* 85:42–66.

Symonds, A. (1974). The liberated woman: healthy and neurotic. *American Journal of Psychoanalysis* 34:177–183.

Tannen, D. (1990). *You Just Don't Understand*. New York: William Morrow.

——— (1994). *Talking from 9 to 5. Women and Men in the Workplace: Language, Sex and Power*. New York: Avon.

——— (1995). The power of talk. *Harvard Business Review*, Sept.–Oct., pp. 138–148.

Tavris, C. (1992). *Mismeasure of Woman*. New York: Simon & Schuster.

Taylor, M., and Hall, J. (1982). Psychological androgyny: theories, methods, and conclusions. *Psychological Bulletin* 92:347–366.

Thomas, S., Albrecht, K., and White, P. (1984). Determinants of marital quality in dual-career couples. *Family Relations* 33:513–521.

Tietze, C. (1957). Reproductive span and rate of reproduction among Hutterite women. *Fertility and Sterility* 8:89–97.

Title VII of the Civil Rights Act of 1964, 42 U.S.C.A. Section 2000e et seq.

Tolnay, S., and Guest, A. (1982). Childlessness in a transitional population: the United States at the turn of the century. *Journal of Family History* 7:200–219.

Tolstoy, L. (1948). Quoted in *Leaves of Gold*, revised edition, by D. G. Remley. Allentown, PA : Coslett.

Tyson, P. T. (1986). Female psychological development. *Annual of Psychoanalysis* 14:357–373.

Tyson, P., and Tyson, R. L. (1990). *Psychoanalytic Theories of Developement: An Integration*. New Haven: Yale University Press.

Ury, W. (1991). *Getting Past No: Negotiating Your Way from Confrontation to Cooperation*. New York: Bantam.

U.S. Bureau of the Census (1995). Statistical Abstract, 115th ed. Washington, DC.

U.S. Small Business Administration (1989). Office of Public Communications, Fact Sheet 39, p. 4.

Valdez, R. A., and Gutek, B. A. (1987). Family roles: a help or a hindrance for working women? In *Women's Career Development*, ed. B. A. Gutek and L. Larwood, pp. 157–169. Newbury Park, CA: Sage.

Vandell, D. L., and Ramanan, J. (1992). Effects of early and recent maternal employment on children from low-income families. *Child Development* 63(4):938–949.

Wallerstein, J. S., and Blakeslee, S. (1995). *The Good Marriage: How and Why Love Lasts*. Boston: Houghton Mifflin.

Walsh, E. (1995). *Divided Lives: The Public and Private Struggles of Three Accomplished Women*. New York: Simon & Schuster.

Walster, E., Walster, G., and Bershide, E. (1978). *Equity: Theory and Research*. Boston: Allyn and Bacon.

Walter, C. (1986). *The Timing of Motherhood*. Lexington, KY: Lexington Books.

West, M. (1994). Gender bias in academic robes: the law's failure to protect women faculty. *Temple Law Review*, vol. 67, No. 1.

Westerbeek, J., and Brinkgreve, C. (1994). From mother to daughter, academic mothers and their daughters on the combination of work and family. *Sociologisch Tijdschrift* 21(1):100–120.

Widerberg, K. (1991). Reforms for women—on male terms—the example of the Swedish legislation on parental leave. *International Journal of the Sociology of Law* 19(1):27–44.

Wilkie, J. R. (1988). Marriage, family life, and women's employment. In *Women Working*, ed. A. Stromberg and S. Harkness, pp. 149–166. Mountainview, CA: Mayfield.

Williams, J. E., and Best, D. L. (1990). *Measuring Sex Stereotypes: A Multinational Study*. Beverly Hills, CA: Sage.

Wolfman, B. R. (1984). Colloquium: women and their many roles. Dissertation, 83–03, 1–8.

Woolf, V. (1942). Professions for women. In *The Death of the Mother and Other Essays*. New York: Harcourt Brace.

Wortman, C. (1988). Domestic chore distribution. In *Psychology*, ed. E. Loftus and M. Marshall, pp. 66–77. New York: Knopf.

Wortman, C., Biernat, M., and Lang, E. (1991). Coping with role overload. In *Women, Work and Health: Stress and Opportunities*, ed. M. Frankenhauser, U. Lundberg, and M. Chesney, pp. 85–109. New York: Plenum.

Xuewen, A., Stockman, N., and Bonney, N. (1992). The dual burden: east and west. *International Sociology* 7:209–223.

Yalow, R. (1977). This world. *San Francisco Chronicle*, p. 2.

Yogev, S. (1983). Judging the professional woman: changing research, changing values. *Psychology of Women Quarterly* 7(3):219–234.

Zuckerman, H., Cole, J., and Bruer, J. T., eds. (1991). *The Outer Circle: Women in the Scientific Community*. New York: Norton.

INDEX